ALEX HALEY

ALEX HALEY

AND THE BOOKS THAT CHANGED A NATION

ROBERT J. NORRELL

St. Martin's Press
New York

ALEX HALEY. Copyright © 2015 by Robert J. Norrell. All rights reserved. Printed in the United States of America. For information, address St. Martin's Press, 175 Fifth Avenue, New York, N.Y. 10010.

www.stmartins.com

Library of Congress Cataloging-in-Publication Data

Norrell, Robert J. (Robert Jefferson)
    Alex Haley and the books that changed a nation / Robert J. Norrell.
        pages cm
    ISBN 978-1-137-27960-6 (hardback)
    1. Haley, Alex. 2. African American journalists—Biography. 3. Authors, American—20th century—Biography. 4. Haley, Alex. Autobiography of Malcom X. 5. Haley, Alex. Roots. I. Title.
    E185.97 .H24N68   2015
    973'.0496073—dc23

                                                                                    2015016043

ISBN 978-1-137-27960-6 (hardcover)
ISBN 978-1-4668-7931-7 (e-book)

Design by Letra Libre, Inc.

Our books may be purchased in bulk for promotional, educational, or business use. Please contact your local bookseller or the Macmillan Corporate and Premium Sales Department at (800) 221-7945, extension 5442, or by e-mail at MacmillanSpecialMarkets@macmillan.com.

First Edition: November 2015

10 9 8 7 6 5 4 3 2 1

For Mary Ann Graham Norrell,
in celebration of her ninety years

CONTENTS

PREFACE

T HIS BOOK TELLS THE STORY OF ALEX HALEY, A
tale whose significance is larger than one man's biography. It is
the story of the remaking of American society's understanding
of the black experience. Haley wrote the two most influential
books on African American history in the second half of the twentieth century. Each of his books sold at least six million copies, and the
films made from them were viewed and appreciated by the masses of
Americans. Haley sold more books than any other African American
author and all but a few white ones.

He shaped the racial sensibilities of more Americans than any
other writer, black or white. Although he was not himself a black
nationalist, his works, more than any other writing, gave texture and
substance to black nationalism. Haley and his work deserve to be
recognized as seminal influences on black identity and American
thought about race.

The Autobiography of Malcolm X gave millions of Americans a
look into the world of blacks in twentieth-century ghettos and especially the anger that life there engendered. The book made Malcolm into an icon of black manliness and resistance to oppression.
Haley's rendering of Malcolm created an archetype that challenged
the image of the loving, nonviolent black male personified by Martin
Luther King Jr. After Malcolm's assassination in 1965, his influence

on the popular imagination grew steadily, helped always by his auto-biography, written by Haley.

Roots cast slavery and the black family in an entirely new light. Haley retrieved the African past of black Americans for the benefit of all people, adding new depth to our understanding of the experiences of African Americans. He created memorable characters that live today in the minds of those who read *Roots* or who saw the television productions based on the book. He opened the eyes of millions of whites to the hard realities of black life over the generations and spurred a national movement among Americans, regardless of race or ethnicity, to seek their family origins. Along the way, Haley taught us that our families' experiences actually composed the nation's history.

Despite the publishing success and the celebrity that came with it, controversy enveloped Haley soon after the publication of *Roots* and plagued him for the rest of his life. He was castigated personally and accused of malfeasance as a writer. The controversy hurt Haley's professional reputation and to some extent undermined his works' influence on American culture. This book tries to explain how and why that happened—and also why Haley should still be remembered and his books still read.

ACKNOWLEDGMENTS

A GRANT FROM THE SOCIAL PHILOSOPHY AND POL-icy Center at Bowling Green University in Ohio boosted this project at an early stage. Jeffrey Paul's continuing interest in my work has been gratifying. W. Fitzhugh Brundage at the University of North Carolina and Daryl Michael Scott at Howard University clarified my thinking about the issues raised in this book. Josh Durbin gave extensive help in the early stages of research, and Alicia Maskley aided at the end. Tracey Hayes Norrell and Jay Norrell each made many helpful editorial suggestions. Geri Thoma at Writers House found a home for the book. I am particularly indebted to Lisa Drew, George Berger, and Bruce Wheeler for advising me on particular issues in the research.

1

GRANDMA'S BOY

ON A SEPTEMBER EVENING IN 1921, SIMON AND BERtha Haley drove into Bertha's hometown of Henning, in western Tennessee, a village of five hundred souls lying in the lowlands not far from the Mississippi River. Bertha brought a present for her parents, Will and Cynthia Palmer. When Cynthia opened the door that night, Bertha thrust a blanketed bundle toward her mother, saying, "Here's a surprise for you." It was a six-week-old baby boy. Bertha had kept her pregnancy a secret from her parents. The concealment was odd, especially because Bertha enjoyed a loving relationship with her parents, and it probably indicated ambivalence about having a baby in her early twenties.[1]

Simon and Bertha had traveled a thousand miles from Ithaca, New York, where Simon was a graduate student at the Cornell University School of Agriculture. They were newlyweds, having met at all-black Lane College in Jackson, Tennessee, and married the previous year at the New Hope Colored Methodist Church of Henning. The nuptials had been grand by Henning standards. Will Palmer had bused in the Lane choir to perform at the wedding of his only child, a sign of the prosperity Will had enjoyed during his twenty-five years as proprietor of the W. E. Palmer Lumber Company. The clearest indication of Will's wealth was the new, twelve-room house to which Simon and Bertha brought their son.

Will and Cynthia were overjoyed with their grandbaby, called Palmer but also named Alexander for Simon's father and Murray for Cynthia's father, Tom Murray, who had established his family in Henning in 1874. Will Palmer had longed for a son. His and Cynthia's own firstborn, a boy, had died as an infant. Will immediately began minding little Palmer. He built a crib and installed it at the lumber company in order that he might take the baby to work with him. Cynthia doted on the little boy almost as much. Early on, she took over much responsibility from Bertha for rearing Palmer.

A tall, brown-skinned woman with flowing dark hair, Bertha considered herself a musician above all. She had studied with a white teacher from Memphis, then at Lane, and at the music conservatory at Cornell during the previous year. In his new house, Will built a music room from which Bertha conducted Saturday afternoon recitals for residents of Henning, black and white. Simon, the grandson of two Irish immigrants who fathered children with slave women, was light enough to pass for white. He grew up in poverty in Savannah in western Tennessee, but he intended to move up in the world. After Lane, he graduated from North Carolina A&T in Greensboro. He enlisted in the military, serving in World War I and rising to the rank of sergeant in an all-black unit that fought at the Argonne Forest, where they were gassed. Simon enjoyed taking Henning residents into Will Palmer's vegetable garden and identifying okra and cabbage by their Latin names. At the New Hope church, Simon had sung "In the Garden" with Bertha's accompaniment, and he liked to opine after services on subjects about which he was expert, all the while twirling the Phi Beta Kappa key attached to the lapel of his three-piece suit. "Dad would start talking all kind of wisdom, using big words that not a soul in the crowd understood a syllable of except him," Palmer recalled. "After a while all eyes in the crowd were on that little key." Sister Scrap Scott, a feisty local woman, always stood directly in front of Simon as he pontificated. One day she pointed at the key. "'Fessor Haley, what is that?" He explained in Greek and Latin phrases about the Phi Beta Kappa honor society. Sister Scrap was not satisfied. "But 'Fessor Haley, what do it open?"

Palmer, who would become the writer Alex Haley, had been born into an African American family atypical in the early twentieth century. Both of his parents had been to college, and his father would earn a graduate degree from an Ivy League university. Also unusual was Will Palmer, who in 1895 had been asked by white men in Henning to take over the lumber company at which he worked from the drunken white man who had driven the business into bankruptcy. Will proceeded to make the company into a thriving enterprise highly valued by local whites. He was well-to-do and occupied the finest new house in the town, set amid white neighbors. He spoke deliberately, and everyone paid attention to what Will Palmer said and did. He was something of an autocrat from his living room rocking chair. When Will spoke, his grandson later said, "nobody dared utter a whisper. . . . You just listened to grandpa. . . . And when he would quit speaking, there would generally be a respectful little lull . . . before anybody else would venture something."

These unusual circumstances occurred in a time of terrible discrimination against African Americans. Lauderdale County was typical of the Mississippi Delta with its large population of black sharecroppers. Henning sat fifteen miles from old Fort Pillow, where in 1864 General Nathan Bedford Forrest and his Confederate cavalry massacred hundreds of black Union soldiers after they had surrendered. In 1866 blacks were murdered during rioting in Memphis, fifty miles to the south. Blacks were disfranchised throughout Tennessee in 1889 and relegated to inferior schools and public accommodations. African Americans were often lynched in the South starting in the 1880s, with incidents near Henning in 1917 and in 1931. As far as little

Palmer knew, however, blacks were not treated harshly but were just considered to be different from whites. Society "decreed everything about the two was different."

Bertha was not adept at either cooking or housekeeping, whereas Cynthia was master of all domestic arts and was such a tireless worker that she sometimes accompanied her friends to pick cotton in order to enjoy the sociability of the field. She considered her daughter over-educated and impractical. "You just don't know nothing about raising a young'un," she told Bertha, who saw herself as different from her mother. Cynthia's family stories about slavery embarrassed her. Bertha would say, "Ma, why don't you quit talking about that old-timey slavery mess," to which Cynthia would retort: "If you don't care nothin' about who you come from, I sho' does." In his first years, Bertha and Simon left Palmer in Henning as Simon filled short-term appointments at various black colleges. Palmer grew up more attached to Cynthia than to Bertha.

He entered the Palmer-Turner Grammar School, one of the youngest and smallest children in his class. The first black school in the area, it was named for both his grandfather and Carrie White Turner, its first teacher. Palmer read avidly from an early age. He loved adventure tales and the Bible stories read and told at the New Hope church. Will Palmer's house was the only one in Henning with a library, and he made sure that it was well stocked. A black traveling bookseller would come around, especially in the fall, when people had money from the cotton harvest. Books usually cost one dollar each, except for Bibles, which were more. A local man, Lewis Young, claimed to have read a hundred books.

In 1926, when Palmer was five, his grandfather fell gravely ill. "He real low," visitors whispered after sitting at his bedside. Cynthia showed her stress by being unusually irritable with little Palmer. He fled outdoors and hid beneath honeysuckle vines outside the window of the sick room, wanting to be in calling distance if his grandpa needed him. Under the honeysuckle, he found a crippled cricket, for which he made a tiny splint. He hoped both the cricket and Grandpa could recover. In his hideaway Palmer also watched a hummingbird that he imagined moved like the angels he had heard described in Sunday school and that he feared might be coming for his grandfather. "Grandpa was so heroic in my world that I just equated him with God," Palmer later said. Finally, he watched the doctor try without success to resuscitate Will, after which the boy ran to the lumber mill, shouting, "Grandpa's dead!" His grandfather's passing was the most momentous event of Palmer's early life.

With Will's death, Bertha and Simon returned to Henning to live. Simon took over the running of the lumber company to get it ready to sell. Bertha taught at the Palmer-Turner Grammar School, where Palmer began first grade. A second son, George, had arrived, and in 1929 would come a third, Julius. Simon discovered that the lumber company had debts enough to reduce its worth below what they hoped to get to secure Cynthia's future. Meanwhile, Cynthia's grief was intense. She neglected cooking and housework and sat for hours on the front porch, staring outward, often with baby George in her lap. Passersby asked how she was doing. "Just settin'," she answered. Palmer played at the edge of the porch, "feeling that I needed to stay protectively near her because Grandpa was gone now." The family assembled after supper on the front porch, where Simon "said light and funny things just in an effort to see if he could get Grandma to laugh." It seemed to Palmer that she never smiled anymore.

Simon had finished his master's degree and yearned to get back to academia. He landed a position teaching poultry science at Lane College, his and Bertha's alma mater. Suddenly, Cynthia came out of the fog of her grief and returned to frenetic bouts of housekeeping, cooking, gardening, and vegetable canning. "With her big black pots steaming atop the wood-burning cast-iron stove," Palmer remembered, she began to "ladle wonderful-smelling things into freshly-scaled quart-sized Mason jars, until rows upon rows of them were stacked in the cool, dark basement."

Cynthia also found comfort in writing letters to family members. She had five sisters and many nieces widely scattered, a reflection of the migration of blacks from the South after 1910. Every afternoon she put pencil to paper and composed a letter. "She would call out a word and then she would call out the spelling," Palmer later recounted. "And if that spelling didn't please her, then she would try another spelling until one sounded right. And then she would start writing character for character. And whenever she finished one word, she would put the tip of this little nubby pencil up to her lip or up to her tongue as if to recharge it." The next morning, as she addressed the envelope, she called out the place where the letter was going, "backed it" with her return address, and walked to the Henning post office to buy a two-cent stamp. Palmer learned his "first concept of communication": if you write a letter, "probably somebody would write to you." This lesson made Palmer a lifelong, habitual letter writer. In the spring of 1927, having overcome her worst grief, Cynthia began to invite the women of her family to visit. Palmer remembered the excitement that always accompanied a letter from a relative announcing her time of arrival. He would go with Grandma to the Henning train depot to "welcome them in a welter of kissings and huggings." The visitors included Mathilda Merriwether, "Aunt Till," from Jackson, Tennessee, wife of a prominent minister; "Cousin Pie" from Chicago, daughter of a long-dead sister, who taught school and spoke with a northern accent; Aunt Mattie Fisher from Carbondale, Illinois; Aunt Posey from St. Louis, actually Cynthia's sister-in-law; and Cousin Millie Brooks from Louisville. Cousin Georgia Anderson from Kansas City talked so fast and said so much that she often exasperated the others. She brought along her teenaged daughter, who played with Palmer.

Cynthia was closest to her sister Elizabeth Murray, who came from Oklahoma, where she was an "old-maid" schoolteacher. "Aunt Liz" was thought to reveal the Indian blood in the family tree. She had long, straight, black hair that she braided and dyed jet-black and high cheekbones and copper-toned skin. The other women were various shades of brown. Elizabeth had never married; her family rejected her suitor because he was too light-skinned—certainly an irony given the complement of white blood that had entered the family line during slavery. She carried herself so proudly that people in Henning speculated that she was wealthy from Oklahoma oil. Having retired, Aunt Liz was moving to live with Cynthia permanently. She became almost as much a fixture in the lives of the Haley boys as their grandmother.

After supper, the Murray women gathered on Cynthia's broad front porch. Palmer crouched behind Cynthia's chair, and the women rocked back and forth like "so many metronomes."[2] They dipped sweet Garrett snuff. "They'd pull out their lower lips and load them up," Palmer remembered, and in a while one of them would tilt her head, lift her chin, say "skeet," and let go a stream of snuff juice. The champion spitter was Liz. "There in the gathering darkness, she would knock a lightning bug on the fly." At first Palmer did not understand the stories the women told on the porch. What was an "Old Massa" and a plantation? "Early I gathered that white folks had done lots of bad things to our folks, things I couldn't figure out why." He began to imagine scenes in the stories, just as he visualized "Noah and his ark, Jesus feeding that big multitude with nothing but five loaves and two fishes." The great protagonist of the women's stories was the one remembered as "the African." They told how he was kidnapped and brought in chains to "Naplis," where he was bought by a planter named Waller and taken to a plantation in Virginia. The African tried so often to escape that a slave catcher finally cut off part of his foot.

Palmer did not understand why people were so mean to the African. The women exclaimed against the cruelty, and Cousin Georgia sprang from her chair, "her small eyes flashing," as she enacted how the African walked with only the rear half of his foot. Palmer said the women practically stood "my hair on end" as they whispered that slave nurses stuck "darning needles into the heads of their massa's infants." The planter's brother, a doctor, saved the African by buying him. He named the African Toby, and that angered the African, who insisted he should be called "Kin-tay." Eventually the African "jumped over the broom" with a cook named Bell, and they had a girl named Kizzy, whom Kin-tay taught African words. He called a banjo "ko" and a river "Kamby Bolongo." Kizzy was sold away to a white man who "vi-lated" her. She handed down the information about the African to her son, George, who was the source of endless fascination to the ladies on the porch for his clever tongue, quick mind, and insatiable appetite for female flesh. George was the father of Tom Murray, who migrated to Henning in 1874 and was the father of Cynthia and her sisters.

For Palmer, the story became "nearly as fixed in my head as in Grandma's." Palmer took the family story with him when he went to play with Arthur and George Sims, Fred Montgomery, and various white boys in Henning. "What a happy crew we were! . . . racing down by the tracks of the Illinois Central Railroad," waving and shouting at the passengers. They played baseball and hide-and-seek and shot marbles. When it rained, the boys—fifteen or twenty of them, most of them black but with six or so white boys, too—gathered in a barn or in the crawl space under a church. When Palmer told his family story, his playmates began to pay him special attention. That was his "first time in life to be 'somebody,'" and he liked the feeling. He told how the masters and overseers were "all the time beating on the slaves until sometimes the slaves ran blood, or sometimes died of beating right on the spot." Then Palmer told the boys about the time the white master hit the African's daughter, Kizzy, and she grabbed him and shouted: "You sucked your baby milk from my black titties! I'll whip you to death."

Eventually the father of one of the white Henning boys appeared at Cynthia Palmer's door demanding an explanation for Palmer's stories. They were the truth as her family knew it, Cynthia answered.

After that, none of the white boys came around. Good stories, Palmer discovered, told of conflict and violence, had heroes and villains, and inspired awe in some and discomfort in others.

Most of Palmer's childhood memories were from the time he spent at his grandmother's side. The two of them were often together in her kitchen—she cooked, and he sampled her culinary art. Cynthia constantly touched and petted him. "Even when she was grumbling something," Palmer later said, "like 'Boy, you've gotten all dirty,' her fingers would still be moving lightly and deliberately as if she were saying with them, 'I care for you; I love you.'" Palmer was a grandma's boy, and the fundamental security of his psyche was rooted in their relationship.

*　*　*

ABOUT A YEAR after Will Palmer's death, Palmer began to live most of the time with his parents, outside Henning. As he grew, he resembled Bertha, with his brown, fleshy face, as opposed to Simon's narrow, light-complected one. Simon, an extrovert and a performer, showed Palmer that storytelling was not just a feminine art. He loved to spin yarns that featured his own prowess. His sons would prompt him to tell about when General Black Jack Pershing sent for Sergeant Haley to save the day at the Western Front or when Simon scored the winning touchdown in a college football game. In time, the boys joked about the likely exaggerations, but they never doubted Simon's strong character.

With the sale of the lumber company, Simon embarked on a peripatetic life through black colleges in the South. The jobs he found paid poorly, and there was scant security at the often-unstable little colleges, which were mostly dependent on meager state funding and, sometimes, Christian denominational support. Simon taught first at Lane College, just forty-seven miles from Henning. The family returned to Cynthia and Aunt Liz most weekends. It felt to Palmer as if they never really left Henning. But in 1929, they moved more than five hundred miles to Oklahoma Colored Agricultural and Normal University in the all-black town of Langston, Oklahoma, where Simon was appointed to a better position in the school's Department of Agriculture. Palmer recalled the strangeness of living where no one knew his family but also the fun of making new friends in Oklahoma. The hard, snowy winters, when jackrabbits froze to death under their house, also made a strong impression on him. The Great Depression descended so heavily there in 1930 that Simon was paid not in cash but in state-issued coupons. "I don't think my mother was very well adjusted to it," Palmer remembered. Not far into their time in Langston, Bertha fell seriously ill, and Simon had to hire a woman to help tend to the children.

People had started to wander the roads in Oklahoma. One evening a white man knocked on their door and asked if Bertha had any work for him. No, she answered, but she could give him a plate of food. Sometime later, the Haleys were driving eastward through Oklahoma on their way to Tennessee when Bertha got very sick. Simon drove to a strange house in the dark and asked for a place for his wife to rest. The man of the house was the same man Bertha had fed. Palmer later remembered that evening as "being a very warm, almost religious experience." Palmer often returned to that story as evidence of the inherently caring human relations of the South of his childhood.[3]

In 1931 Simon accepted a significantly better position as dean of agriculture at Alabama Agricultural & Mechanical College, the state's black land grant college, near Huntsville, Alabama. The campus sat on a wooded area that the school claimed presented "a beautiful picture" to passengers traveling past it on the tracks of the Southern Railway. "Large limestone boulders, wooded areas of cedar, hickory, walnut and poplar, and sparkling water" from a mountain spring lent a "charm and picturesqueness surpassed by few school locations." Local whites tagged it "Nigger Normal"—*normal* was the term used to designate a teacher's college.

Conditions at the school were not good when the Haleys arrived. Simon's annual salary was $1,800, about $26,000 today, but Simon was told that the financial situation in Alabama "may render it impossible for salaries to be paid promptly." The state superintendent of education declared that "financial chaos . . . aptly describes our situation." Schools depended mostly on taxes on property whose value had plummeted. In 1931 the state of Alabama was issuing warrants instead of cash to Alabama A&M, and the college was not able to pay its faculty their meager salaries for the first half of 1932. In some cases, schools issued state-backed scrip that teachers like Simon usually had to sell to speculators at deep discounts to get cash needed at the moment.[4]

The family moved into a small campus bungalow, one corner of which Simon turned over to an indigent student. "Dad would always find some way to cram somebody else in the house so they could get through school," Palmer said. Ten-year-old Palmer and six-year-old George attended a small elementary school on the college campus. Simon relished his position as dean of agriculture. He put his students to work growing vegetables and raising livestock and poultry to feed those at the college. He taught them how to castrate male chicks and watch the capons grow to be as big as turkeys. He wanted more than anything to improve the farming practices of black sharecroppers in that part of Alabama. Simon often drove through the country, with Palmer seated beside him, visiting with local black men. "They received Dad in much the same way as Dad might have reacted if the Commissioner of Agriculture from Washington had arrived at our house." Simon was evangelical about scientific agriculture. He preached a gospel of rotating crops, planting legumes, and applying lime to the soil, while Palmer played with the farmers' sons. "If Dad ever so slightly suggested something," Palmer remembered, "the response would be polite, its phrasing and tenor such that you knew good and well the farmer wasn't going to do any such thing." Such practices might work at the college on the hill, they finally said, because the school had lots of state money to spend on fancy farming—none of which these sharecroppers would ever have. They said to Simon, "'Fessor, that college ain't out here trying to make no living."

Even so, Simon had Palmer keep a list of every farmer they visited, along with their wives' and children's names and their mailing addresses. After the crops were laid by in the late summer one year, he invited all the local farmers to the First Annual A&M Seminar of Farmers, a convention on the college campus, where he treated the sharecroppers as visiting dignitaries and presented demonstrations of scientific farming. At the end of the meeting, he gave each farmer a postcard to mail back, setting a time for a visit from the A&M faculty to advise him on farm problems. To Simon's great disappointment, no postcards were returned. His next strategy was to gather the sons of farmers and have each boy ask his father for the least productive acre on his farm; Simon would then teach the boys scientific farming methods, such as gathering humus from forest floors and collecting cow manure to enrich worn-out soil. Not much came of this effort either.

The single-crop, sharecropper existence offered almost no hope for improving material circumstances; most black farmers were trapped in a downward cycle of indebtedness and desperate poverty. Sharecropping was a cruel, hopeless system essentially immune to all efforts to improve it.[5]

"Dad had his heart set on raising at least one of his sons to be what he called a 'scientific farmer,'" Palmer later wrote, "and as I was the oldest I was his principal target." Simon drove Palmer all the way to Tuskegee so that he might meet the great Dr. George Washington Carver, in the hope of encouraging his son to follow in those steps. Watching Simon's persistence in trying to improve the farming practices of poor black farmers in the Great Depression instilled in Palmer admiration for his father's determination and self-sacrifice, but Palmer did not share his father's ambition. He never actually worked on a farm and apparently never had any inclination to do so. What the boy took from the experience was an appreciation for the goodness and intelligence of rural southern people.

Soon after they settled in Alabama, Bertha again fell seriously ill, this time with a throat malady. She was hospitalized but got no better, and Simon had to bring her home. One morning a student of Simon's appeared at six-year-old George's first-grade classroom and led the boy home and into the room where his mother lay. Palmer remembered hearing "an awful, awful sound"—the death rattle. Soon the doctor said, "Well, she's dead." Nobody said anything until George looked at his father. "Well, Dad, how can Mama be dead when her eyes are open?" Simon grabbed George into a tight hug and started crying. To little George, "it looked like the whole world was crying . . . the doctor and everybody." George later said that his first real experience with God was one of fear. "That He would take from me . . . the person that I loved. . . . He certainly demanded my respect, God did."

Palmer later said he suffered relatively little emotional trauma from his mother's death, because Bertha had not shown him much affection. At that time, "what I lived for was to get back to Grandma. She was the answer to everything." That did not mean, however, that Bertha's funeral was easy for him. The worst part for Palmer was seeing his father crying uncontrollably. Bertha's casket was put in her music room at her parents' house to wait for the arrival of distant family members, several of whom emitted piercing screams through the nights of her wake that traumatized the little Haley boys. Bertha's funeral was held at the Baptist church, because the New Hope church was too small to accommodate the crowd of mourners.

When Simon and the boys returned to Alabama, his mother, Queen, came to help attend to the boys, but she "just didn't have much to say," Palmer remembered. Various women began to pay attention to the handsome and pleasant young widower. He surely needed a helpmate. The woman Simon chose was a fellow Alabama

A&M faculty member, an English teacher, Zeona Hatcher. A small, highly disciplined woman with a master's degree from Ohio State University, Zeona married Simon within a year of Bertha's death. The Palmer family, including Cynthia, was upset about his marrying before Bertha "got cold in the grave."

Over the next few years, the Haley boys adjusted to Zeona with varying degrees of acceptance. For Julius, only two when Bertha died, Zeona was the only mother he knew; he was raised with Doris Ann, born about two years after Simon and Zeona married. George, well-behaved and studious, conformed to Zeona's expectations of good conduct. He called her "Mother" to distinguish her from his late "Mama." Yet years later he could not remember Zeona ever having hugged him. Palmer did not use any name for Zeona and often was at odds with her. He was an indifferent student, which Zeona knew firsthand because she taught his English class in high school and caught him cheating. Her favored form of punishment was to make him memorize Bible verses. She liked Palmer least among Simon's boys, which the adolescent surely sensed. She thought he was lazy. During the summer when they were in Henning, she required that they write letters to her and Simon, which she marked for errors and returned to them. George later observed that "Mother" was greatly concerned with what "the public"—meaning the black folks in the college community—thought of her boys. Zeona enforced strict discipline on such matters as table manners. She instituted a system of rewards and punishments regarding the use of eating utensils and dinner napkins. She had high expectations for maintaining a good appearance. George, while recalling later that Simon was forced to watch Zeona's harsh ways toward his children—"he sometimes really suffered under that, trying to keep the whole thing going"—thought that his father endured too much of his Zeona's harshness in silence.[6] Although he was the least cooperative of the boys while living with Zeona, Palmer later credited her with teaching him household skills and the virtues of discipline. "She was very strong in teaching us manners and in how to live in a personal orderly way." His munificent memories, given many years later, probably glossed over their conflicts during his adolescence. By the time he was a teenager in Alabama, Palmer was practicing the art of avoiding conflict.

A duality had emerged for Palmer between the structured life of school, closely monitored by Zeona and Simon, and the free existence of Henning, where Grandma doted on him and Aunt Liz entertained him with her stories. Little wonder that he later remembered life in Henning as an idyllic existence—and the other places scarcely at all, as if he had blocked them from his memory. In Henning Palmer read books and played with his local friends, including a white boy named Kermit. "We ate in each other's homes, slept on pallets on the floor, got spanked by our respective mothers from time to time." Palmer later said such an interracial friendship was typical in the South in the 1930s. But perhaps also typically, their relationship came to a quick end when Palmer was about twelve. One day Kermit said to Palmer, "Pretty soon, you're gonna have to call me Mister." Palmer later said he "froze at the remark and began to withdraw."[7]

Palmer was a dreamy boy, not a good student like George. He was happiest while cruising the stacks of the Alabama A&M library, looking for books of adventure. In school, he often drifted into an imaginary world. "I was given to creating fantasies of all kinds that I would never tell anybody," he recalled. He liked classes that required writing, though he was never asked to write more than the simplest narrative. Simon had insisted when Palmer was eight that he learn to type, which may have been the most useful skill he acquired in his formal education. He was always younger than the other students in his class, finishing high school in Alabama at age sixteen. He was small in stature and shy around girls. "Instead of being the one who was kissing the girls," he said, "I was the one who took love notes from the girls I wished I could kiss to somebody [else]." Palmer later remembered a particular girl in Alabama, a "big, hefty, kind of a cotton field type girl," who pulled him under the school stairs when he was in the eleventh grade. "I was so mortified, embarrassed, and she just grabbed me all about the ears" and kissed him.

In 1937 Palmer graduated from high school in Alabama and went with his father to Alcorn A&M in the Mississippi Delta. Why Simon left Alabama A&M is not clear, nor do we know why he quit the Alcorn job before starting it. Zeona had gone with the other children to Elizabeth City College in North Carolina, and Simon followed her there. Palmer stayed at Alcorn for his freshman year. He liked being on his own, living in a dormitory, and being free of Simon and Zeona's supervision. He was water boy on the football team but a mediocre student who failed French. He was interested in girls, but he was young and looked it. Slight of frame, he had reached his full height of five feet, seven inches.

In 1938 Palmer joined his family at Elizabeth City College, where he again did poorly in his studies. Simon had high expectations for his children's education: he wanted each of them to earn a bachelor's degree, then graduate degrees, and he hoped that they would also become college professors. But Palmer "didn't have any ambition to be a teacher," he said later. "I was for three weeks going to be an aviator and then the next week I was going to be something else." Writing and journalism never occurred to him as a career. "We just didn't have writing in our immediate world. There were no role models." When Palmer's performance in school fell short of his father's expectations, Simon spanked the boy. Still only eighteen years old, Palmer agreed with his father that he would benefit from time in the military, after which he might have the maturity to do better in higher education. The military would also give him another chance to be on his own. Palmer liked the uniforms of the Coast Guard, and in 1939 Simon oversaw Palmer's enlistment for three years. Thus began an entirely new phase of his life—as a cook.

2

THE COOK WHO WRITES

P ALMER'S FIRST SHIP WAS THE CUTTER *MENDOTA*, A patrol boat out of Norfolk, Virginia, and on his first voyage, to Bermuda, he got "sicker than hell." The Coast Guard's long history of skilled black service had, in the decades leading up to World War II, devolved into a near-perfect caste system. Virtually every black man in the Coast Guard was either a steward or a mess boy. At any one time, there were between six and ten black seamen on the *Mendota*. Filipinos made up the rest of the mess staff. Every day the mess boys shined shoes and brass, cleaned staterooms, made the officers' bunks, and scrubbed and waxed the wardroom floor. Then they showered quickly, dressed in their white jackets, set the dining table with china and silver, and served the officers' dinner. "A mess-boy was the lowliest of creatures," Palmer later said. "We were domestics." The system was unfair, but Palmer "didn't see it was unfair then because that was the way things were outside [of the military] at the time." Some mess staff thought their jobs were better than those on deck. "You ate well, you were clean, you were kind of protected, shielded," Palmer later said. Roy Byrd, one of Palmer's black shipmates, who had grown up in poverty and racism in Georgia, said that life in the Coast Guard was the best he had known. To be sure, there was discrimination, but there were three square meals every day and opportunities for further education. "We found a home in the military. . . . We just did what we were told," Byrd said.[1]

The *Mendota* patrolled the coast from New Jersey to North Carolina. The crew constantly performed drills—collision, fire, man-overboard maneuvers. But it was not all work: seamen played chess and pinochle and watched movies many nights. The greatest excitement of Palmer's time in the Coast Guard was the rescue of German sailors whose cargo ship had broken up near Cape Hatteras, North Carolina. The *Mendota* recovered the bodies of several dead seamen.[2]

Palmer liked the military. "I was on my own," he said later, which did "a great deal for my self-image." In the Coast Guard, there were still people telling him what to do, but it was not like being ordered around at home. He was thrilled to awaken at sea and stand at the rail, looking at the ocean. He liked the smells of paint and steam and of coffee. He enjoyed talking with his shipmates. In recognition of his new condition, he began to identify himself as Alex Haley.

In Norfolk, where there were thousands of sailors, Haley joined the shore liberty forays of older mess boys and stewards. Prostitutes captured his attention in the black area of Norfolk known as "Trick Street." Women were "the number one objective of almost every red-blooded sailor that I ever knew." Haley had his first sexual encounter when he and a buddy got drunk, and the friend took him to a prostitute called Chow-Chow, telling her, "My friend here wants a piece-a-ass." Haley followed her upstairs as Ella Fitzgerald sang "A Tisket, A Tasket" on the jukebox.[3]

One fellow seaman remembered that Haley was different from the other mess boys, more educated and able to converse with white officers.[4] That ability was both a blessing and a burden for him. Lieutenant Junior Grade Murray Day, from South Carolina, noted Haley's intelligence and college training and ordered him to do the work for Day's college correspondence courses. Day was pleased when Haley won him high grades, but when he got a C in a meteorology course, Day became enraged at Haley and cursed him. Haley responded that Day was a "stupid son-of-a-bitch." At the point of blows, they both pulled back. Haley left the confrontation expecting to get court-martialed, but when the two were summoned to meet with the captain, Day said to forget it. He did not want the story to get out about a black sailor doing his work for him.[5]

When Haley developed a pen-pal relationship with a young white woman, he made the mistake of showing her picture to his mates. News of his white female friend got around the base, and he was transferred out of Norfolk to Beaufort, North Carolina, and assigned to the USCG *Pamlico,* an old cutter that patrolled the North Carolina coastline. In Beaufort he advanced from mess boy to mess attendant first class, got an increase in pay, and cooked for a small group in the officers' mess. Isaiah "Pop" Robinson, a veteran Coast Guard cook, taught him to stew meat and crumble egg yolks and parsley into the mix for appearance's sake. Officers thought they were gourmets, Pop advised; they ate with their eyes, whereas enlisted sailors ate with their bellies. Haley was helping Pop clean up the galley after lunch on the first Sunday in December 1941 when a sailor rushed in and blurted: "The radio says the Japs just bombed the hell out of us—somewhere called Pearl Harbor!" The next day Haley knew the world had changed: the crew had to rescue a Filipino shipmate from a group of red-faced, cursing white boys who were chasing him up the gangplank shouting, "Jap! Jap! Jap!"[6]

Just as the war broke out, Haley was driving around Beaufort and spotted a beautiful, light-complected young girl on the street. "She had a doe look about her," Haley recalled. "She was young and lovely and shy." He did not introduce himself then, but afterward he searched for her and finally found Nannie Branche at a dance. "Her voice was soft, with a gentle accent," Haley recalled. He pursued Nan vigorously, meeting her at a joint called The Quick Lunch, where one could get a baloney sandwich and a Pepsi for a nickel each and then play the jukebox for the same price. As the necessities of war pressed on the couple, "we were in such a state of love that the very idea of leaving her appalled me . . . and it was mutual." They were dancing to "Stardust" one night in early 1942 when Haley asked Nan to marry him. "Sure," she answered. It was, Haley recalled, "a kind of marrying time for military people."

But before they married, he took her to Henning to meet his family. By 1942, Simon had moved to Arkansas A&M in Pine Bluff, but Zeona had left him there to teach at LeMoyne College in Memphis, and after that they lived apart. When she met Nan, Zeona took the opportunity to warn her that marrying Alex would be the worst mistake she ever made. Nonetheless, the two got married in North Carolina, with Haley using his last four dollars to pay the minister. They lived together long enough for Nan to become pregnant with their first child, Lydia, born in 1943. Alex Haley had gotten married at age twenty without much sense of marital responsibility, without much experience when it came to women, and probably without a good example of a successful marriage to guide his behavior. He could not remember much about his grandparents' loving marriage. His parents' union had seen difficult circumstances, with Bertha's bad health and Simon's frequent moves. Simon's marital relations with Zeona were marked by acrimony; she freely expressed her distaste for Simon to Nannie Branche.[7]

In September 1941, in anticipation of war, Coast Guard personnel were put under the naval command. Not long afterward, when the United States entered the war, Haley was shipped to California, and in 1943 he was assigned to a supply ship, the *Murzim,* which carried shells and ammunition to the South Pacific. The crew of 250 was white except for eight blacks and eight Filipinos in the mess. The *Murzim* left San Francisco in July 1943 and arrived a month later at the island of New Caledonia, off the eastern coast of Australia. Haley was aboard the ship for eighteen months as it ferried supplies to Australia, New Zealand, New Hebrides, the Fiji Islands, the Solomon Islands, New Guinea, and the Philippines.

It was hazardous duty, though men on the *Murzim* thought little of it, Haley later said, after the first days at sea, when every whitecap sent tremors of fear about Japanese submarines. The crew was forced at one point to abandon the ship when a fire broke out on board and threatened to result in a catastrophic explosion. Indeed, that happened on the *Murzim*'s sister cargo ship, the *Mount Hood,* whose explosion in 1944 killed nearly the whole crew. Haley's big problem during the long nights at sea was not fear but loneliness and boredom. He had made the fateful decision to take a portable typewriter on his Pacific service, and he got into the nightly habit of writing letters to family, schoolmates, and even to teachers. "It wasn't uncommon at every mail call for me to receive maybe 30 or 40 letters," he recalled. Shipmates took notice.

Haley's boss on the *Murzim* was Steward First Class Percival L. Scott, a black, twenty-five-year veteran of the Coast Guard, a man whose height and breadth dwarfed Alex's. Their relationship was tense at first. Haley said that Scott was "a hostile old sea dog from the day I entered his galley." Scott once looked down at Haley with a smirk and said in his growling bass voice: "Us bein' the same race ain't gon' get you by. Damn civilians done ruint the service." Haley saw a letter that Scott wrote to his wife: "Haley he the steward second-class, supposed to be my assistant. Ben to college and can tiperite but schur is stooped. Can't boil water."

At first Haley's nighttime typing in the pantry annoyed Scott. But "after haranguing me all day," Haley later said, Scott "was irresistibly lured to watch me 'tiperite.' I'd make the portable rattle, certain it angered him that a subordinate had a skill he hadn't." But after a time, it emerged that Scott had thought of how he might deploy Haley's skill. "Looker here, boy, you ever seen the Cap'n talk letters to his yeoman?" The yeoman took shorthand, but Scotty thought that was unnecessary. "Fast as you run that thing, you might make a yeoman. I'll help you practice; I'll talk you some letters." Haley's initial response was dismissive, since "the idea of this ungrammatical clown hijacking my offtime to dictate to me was hilarious." Scott replied: "You're real wise, ain't you?" The next day Scott ran Haley ragged with orders to shine steam kettles and scrub garbage cans. Haley realized that he could resist Scott further and perhaps end up in the brig, or he could type Scott's letters. "You got the message?" Scott asked, to which a still-angry but conflict-shy Haley nodded. "You a smart boy."[8]

That night Scott followed Haley to the pantry. Scott's first letter was to an old colleague on another ship. "I typed one garbled, ungrammatical cliché after another," Haley recalled, and then Scott signed it as though "it were the Emancipation Proclamation." The next morning Scott assembled five mess boys, telling them, "Never forget, Haley give order, it's the same as me!" From then on, Haley was free of drudgery in the mess, and every night he typed letters. Eventually, Scott arranged for Haley to spend time on the bridge of the ship, where he learned to read flags and blinker lights, thus gathering war news that he reported to Scott. Then Scott would "predict" the next big happening in the war.

Scott had appointed himself officer in charge of sailors' morale. His gruff demeanor belied a tender concern about the happiness of all the men, black and white, on the *Murzim*. He got angry when a young seaman received a "Dear John" letter from a girl back home. One night he brought an upset sailor to Haley and demanded that Haley read the break-up letter. "I'm goin' to set her straight," Scott told Haley, and he began dictating a letter to the miscreant girl. "Here I set on a ship full of 500-pound bombs in a ocean full of subs and sharks. You don't even wait to see if I get back. I bet you grabbed some disanimated 4-F. It ought to be him out here doin' your fightin' and dyin'." A mortified Haley typed it all, and it would not be the last time Scott's tongue and Haley's typewriter lashed an unfaithful woman. At the next port of call, recipients of break-up letters began to get missives of repentance and pleas for forgiveness.

With Scott's sponsorship, Haley began writing and publishing the ship's newspaper, the *Seafarer*, a mimeographed sheet of news, human interest stories, and jokes. He wrote an admiring description of the work of the Seabees, the naval construction force: "Born of thousands of veterans of hundred-odd industrial trades that would net them top-flight salaries in civilian life today, the Seabees who volunteered in silent aid of their country's cause have proven their worth time and time again under conditions that, to say the least, are too often unpleasant. . . . Murzimites know them best for their cargo handling techniques, at that, they're superb."[9]

Scott watched the *Murzim*'s irregular mail calls carefully. He knew when a sailor had lost a girlfriend or was being neglected by his family. He pointed out two crewmen to Haley. "Poor guys don't never get no mail." Scott ordered Haley to get the neglected sailors listed in pen-pal ads. These crewmen suddenly began to get letters. In the *Seafarer*, Haley wrote a poignant article titled "Mail Call," which he intended not just for the crew but also for folks back home. The story's scene was set with the ship's loudspeaker booming for sailors to come to the number three hatch. Haley recounted the chatter on the stairwells up to the deck:

Geez, I sure hope I hear from Mom today . . .

I wanna hear from Jean.

I didn't get any mail the last two calls . . .

I just wanna hear from somebody, that's all.

When the mail sacks were opened, names were called. "Jones . . . Barker . . . Taylor." Men pressed forward toward the caller. Then Haley shifted his lens to the outer limits of the group, where men kept their eyes, full of hope, on the caller's lips, but "always their faces drop after each name." Everyone knew which sailors usually did not get mail, and when one of them happened to get a letter, a cheer went up. Afterward the lucky ones hung about sharing pictures received from home, but the unlucky left with their heads down. "They manage a brave smile if they see you watching . . . but if you'll notice, the smile fades quickly and maybe they'll amble over to the rail and look out over the side, at the sea and the horizon." They never looked toward land but always out at the ocean—"the direction home is in." Haley concluded with an admonition: "Now, folks back home, is he someone you should be writing to?" Keep our mail bags full, Haley promised, and "we'll do the rest." Many crewmen did, in fact, send "Mail Call" home, and it was reprinted in hundreds of stateside newspapers. For years afterward Haley was identified as the fellow who wrote "Mail Call."[10] Haley's writing in the *Seafarer* revealed that he had excellent instincts for public relations. He had a gift for describing a scene and setting a mood. Indeed, his work reflected remarkable skill for an untrained and mostly inexperienced writer.

In the meantime, Haley was secretly attempting to write magazine articles, mostly romance stories for women's confession magazines. He wrote from the perspective of a woman treated badly by a man. The stories were rejected, but Scott discovered them and put them to use in a new morale-building mission. He began dictating love letters to women whom crewmen had met in Australia, cribbing passages from Haley's stories. Soon crewmen began to receive adoring letters. Haley later wrote that after a shore leave in Brisbane, "Scotty's clients wobbled back, describing fabulous romantic triumphs. . . . Three cheers for the old sea dog rang out regularly. Scotty was fit to split with bliss."

Crewmen asked Haley to help them with letters to women at home. Soon there was a line of waiting men each night. For a dollar, he interviewed a sailor, got information about the girl's eyes and hair, and banged out a letter. If she was a blonde, Haley might write: "Your hair is like the moonlight as it reflects on the rippling waves away [*sic*] out here where I am only awaiting the next chance to see you." All the sailor had to do was copy the letter in his own hand and post it. Soon Haley no longer cooked at all. All he did was write love letters and edit the *Seafarer*. "It was a pleasant and rather startling discovery: that one could make his living doing nothing else but writing." By the time his tour of duty on the *Murzim* ended, Haley knew he wanted to be a writer. Many noteworthy Americans emerged from the war with similar intentions. A brief list of war veterans who became successful fiction writers includes Joseph Heller, J. D. Salinger, James Jones, Norman Mailer, Kurt Vonnegut, Leon Uris, James Michener, and Gore Vidal. Haley did not often use the war experience as the subject of his writing, but military service made him a writer just the same.

*   *   *

IN EARLY 1945, as the war was winding down, Haley decided to re-enlist. Staying in the Coast Guard gave him something to do rather than return to college, as his father wanted. The service had provided him with good opportunities, and it had made significant strides during the war toward fair treatment of black seamen. Haley was posted to the Coast Guard demobilization center in Brooklyn, New York. There he produced Coast Guard publications and handled public relations. In the late 1940s Haley was transferred to the Coast Guard's district headquarters in Manhattan. He still performed public relations duties, but he also served as steward to Admiral Edward H. Smith, who had founded the International Ice Patrol. "Iceberg" Smith was the most famous officer in the Coast Guard. One day when Haley was serving him coffee, the admiral said, "Haley, I just read an interesting article by a colored fellow." Haley looked at the article and replied, "Yes, sir, I wrote it."

Smith then arranged for the creation of a new Coast Guard rating for journalists. In late 1949, at age twenty-eight but now sporting a thin mustache that made him look a bit older, Haley was made a chief petty officer with the title Chief Journalist of the Coast Guard. That development was good public relations for the Coast Guard: in 1947 President Harry S. Truman had ordered the desegregation of the U.S. armed forces.[11] But Haley's success owed much to his likable manner. "All officers liked Alex," a black colleague later said, but he was also popular among his fellow blacks, who knew him as an easygoing person and looked at him as a role model.[12]

His public relations work brought Haley in touch with influential press people. A New York newspaper reported that "the amiable, industrious and ever helpful Alex Haley" was the one to call "when there's a ship in distress along the Atlantic coast, a plane down at sea, a fishing party marooned." In 1950 explosives detonated at South Amboy, New Jersey, during the loading of volatile material from ships onto railroad cars. The Coast Guard had responsibility for the work. The explosion killed thirty people, injured many more, and destroyed $20 million in property. Haley handled the Coast Guard's press relations during the catastrophe.[13]

By then, Alex and Nan lived at 419 West 129th Street in Harlem, in a nice apartment that Haley got by paying money "under the table" to a realtor. The couple's son, William, known in the family as "Fella," was born in 1945, joining Lydia, now age two. The family arrived in Harlem in the aftermath of the 1943 riot there, provoked by a policeman's shooting of a black soldier who intervened when the cop was beating a black woman. A crowd of three thousand formed around the policeman, a rumor spread that the soldier had died, and two days and nights of property destruction ensued. The event so disturbed New Yorkers and riveted local attention that Langston Hughes, Ralph Ellison, Richard Wright, and James Baldwin—all residents of Harlem at the time—recorded their observations and feelings about the violence in their writing.[14] In the eyes of whites, Harlem had become a kind of no-man's-land where crime and violence were ever present.[15] Many Harlem residents felt a keen alienation from the mainstream of American society. A government survey taken in Harlem in the spring of 1942 had discovered that most black residents believed they would be as well or better off if the Japanese won the war.[16] But racial separation and hostility marked all of New York in the 1940s. Whites expected blacks to remain apart in their enclaves in Harlem and Brooklyn, and the few integrated neighborhoods were tense places. In the predominantly white areas of Manhattan, few hotels or restaurants welcomed blacks. On the other hand, the city was home to many black intellectuals and radicals, and it was an environment where discussion of race was continuous—a place where a black writer found rich material.

Now finally reunited with Alex, Nan expected his attention to focus on her and little Lydia and Fella. But she soon felt that he neglected them, and she found his response to her feelings unsatisfactory. Alex usually avoided conflict with Nan, but during an argument in 1947, she slammed the bathroom door in front of him and he reached in and pulled her out roughly. His feelings for Nan were secondary to his professional ambitions. He came back from the war intent on being a writer. "Every night that the Lord brought I was writing," he said of that time.[17]

Simon still wanted Alex to go to college. "Improve your education" was his constant admonition. Now almost thirty years old, Alex felt his father's disappointment acutely. He was the black sheep of the family. By this time, his siblings were college graduates, headed to professional careers. "It was unthinkable," he wrote later, "that his son would not go to college . . . it was in fact a disgrace. Worst of all, the first son." Simon was "always drumming into me that everybody in the family had struggled to be somebody—and what was I thinking now[?]"[18]

Service in the war, pursuit of a second career in New York, and perhaps Simon's disapproval separated Alex from his southern roots. He was busy and a long way from Henning, and he did not often return there in the 1940s or 1950s. Lydia later said that her father never took her to Henning. In 1949 Alex's beloved Grandma died, and his memorable Aunt Liz shortly followed her to the graveyard.

*   *   *

AS HE WROTE for Coast Guard publications, Haley also spent the decade between 1944 and 1954 trying to break into writing for national magazines. The 1920s and 1930s had brought the heyday of mass-circulation publications. The most prominent weekly magazines, like the *Saturday Evening Post* and *Time,* had circulations of two to three million in the 1950s, and the monthly *Reader's Digest* went to ten million addresses at that time. Many middle-class American homes subscribed to three or four magazines, and along with newspapers, they were the main portals to American news, opinion, and popular culture.[19] For freelance writers, there were two tiers of magazines to contribute to. At the top were older weeklies that published the leading fiction and nonfiction writers in the country. These included the *Saturday Evening Post, Collier's, Atlantic Monthly, Women's Home Companion,* and *Ladies Home Journal; Time, Life,* and *Look,* which were focused on news and were written mostly by full-time staff members; and *Reader's Digest,* which was known for its feel-good stories about American life *and* was unique in that its content was mostly reprinted from other magazines, though it published some original pieces by freelancers. These magazines were well illustrated and printed on glossy paper. Less prestigious were magazines called "pulps" for the rough grade of paper on which they were printed. They included the men's adventure publications *Argosy* and *True* and the women's romance magazines *Love Story, Modern Romance,* and *True Confessions.* The hundreds of pulps published in the 1930s and 1940s relied on freelancers and typically paid them a penny a word.

Haley's apprenticeship as a magazine writer was arduous. He had submitted stories to the pulp magazines in his early days in the Coast Guard with little success. At one point he papered a wall with rejection notices, reflecting years of trying. His brightest moment was when he received a postcard from an editor that read simply, "Nice try." That note was the only encouragement he had received, he said, "but it was all I needed."[20] In 1946 he sold his first story, "They Drive You Crazy," set in the Coast Guard, for $100 to a Sunday newspaper supplement, *This Week*. The editors rewrote the story, but Halcy got a byline.

Robert Monroe, his Coast Guard commanding officer, had been a sportswriter in Florida. Haley showed Monroe some of his freelance writing, which Monroe began to edit. "I would give him a page and it would come back with chicken scratches with green ink," Haley later said. Monroe was the first person to give Haley a sense that writing was "more than slathering a lot of words over a piece of paper." While he was telling people in the Coast Guard that Haley had real promise, he would say to Alex, "In five years you might learn to write a good sentence." When Haley shared his many rejection slips, Monroe asked, "What the hell did you expect?" But Haley knew that the gruff exterior covered a kind heart. The two became good friends.

Haley's Coast Guard work put him in touch with writers who suggested magazine opportunities. Glenn D. Kittler, a freelance journalist, told him that *Coronet,* a general-interest, digest-sized monthly that featured stories about and by celebrities, was buying one-page historical vignettes. Starting in 1952 Haley wrote several of these for *Coronet* and was paid $100 if they ran under his name, $125 if under the name of some celebrity. Since the early 1920s *Time* magazine had advanced the nation's preoccupation with personal fame through its cover portraits, and its sister publication, *Life*, devoted many of its slick, large-format pages to profiles of entertainment, sports, and political figures. *Reader's Digest* reprinted articles on celebrities and created a variation on the celebrity theme with its feature "My Most Unforgettable Character." Editors presumed that Americans viewed society through the lens of the individual profile.

By 1954 Haley felt that he was making headway. Now he wanted to explore more serious social issues. He was already familiar with the work of Richard Wright, and if he had not yet read Ralph Ellison's *Invisible Man* and James Baldwin's essays, he would do so shortly. Much of the best writing by African Americans was autobiographical, whether fiction or nonfiction. Alex had lived his boyhood immersed in his own family history. If his own story could not match the degradation of Wright's Mississippi background or the religious tension of Baldwin's Harlem upbringing or the psychological tortures endured by Ellison's Invisible Man, Alex had acquired in Henning a rich and original story.

In 1951 he began to imagine a story he entitled "The Lord and Little David." He set it near Vicksburg, Mississippi, during the summer of 1926, in a community that was about half white and half black. The plot centered on the relationship between two twelve-year-olds, David, white, and George, black. Haley wrote that "there was no thought of any race 'problem'" in a community that "ran quite smoothly, all sharing the bond of being poor and living for cotton, both facts as accepted as the seasons."[21] In 1952 he submitted "The Lord and Little David" to the *Saturday Evening Post*. The *Post*'s editors thought Haley's dialogue was good, but they were not sure whether the characters were white or black, nor could they quite follow the plot, which centered on a white church excursion. A while later, Haley sent the manuscript to a "literary consultant," Maryse Rutledge, who confirmed the *Post*'s critique. "It runs off in too many directions and is what I would call too busy," Rutledge said, "confusing to the reader because, although you have sensitive feel of your characters, the story itself seems to get lost." Haley worked hard on his craft. He took twenty-one pages of notes from Maren Elwood's widely used instructional guide *Characters Make Your Story*. And he now embraced autobiographical subjects for his main writing efforts, never to let them go.[22]

* * *

IN 1954 race relations in the United States were changing significantly. This was the year of *Brown v. Board of Education,* in which the U.S. Supreme Court turned American jurisprudence firmly against segregation. The next year the Montgomery bus boycott initiated a direct-action movement against segregation that continued into the mid-1960s. The civil rights movement would create new opportunities for black journalists of Haley's generation. Carl Rowan, another Tennesseean and a navy veteran, covered the movement for the *Minneapolis Tribune* and later the *Chicago Sun-Times.* James Hicks, a veteran of the South Pacific theater, edited the *New York Amsterdam News* and also covered the trial of Emmett Till's killers in 1955 and the Little Rock school crisis in 1957. Lerone Bennett, a Mississippi native, edited *Ebony* and commented extensively on civil rights activism through the 1950s and 1960s. Louis Lomax from Georgia wrote widely about activism and then became the country's first black television reporter.

African American life was covered by John H. Johnson's three magazines: *Negro Digest,* first published in 1942; *Ebony,* begun in 1945; and *Jet,* launched in 1951. A black version of *Life, Ebony* focused on black celebrities and on civil rights activities. *Jet,* a weekly digest-sized newsmagazine in the style of *Time* and *Newsweek,* became for many African Americans the authoritative source for news about civil rights protests and the lives of famous African Americans. Johnson believed that his magazines delivered the message that blacks "were going places we had never been before and doing things we'd never done before" and that his publications had a larger social impact: "You have to change images before you can change acts and institutions."[23]

Though he never wrote for Johnson's publications, Haley in 1954 started to write articles that challenged the negative images white

Americans held about African Americans. Appearing first in the *Christian Science Monitor* and then in *Reader's Digest* was his article entitled "The Harlem Nobody Knows." Haley cast Harlem as a place that defied its reputation as a "sinkhole" of capitalism. He predicated his story on the Cold War assumption that foreigners believed that the largest obstacle to the United States' influence among "the colored races who comprise two-thirds of the world's population is discrimination against the American Negro, seemingly typified by this over-crowded, dilapidated area." To counter the image of black degradation in Harlem, Haley emphasized that the area was filled with businesses run by blacks who had overcome the problems caused by the Great Depression and the 1943 riot. "What we need is a crusade of public relations," one man told Haley. "Harlem's biggest trouble now is that in too many minds the Negro remains a stereotype."

In 1955 Haley published a piece in *Atlantic Monthly* recalling his Aunt Liz. The story is a slice of life with a building plot—the expectation in Henning that the proud and independent Elizabeth Murray had a lot of money and would contribute it to some community cause. Haley displayed a talent for description, as in the case of a service at the Colored Methodist Episcopal Church: "Both the Senior and Junior Choirs sang with inspiration. Then the preacher gave the devil such a beating round the stump that Brother Dandridge's wooden leg was going fortissimo in general bedlam, Sister Scrap Scott shrieked three times in high C and fainted right in the choir stand, and Brother Rich Harrell leaped clear over the rostrum railing to kiss the preacher's hand." Haley wrote in Negro dialect, even though its use was then being condemned for pandering to white racism. He thus took an idiom used to mock black people and made it one that celebrated them. Haley believed it brought authenticity to his writing.

Haley's publishing success undermined the popularity of the man known in the Coast Guard as "the cook who writes." Some officers insisted that "no man can serve two masters," and Haley sought a transfer. He was dispatched to Coast Guard headquarters in San Francisco. Though it meant leaving the center of American publishing, Haley was relieved to get away from New York. "You can't be around people who are perceiving you negatively for too long."

Haley was excited about the journey across the country at a time when such trips were glamorized as the modern American family's ideal excursion. But his years in New York had insulated him from the indignities of the race segregation that still existed. The Haleys' drive to San Francisco was a journey through the humiliations that remained for African Americans in the mid-1950s. They faced constant denial of rooms at motels that displayed "Vacancy" signs. Haley began wearing his Coast Guard uniform to try to get better treatment. At times, the family simply slept in the car on the side of the road.

*   *   *

IN 1955 Haley assumed his duties as press officer for the Coast Guard's Twelfth District, covering activities from California to Alaska to Honolulu. The office was located on Sansome Street in San Francisco, only a few blocks from the Embarcadero, Chinatown, and the North Beach entertainment and arts district. The Coast Guard provided integrated housing for him and his family in the Presidio, the old military barracks, also on the north shore near the Golden Gate Bridge. He performed the same public relations duties there as in New York, and his boss, John B. Mahan, recalled that Haley was the perfect public relations professional, skilled at every task.[24] In October 1956 a Pan-Am flight attempting to circumnavigate the globe ditched in the Pacific, its passengers and crew rescued by the Coast Guard. By the time the survivors were brought to San Francisco, the crash and rescue had become the subject of intense media attention, which Haley managed masterfully, dealing with *Life* magazine and the Art Linkletter television show.[25]

San Francisco then offered a more open racial environment, one far more relaxed than New York. It was a "be yourself, do your thing town," Haley later said admiringly. The city had become home to the "Beats," the movement of avant-garde poets and writers led by Allen Ginsberg and Jack Kerouac in the 1950s. They were keenly interested in ethnic cultures, especially those of Asians and blacks, more than in the mainstream traditions that had until then dominated American letters. The Beats lived public lives in the coffee shops, nightclubs, and bookstores of San Francisco's North Beach.

Early in Haley's time there, a group of Coast Guard public relations men went to Enrico Banducci's famous outdoor café, the Hungry i in North Beach, and one of Haley's colleagues recognized Barnaby Conrad seated nearby. A writer and San Francisco celebrity, Conrad had published *Matador* (1952), a fictionalized biography of Spain's most famous bullfighter. After *Matador* sold three million copies, Conrad wrote other books and articles for *Collier's, Reader's Digest, Look,* and *Saturday Review.* In 1953 he had opened a nightclub in the Barbary Coast section of North Beach called El Matador, which immediately became the place to be seen in San Francisco. Unprompted, Haley's colleague approached Conrad and said that the author needed to meet a fellow writer named Alex Haley. Conrad draped his arm around Alex's shoulder and insisted that he come to El Matador. Haley went there often and saw many famous actors and musicians, but the celebrities who made the greatest impression were the writers. John Steinbeck, Truman Capote, William Saroyan, and Budd Schulberg came through. Conrad made a special effort to have Haley spend time with Schulberg, who became Alex's lifelong friend. Haley later said that Conrad was no "liberal," meaning that he treated him as he did other friends, without the false warmth that some whites showed blacks to display a progressive attitude. Conrad had taught writing, knew the writing market, and edited Alex's work. He later said Haley was "a good storyteller, worked hard at writing every day, read everything about writing and never gave up." Haley spent hours chatting with other writers. "It was the first time I had been in a community of selling writers."[26]

The celebrities most appreciated at El Matador were raconteurs, and Conrad was an accomplished storyteller. Haley had grown up amid good storytellers, and now his appreciation of the art was reinforced. Conrad was also a model for how to act as a celebrity and how to behave toward them. A friend wrote that Conrad made it "his business and pleasure to chat up the celebrity at hand," and soon they went "off into the night, arm in arm, to begin a lifelong friendship." The same could be said of Alex Haley. One of the keys to Haley's success as a writer and celebrity in his own right was his affability. He was pleasant company, quick to offer an entertaining yarn. He was comfortable with whites at a time when blacks and whites had relatively few interactions.

But home life was a different matter. Nan remembered that Alex would come home from work, have dinner, and leave again, saying that he was going to back to his Coast Guard office to work on his writing. He was not always working. His San Francisco friends like Barnaby Conrad knew that Haley saw other women and that he was a self-confessed "womanizer." Haley's good friend C. Eric Lincoln later told an interviewer that he and Haley had caroused looking for women during these years. One evening Nan began hemorrhaging, called Haley's office, and was given a different telephone number to call. The woman who answered called Alex to the phone, but Nan hung up. Her daughter called an ambulance. In 1958 Nan, Lydia, and Fella—the children were now teenagers—went back to her home in North Carolina for a visit, and once there, Nan decided to stay. The marriage was almost over.[27]

The San Francisco experience gave Haley confidence that he belonged in a community of writers, but he did not publish much in those years. That his writing had stalled may have fueled his desire to return to New York when he retired from the Coast Guard after twenty years' service. In 1959, at age thirty-eight, he was going to create his own fame as a writer.

3

PEOPLE ON THE WAY UP

NAN HALEY OFTEN TOLD HER HUSBAND, "YOU'RE married to your typewriter." In June 1959 she gave him an ultimatum. "She banged her hand on the kitchen table and said, 'It's me or that typewriter,'" he recalled. "I thought, 'I wish you hadn't phrased it that way.'" They both moved back to New York in the summer of 1959 but separated for good. Nan settled in Harlem, and Alex moved to a one-room basement studio apartment on Grove Street in Greenwich Village. Maintaining two residences and living on a relatively meager military pension meant that Nan and Alex faced hard financial times. He had not wanted her to work when the children were small. But "when Alex left me, I knew I had to work," she said later. "I had to take care [of] and provide for my children. Because I knew that I could never depend on him." By then she was angry at his financial irresponsibility. "It was always 'when my ship comes in and when things get better, I'm going to do this for you, I'm going to do that for you.' But he never did. . . . He did not do what he was supposed to do." Years later, Nan bemoaned Alex's failings as a husband. "I don't think he ever let me get close to him. Only to cook, wash, have sex, that's about it. . . . He always was secretive." Haley never spoke speak critically of Nan and claimed that they "just sort of drifted apart."[1]

Haley maintained contact with his children but made little time for them. His son, Fella, lived with him for a while in the Village after the teenager was accused of having sex with a minor girl in Harlem in 1962. The disposition of the charge is not clear. Fella entered the army in the mid-1960s and served with the 101st Airborne Division as a paratrooper in Vietnam.[2]

Money problems plagued Haley from his first days out of the Coast Guard. He pursued freelance writing jobs far and wide, but they did not come quickly. "I was literally hanging on by my fingernails, trying to make it as a magazine writer," he remembered. One fellow Coast Guard veteran noted that it was hard for some men to adjust to fending entirely for themselves, saying, "Alex lost control of his finances." A friend told him about a civil service job as a "public information officer," for which Haley was well qualified. The friend, to whom Haley owed money, promised that he could get Haley the job if he agreed to take it immediately. Haley finally said that he wanted to "keep on trying to make it [with] writing." At that point his Greenwich Village cupboard held only two cans of sardines and his pocket only eighteen cents, which he spent on a head of cabbage. He thought, "There's nowhere to go but up."[3]

Haley longed for the writing community to which Barnaby Conrad had introduced him in San Francisco. He wrote to several writers then living in Greenwich Village. He heard only from James Baldwin. "Jimmy, bless him . . . perceived, that I was really crying for a shoulder to lean on." Baldwin walked into Haley's basement apartment, "as if we were old buddies and writing peers, and sat down, cross-legged on the little hassock I had, and talked to me for an hour . . . about nothing in particular, and not that much about writing. But he said to me, in his actions, that he regarded me as a peer. And that did more for me than he could ever know." The two became good friends.[4]

More companionship came from George Sims, a boyhood friend from Henning, a tall, light-skinned man married to an Irish woman at a time when interracial marriages were uncommon. Sims had settled in Greenwich Village and worked as a janitor and bank messenger. He had arranged for Haley to live in the basement apartment of his building. Sims had an avid curiosity about black history that he satisfied by spending nights and weekends at the New York Public Library. He reputedly had a photographic memory. In the early 1960s Sims and Haley spent many late evenings wandering about Greenwich Village. They chatted about Henning, the people they knew there, and the meaning of the lives they had observed. The time spent with Sims in Greenwich Village nurtured Alex's autobiographical instincts. The two men were close companions for the next thirty years, and Sims became Haley's research assistant.

Haley wrote in his diary on New Year's Day 1962 that he was hard at work writing, pausing only a few minutes to have a drink with the Simses before recording his resolutions for the future: "This year, I hope, will see a number of aspirations accomplished, chief among them my first book—at this writing, the book on Henning, and that it will prove a resounding success." This is the first recorded mention of his conscious intention to write about his background.[5]

Years later he wrote an unpublished autobiographical novel in the third person, set during these years in New York. One scene depicted Alex visiting Nan at her job as a waitress. In the novel she works because she enjoys it, not because she has to, and "Alex wishes she wouldn't work." He hands her his pension check, and Nan pushes it back to him. She senses that something is disturbing him but knows that she "probably can't get close to it." She asks about his writing, and "he says a little too much about how well it's going." He will have to "install a bigger mailbox to handle all the checks!" The next scene describes his mailbox as overflowing with rejected manuscripts and unpaid bills. "He hasn't had a sale in too long. . . . turned down by all the best magazines. What's wrong?" George Sims offers to get Haley a job as a messenger at the bank where he works. In the next scene, "Alex is in a messenger's uniform which is too small in some places and too big in others." His white boss is overbearing and condescending, and on the job, Haley is "shunted aside, ignored, treated as though he were a mindless robot." He feels like Ralph Ellison's Invisible Man: "Nothing. Nobody."[6]

He returns home to his basement cell, like the one the Invisible Man occupies, to find his father waiting for him in the hall. Simon Haley looks at the messenger's uniform and asks what Alex has done to himself. "Three sons I've got . . . a lawyer, an architect—and a messenger boy." Simon has let Alex find his own way, but now Simon thinks that was a mistake, and he is "ready to move back into the vacuum." His response to Alex's poor achievement is the same as always: college. Alex refuses, because he is going to be a writer. He tries to make peace with Simon, but his father is bitterly disappointed in him. "And what next?" Simon asks. "A janitor? A shoe-shine?" The next day on the job, Haley lashes out at white women who refuse to acknowledge his presence. "Look at me! I'm somebody, you hear? I'm a person. Look at me!" He angrily quits the messenger job.

Haley's autobiographical novel revealed his fear of failure during his first years after leaving the Coast Guard. His commitment to writing did in fact falter amid his financial struggles. He applied for corporate public relations jobs and included his photograph with his resume, so there would be no awkwardness at an interview. Despite excellent qualifications, he never got an interview. He did work briefly as a bank messenger. Whether or not the interaction with Simon in the novel was based on a real event, it showed his hurt at his father's disappointment in him. It would have been uncharacteristic of Haley to lash out at the white women ignoring him, but the scene he created suggested the kind of anger found in the writing of

Wright, Ellison, and Baldwin. Haley was at work on imagining a narrative of his life that dwelt on the obstacles he had overcome.

In the early 1960s Haley pursued magazine assignments intensively. He queried various magazines about a wide range of story ideas and was forced to develop a thick skin. He renewed connections to *Coronet, Reader's Digest,* and the *Saturday Evening Post.* He discussed story ideas with the editors of the men's pulp magazine *Climax* and talked about possible celebrity pieces for Hugh Hefner's *Show Business Illustrated.* He developed a profile of the comedian Phyllis Diller, whom he had known in San Francisco, where she began her career; he eventually sold the piece to the *Saturday Evening Post.*[7] Haley then began to focus on profiles of black celebrities. He developed a list of what he called "People on the Way Up." He developed stories on Lena Horne, Leontyne Price, Dick Gregory, Leadbelly, Floyd Patterson, and the Olympian Ralph Boston. None of these articles, together representing many months of work in 1960 and 1961, was published. Freelance writing was often a demoralizing pursuit.

In 1962, he did place a long piece on the theme of black achievement in *Cosmopolitan* magazine, at that point still a literary and arts publication. Haley wrote a history of black contributions to American musical culture that touched on the evolution of African traditions through spirituals, minstrels, blues, and jazz, culminating in musical theater in the mid-twentieth century. He connected dozens of black artists to one or another of the musical genres and ended on a triumphal note: "It will be an exciting future indeed when Negro contributions in other fields equal those made in the musical life of America."[8]

Haley began to connect with entertainment celebrities in New York. In February 1961 he attended a performance of *Il Trovatore* with the singer and actress Lena Horne; her husband, Lennie Hayton, a white composer of big band music and Hollywood musical scores, including "Singin' in the Rain"; and the sociologist and social reformer Jeanne Noble, who had recently become a professor at New

York University. Afterward, he had dinner with them at Sardi's, a theater district restaurant. Horne and Noble were members of the black sorority Delta Sigma Theta, and both were involved in civil rights activism. Haley was making contacts with an entertainment elite that might help him on the way up as a writer. But he may also have been having a romance with Noble, a thirty-four-year-old Georgia native. Like Nan, she was a pretty, light-skinned woman who went on to a distinguished career in academics and public service. In his autobiographical novel, Haley describes a relationship he had had with a young, black, and ambitious woman he called "Gwen Richards." He finally breaks off their relationship because he is more committed to his writing than he is to Gwen.[9]

Haley's most successful connection in the world of magazine writing proved to be with *Reader's Digest.* In the early 1920s, DeWitt Wallace had recognized that there was a rapidly expanding middle-brow audience for periodical literature and that there were far too many magazines published for the average person to keep up with all the good journalism. Wallace liked articles that were uplifting, that revealed the tenacity of the human spirit and people's capacity to help others. It may have been at *Reader's Digest* that Haley acquired the maxim he often offered: "Find something good and praise it." In 1960 and 1961 Haley developed a number of stories for the *Digest,* most of them profiles of celebrities, black and white. His most noteworthy article was an adoring piece on Percival Scott, his boss on the *Murzim.* Still, fewer than half the stories he wrote for *Reader's Digest* were published.

The stories that did appear in print were all profiles of talented African Americans who had overcome great obstacles and remained humble, unchanged by great success. Haley wrote about two gold medal–winning Olympians from poor black families, the high jumper John Thomas and the sprinter Wilma Rudolph. Thomas had suffered a terrible injury to his leg but recovered and returned to the top of the field. Haley quoted Thomas's white coach about him: "A kid so nice you'd be proud if he was your own." Wilma Rudolph had been born with what everyone believed were hopelessly crippled legs—everyone except her mother, who was determined that her twentieth child would walk. At great sacrifice, she got her daughter the therapy that enabled her finally to walk at age eight, and by eighteen, Wilma had grown to be a gazelle-like sprinter. She won three gold medals at the Rome Olympics in 1960 and then returned to her small Tennessee hometown and prepared to be an elementary school teacher. Haley's profile of Mahalia Jackson, "She Makes a Joyful Noise," tells of the singer's rise from humble beginnings in New Orleans, where her gift of a powerful soprano voice was spotted early. Jackson often turned down lucrative deals that would have meant switching from gospel music to blues and jazz. Haley placed her in the context of black Christianity and portrayed her loyalty to gospel music as her chief virtue.[10]

In 1963 Haley turned to his family experiences in "The Man Who Wouldn't Quit." Here he told the story of his brother George's struggle as one of the first blacks to enter the University of Arkansas law school in the early 1950s. George was a model young man, a war veteran and an outstanding college student, the academic star of the Haley family. Simon Haley, now teaching in Arkansas, had persuaded George to be a pioneer of desegregation. George suffered abuse from other students and isolation from the law school community, and in his first year he wanted to quit. But he endured the hardships, finally made a white friend, Miller Williams, and ended his legal education on the school's law review. At the end of his piece, Haley announced proudly that George was a successful lawyer and a rising star in Republican politics in Kansas—and revealed that George was his brother.

This story ran in spite of the angry opposition of Miller Williams, who in 1963 was on faculty in the English Department at Louisiana State University, having forsaken law for poetry. Williams feared the possible impact that public exposure of his support for racial integration in Arkansas would have on him and his family, given the volatile racial atmosphere of Louisiana. He had originally been asked to collaborate with Haley on the article, but after traveling to Kansas City to interview George, Williams was cut out of the process, he said, without compensation. Alex, he said, nonetheless promised that Williams would have a chance to review anything said by or about him before it went into print. But Williams said that he was not given that chance and that George ignored his pleas for help. After threatening Alex Haley and *Reader's Digest* with a lawsuit, he was sent galley proofs for the article, which was due out in days. Miller then informed Alex that one anecdote in the story was fabricated: "I get the impression that your attitude has been, 'What does it matter, so long as I got the information I needed, and so long as I get me a good story?'" He demanded that Haley "get rid of my name and my teaching at L.S.U." Furthermore, "the remarks attributed clearly to me are self-disparaging, they are inane, and they are false." But the story ran with Williams's name, his affiliation with Louisiana State, the allegedly false anecdote, and a quote attributed to Miller asking George to be the godfather of his daughter Lucinda. Alex Haley wrote to the *Reader's Digest* legal department that Williams was upset that he had been cut out of a byline and that his need for money could explain "his seeming anxiety to file some potentially lucrative suit."[11]

There was a postscript to this situation: in a few years, Miller and Lucinda Williams got away from Louisiana unharmed and settled at the University of Arkansas, where he established a university press and became a nationally renowned poet. Lucinda became a celebrated singer and songwriter, nominated fifteen times for Grammy Awards and winning three. Bill Clinton asked Miller Williams to read his poem "Of History and Hope" at the 1997 presidential inauguration. And in 1998 Clinton appointed the staunchly Republican George Haley ambassador to the Gambia.

By 1962 Haley's freelance career was taking off. His work benefited from extensive critiques by *Reader's Digest* editors, especially a senior editor, Charles Ferguson. In 1963 the *Digest* arranged to pay Haley a monthly stipend of $300 and to cover his travel expenses as he scouted for stories. It was an unusual—and fortunate—arrangement for a freelance writer. The *Digest* paid him $12,000 in 1963. He wrote ten articles, of which the editors bought only two, for $4,000 each. He began to place stories with other magazines too. "I got to the point I'd sell one in every five and then gradually one in every four. Eventually I became able to sell just about whatever I wrote, particularly after I began to be assigned stories by editors who had. . . . acquired a certain amount of confidence that I could execute an assignment. I could make a month's pay with one article."[12]

*   *   *

HALEY'S RISE as a freelance writer was linked in part to the growing notoriety of the Nation of Islam (NOI). He had first heard of the Nation when a black musician he knew in San Francisco went home to Detroit, was converted to the sect, and returned saying, "The white man is the devil." In July 1959, about the time Haley got back to New York, Mike Wallace produced a sensationalist depiction of the group, *The Hate That Hate Produced*, for a local commercial New York station. Widely viewed, the report introduced the Nation to a white population previously unaware of it. The Nation had mosques in fifty American cities, and Wallace showed that some blacks had embraced the "flagrant doctrine of black supremacy." Elijah Muhammad, known by his followers as "the Messenger" of Allah, led the Nation. Muhammad declared that blacks were not originally or naturally Christians. Among the sensational statements Wallace highlighted was the Messenger's promise "to give the call" for destruction of the white man by 1970. *The Hate That Hate Produced* also brought before the camera Malcolm X, a handsome, red-headed, copper-skinned man whose speeches riveted listeners, whether they agreed with him or not. Malcolm was brilliant at the podium and on television. His crackling baritone voice and his razor-edged opinions about white society's hypocrisies made for irresistible listening. In 1958 an FBI informant reported that Malcolm was an "expert organizer and an untiring worker" whose hatred for whites was not likely to "erupt in violence as he is much too clever and intelligent for that."[13]

Malcolm recounted the Nation's creation story: the serpent in the garden with Adam and Eve was Yacub, a white man, from whom the pale races of men evolved. African civilization was originally superior to European civilization, and only through millennia of oppression had people been led to believe otherwise. Blacks were not really in favor of integration, Malcolm insisted, because it polluted black interests. The NAACP was a "black body with white head." Malcolm was most compelling when he justified the Nation's hatred of "the white devil." Whites' characterization of members of the Nation as subversive was outrageous, he said: "Here is a man who has raped your mother and hung your father on his tree, is he subversive? Here is a man who robbed you of all knowledge of your nation and your religion and is he subversive?"[14]

Malcolm had moved to Harlem in 1954 and transformed NOI Mosque No. 7 into an exciting place with a growing membership. Harlem residents seemed irresistibly drawn to him. His duties soon included expanding the Nation along the East Coast, which he did with astonishing success. He later claimed that the national membership of the Nation was only about four hundred when he began preaching but numbered in the tens of thousands by 1959. Malcolm and the Nation's message of strict personal conduct appealed to a growing number of residents of dangerous black ghettos.[15]

Haley interested *Reader's Digest* in a piece on the Nation, and he wrote Malcolm several letters that went unanswered. Finally he went to the Muslim restaurant in Harlem that served as Malcolm's office. Haley showed Malcolm a letter from *Reader's Digest* requesting a story on the Nation. "You're a tool—you're a white man's tool," Malcolm responded, but he kept talking to Haley. Haley responded that he intended to write an objective piece, to which Malcolm replied that a white man's promise was worthless but that he would consider cooperating. Later Malcolm said that Haley would need the permission of Elijah Muhammad. Haley went to Chicago and had dinner with the Messenger. Nothing was said about the article, but when Haley returned to New York, Malcolm agreed to help. Haley began attending Mosque No. 7 in Harlem, and he traveled to NOI temples in several other cities. His easygoing demeanor and enthusiasm for research allayed at least some of the natural suspicions among the NOI men.[16]

Malcolm introduced Haley to Louis Lomax, the black television reporter who had collaborated with Mike Wallace. Lomax personally rejected the NOI's separatism but believed that 80 percent of blacks "vibrate sympathetically" with its open hatred of whites. Haley's friend James Baldwin held a sympathetic view of the Nation. In 1961 Baldwin wrote that "the Muslim movement has all the evidence on its side. . . . This is the great power a Muslim speaker has over his audience. His listeners have not heard the truth about their daily lives honored by anyone else. Almost all others, black or white, prefer to soften the truth, and point to a new day which is coming for America." In a 1962 *New Yorker* article, later published as the longer of the two essays in his celebrated book *The Fire Next Time,* Baldwin wrote that Elijah Muhammad had done "what generations of welfare workers and committees and resolutions and reports and housing projects and playgrounds have failed to do: to heal and redeem drunkards and junkies, to convert people who have come out of prison and to keep them out, to make men chaste and women virtuous, and to invest both the male and the female with a pride and a serenity that hang about them like an unfailing light."[17]

Probably the greatest influence on Haley's understanding of the Nation came from C. Eric Lincoln. Haley and Lincoln were about the same age, had grown up in Alabama at the same time, and both had backgrounds in the AME church. They spent time together in Greenwich Village while Lincoln finished his dissertation, the first scholarly treatment of the Nation, *Black Muslims in America,* published in 1961. Lincoln placed the NOI within the historical context of black nationalism. Lincoln began with William Edward Burghardt Du Bois, who in 1903 published *The Souls of Black Folk.* Du Bois argued for the existence of an Afro-American folk spirit, writing that "the Negro is a sort of seventh son, born with a veil, and gifted with second-sight in this American world. . . . Negro blood has a message for the world." Du Bois defined black nationalism as including a sense of alienation from white power and dominant white values. He emphasized blacks' common history—a glorious African past, the horrors of slavery, the disappointments of emancipation—and the myths that blacks built on them. Black nationalism included the celebration of African American culture and the belief that blacks' spirit as a people arose from their cultural distinctiveness. For Du Bois, whites, in essence, were selfish and violent, and blacks in their essence were gifted with higher sensitivity, a distinctive humaneness that whites lacked.[18]

Lincoln noted that most older members of the Nation of Islam shared a background in Marcus Garvey's Universal Negro Improvement Association (UNIA), which had attracted millions of American members in the 1920s. Garvey insisted the United States was far too racist and undemocratic to ever include blacks as equals, and he cited the mistreatment of blacks during and after World War I to justify a plan for blacks' wholesale migration to Africa. Few of Garvey's followers actually intended to emigrate, but all responded to the movement's promotion of race pride. Unlike the NOI in its condemnation of Christianity, Garvey reconciled evangelical Christianity with black nationalism by portraying God and Jesus as black. It worked: many of the UNIA's most devoted organizers were Christian ministers, including Malcolm's own father. Garvey's influence among blacks raised the suspicions of the U.S. government, which believed rumors of armed Garveyites preparing for race war. In 1925 Garvey was convicted of mail fraud, sent to prison for several years, and then deported. The UNIA went into decline, but some of its supporters joined the Nation of Islam when it emerged in Detroit in the 1930s.

"Mr. Muhammad Speaks" appeared in *Reader's Digest* in March 1960. The article began with a tone similar to that of *The Hate That Hate Produced*. Blacks across America, the piece noted, were talking about Elijah Muhammad and the Nation, which Haley described as a "vitriolically anti-white, anti-Christian cult that preaches black superiority." The Nation was building businesses and schools intended to end black dependency on whites and to help blacks in cities find "a new way of life—a militant and arrogant black unity." He quoted Malcolm: "When I was a Christian, I was a criminal. I was only doing what the white man taught me." This rejection of white society, Haley wrote, arose from discrimination against blacks, and his article turned more sympathetic to the Nation. He noted: "Old friends of new Muslims are astounded at the incredible changes of personality which take place as converts swap lifelong habits for new spartan standards." He quoted black sources who understood the Nation's growth as a response to bad social conditions for blacks. He concluded that it was "important for Christianity and democracy to help remove the Negroes' honest grievances and thus eliminate the appeal of such a potent racist cult."[19]

* * *

IN 1961 Haley made a connection with a new magazine, *Show Business Illustrated*, published by Hugh Hefner and the *Playboy* enterprise. Haley developed a story about Miles Davis, the brilliant jazz trumpeter, a man known for his hostility to the media and his racial edginess. Davis routinely refused to talk to white journalists, but he gave the affable black journalist an interview. Before the article could be published, however, *Show Business Illustrated* folded. A. C. Spectorsky, Hefner's editorial director, was transforming *Playboy* from a girlie magazine into a publication with serious literary content and social criticism, including a concern for American race relations. Hefner was sympathetic to civil rights activism. He forced the desegregation of Playboy clubs in southern cities, and he and Spectorsky instilled a pro–civil rights message in the magazine. In July 1962 *Playboy* ran a long article, "Through the Racial Looking Glass," by Nat Hentoff, the jazz critic for the *Village Voice* and a writer in close touch with black intellectuals and artists, that explored black anger. Hentoff quoted the jazz trumpeter Dizzy Gillespie as telling a group of white jazzmen, "You people had better just lie down and die. You've lost Africa and Asia, and now they are cutting out from white power everywhere. You'd better give up or learn how it feels being a minority." James Baldwin asserted for the article that "the American Negro can no longer be, and will never be again, controlled by white America's image of him." Hentoff also quoted the comedian Dick Gregory: "I'm so goddamn sick and tired of a white man telling us about us."[20]

In 1962 Spectorsky appointed Murray Fisher to develop the magazine's interview series. Fisher, tall and muscular and about thirty years old at the time, was described by Playboy colleagues as abrasive, combative, and even a bully. Fisher found Haley's unpublished piece on Miles Davis in the files of *Show Business Illustrated* and asked him to develop it into the first *Playboy* interview. Davis had liked Haley since the writer showed up at Davis's boxing gym and put on gloves to spar with him. "In a clinch I agreed with Davis that writers and reporters were a hateful, untrustworthy breed," Haley recalled. Davis laughed and later gave Haley a series of illuminating interviews. He dwelt on the perils of being a black celebrity; he believed he had been mistreated by white critics and disrespected by white audiences at his performances, and unlike most black entertainers in the past, he did not keep his resentments to himself. Davis had long rejected bookings in the South. "I ain't going to play nowhere in the South that Negroes *can't* come. But I ain't going to play nowhere in the North that Negroes *don't* come." Davis concluded by saying, "This whole prejudice mess is something you would feel so good if it could just be got rid of, like a big sore eating inside of your belly."[21]

The Miles Davis piece established Haley as a gifted interviewer. Haley's affability and his reticence about his own political and social views lent an empathetic tone to his profiles. "I like to study the person," he later said, "study what they've done, be low-key in my approach with them . . . project by my manner and my sincerity, which really has to be sincere, that I was genuinely interested in what they did and how they did it." But in the Davis interview, Haley's questions did not exhibit overt sympathy; they might have come from a polite, white skeptic.

In January 1963 the *Saturday Evening Post* published another profile of the NOI titled "Black Merchants of Hate," which Haley co-authored with Alfred Balk, a white investigative reporter on the *Post* staff. Balk and Haley presented themselves as an interracial investigating team that discovered things both "heartening" and "deeply disturbing." During their research, Balk was reporting to the FBI on his and Haley's research and getting information from the Bureau with the promise that he would not attribute it to the FBI. This was a common tactic at the Bureau in investigating organizations suspected of "un-American" activities.[22] Haley and Balk's story began with how, in 1957, Malcolm dispersed a Harlem crowd assembled to protest the beating of an NOI member. "No man should have that much power," a white policeman observed. Police in Chicago insisted that the NOI was not a mere cult but "a mass movement on a national scale." Haley and Balk described an NOI meeting of five thousand that put them in mind of the "huge meetings at which Hitler screamed his doctrines of Aryan supremacy." As quoted in the article, Elijah Muhammad declared that whites were corrupt and their civilization doomed: "Get away from them! . . . They was taught to do *evil!* They was taught to *hate* you and me! Stand up and fight the white man! . . . *We will rule!*" Haley and Balk quoted C. Eric Lincoln's characterization of NOI members as having been uneducated, unskilled, isolated from "the common values of society," "shunned by successful whites and Negroes alike," and hopeless until they heard Muhammad's prophecy of race supremacy.[23] The article delivered the message of black subversion of traditional authority, which the FBI consistently advanced about black groups, including civil rights organizations.

"Black Merchants of Hate" carried a harsher tone about the NOI than Haley's 1960 *Reader's Digest* piece. The *Post* had a history of racist fiction and edgy investigative journalism. It probably reflected the influence of Balk, and perhaps through him the anti-black views of J. Edgar Hoover and the FBI. Haley had certainly been exposed to a much more complex understanding of black anger than was reflected in the *Post* piece.

The other noteworthy difference between the *Reader's Digest* piece and the *Saturday Evening Post* article was the latter's much more extensive focus on Malcolm X. He was portrayed as the most influential Black Muslim. The media attention contributed to a growing opposition to Malcolm in the close circle around Elijah Muhammad, especially on the part of Muhammad's aide John Ali, formerly a protégé of Malcolm, and of Muhammad's daughter and son-in-law, Ethel and Raymond Sharieff. In 1960 and 1961 Muhammad had disapproved of Malcolm's meeting with Cuban leader Fidel Castro and his public criticism of President Kennedy; the Messenger discouraged any activity that invited closer scrutiny and harassment by the federal government. Muhammad downplayed his unhappiness with Malcolm when they met, but the inner circle schemed against Malcolm with Muhammad's tacit approval. At the same time, people within the sect had been whispering that Muhammad had fathered a number of children with secretaries in the organization. The gossip was true, but Malcolm tried to ignore it. He saw himself as a loyal servant of the Messenger and wanted to be seen as such by others, even as his fame as the main public representative of the NOI grew.[24]

* * *

HALEY'S POSITIVE RELATIONSHIP with Malcolm X seemed not to suffer because of "Black Merchants of Hate." When Haley asked him to do a *Playboy* interview, Malcolm and Muhammad again agreed. Spectorsky, who was Jewish, objected to the interview, probably because of the vicious anti-Semitism Malcolm expressed. Hefner overruled him, and the editors justified the interview on the grounds that "knowledge and awareness are necessary and effective antitoxins against the venom of hate." Introducing the interview, *Playboy* characterized Malcolm as Muhammad's erudite disciple, who wielded "all but absolute authority over the movement and its membership as Muhammad's business manager, trouble shooter, prime minister and heir apparent."[25] In the interview, Malcolm said there had never been a sincere white man, ever, in history. Whites had brainwashed blacks, but now blacks had seen the truth of the white devils' malevolent influence, and the white man's influence in the world was finished. Christians of all varieties were evil, especially Catholics, who produced fascist and communist dictators. Jews liked to advise the black man, he said, "but they never advise him how to solve his problem the way Jews solved their problem." Elijah Muhammad "cleans us up—morally, mentally and spiritually" from the "the mess that white men have made." Blacks should be given their own territory in the United States. Muhammad taught that it was God's intention "to put the black man back at the top of civilization, where he was in the beginning—before Adam, the white man, was created." Bourgeois Negroes pretended to be alienated from the Black Muslims, "but they're just making the white man *think* they don't go for what Mr. Muhammad is saying."

Throughout the interview, Haley challenged Malcolm's interpretations of history and motive, but the minister never backed away from the anti-white doctrines of the NOI. Malcolm insisted to Haley that *Playboy*'s editors would never print the interview as he gave it, and he was taken aback when in fact they did. Haley and Malcolm had created a seminal document of American history and a memorable expression of black alienation. The interview changed the course of both men's lives.

4

THE FEARSOME BLACK
DEMAGOGUE

IN EARLY 1963 CHARLES FERGUSON, HALEY'S EDITOR
at *Reader's Digest,* arranged for him to meet the literary agent Paul
Revere Reynolds Jr. Ferguson and Reynolds were good friends and
neighbors in the Westchester County town of Chappaqua, home of
Reader's Digest. Reynolds, tall with silver hair, in his late fifties, gave
the strong impression of a proper Yankee gentleman. Son of the first
American literary agent to represent English writers in the U.S. market, including Winston Churchill, H. G. Wells, and Arthur Conan
Doyle, Reynolds was now one of the most influential literary agents
in New York. He represented Irving Wallace, Morris West, William
Shirer, and Howard Fast and had nurtured Richard Wright's career
with sensitivity to the racial indignities that he endured. Reynolds
agreed to take on Haley as a client. Haley sent Reynolds two hundred pages of what he called "advance material" for the book he entitled "Henning, U.S.A." This was Haley's original attempt to treat
life in his Tennessee hometown as representative of race relations in

the South. Reynolds's response was not encouraging. "I've got to be pretty pessimistic about this manuscript. I'm keen about you as a writer, about your ability as a writer. But these vignettes would be very difficult for a book publisher to sell in my opinion." Haley was undaunted by the critique: "I have heard so much of the caliber of your judgment, and of the publishing field's respect for you, that I now feel as though a milestone has been achieved when my efforts at a book cause you to want to discuss it."[1]

In late April 1963 the *New York Times* ran a story titled "Assertive Spirit Stirs Negroes," written by M. S. "Mike" Handler, who had just returned to the United States from three decades of reporting on the origins and aftermath of World War II in Europe. Perhaps because he was out of the United States during the popular demonization of the Nation of Islam, Handler offered a more dispassionate evaluation of the black mood than it had received in the American media so far. Thirty years of experience in Europe had taught him that powerful forces in a struggle were frequently "buried beneath the visible surface and make themselves felt in many ways long before they burst out into the open." He believed that ideas had more power than Americans typically afforded them, and he sensed that the opinions most influencing black thinking at the moment came from "those working in the penumbra of the [civil rights] movement—'underground,' so to speak." Handler defined Black Nationalism—giving its name in the upper case—as an assertive mood represented by the Nation of Islam and in particular by Malcolm X. All segments of the black population shared some of the black nationalist anger, but only the Black Muslims renounced integration with whites. Handler called Malcolm X "the dynamic leader" of the Black Muslims and said he now overshadowed Elijah Muhammad. Malcolm articulated black anger more powerfully than anyone else. Handler gave Malcolm the last word: "You cannot integrate the Negroes and the whites without bloodshed. . . . The only peaceful way is for the Negroes and whites to separate." The story ran while Martin Luther King Jr. demonstrated in Birmingham, but his leadership of the civil rights movement was peripheral in Handler's story.[2]

The Handler story coincided with the publication of Haley's *Playboy* interview with Malcolm. A great many Americans in 1963 would believe something was true only if they read it in the *New York Times,* and now Haley had that validation. He wrote to Reynolds about the man Haley now referred to as "the fearsome black demagogue." He thought the combination of his *Playboy* interview and the *Times* article created a "tailored package to impress upon a publisher what Malcolm's signed book would offer." Haley had that day discussed with Malcolm the idea of collaborating on a book. Malcolm was happy with the responses to the *Playboy* interview and said that he had Elijah Muhammad's tentative consent for the book but Haley would have to discuss the matter with the Messenger. Haley went to Muhammad and was told, "Allah approves."

With that, Paul Reynolds made his way to the NOI restaurant for an audience with Malcolm. Reynolds recalled that Malcolm was an "erudite man" who quoted Shakespeare to him, which prompted the agent to respond, "Now will the winter of thy discontent be made into glorious summer by the writing of Haley." That's from *Richard III,* Malcolm noted. Reynolds and Malcolm chatted amiably about the book contract. Haley later shared with Reynolds Malcolm's comment that "that White Devil himself hath class." In a written agreement Malcolm and Haley set clear ground rules for the content of the book. Malcolm promised to give Haley enough time to elicit material sufficient for a hundred-thousand-word book. Nothing could appear in the book that Malcolm did not approve of, and anything Malcolm particularly wanted in it would be included. When Malcolm signed the contract, he said to Haley, "A writer is what I want, not an interpreter." Later Haley got Malcolm to give permission for him to write his own comments at the end of the book, without Malcolm's review. Haley decided not to be listed as Malcolm's co-author because he thought that would imply that he shared Malcolm's views, "when mine are almost a complete antithesis of his." The book would be by Malcolm, "as told to Alex Haley."[3]

Why did the NOI open itself to book-length scrutiny at a volatile time in American race relations? Haley was only vaguely aware that all the media attention given Malcolm had antagonized Elijah Muhammad and his inner circle. According to Manning Marable, Malcolm believed the autobiography would give him a means to reconcile with Muhammad by demonstrating in print his fealty to the Messenger. Both Malcolm and Muhammad tolerated negative interpretations of their movement for the sake of the publicity that men like Haley brought the NOI.[4]

Reynolds set the price of the book for prospective publishers—$20,000. He soon had an offer from Doubleday and Company. "They are a large house, a conservative house, a conscientious house, and publish quite a lot of distinguished writers," he explained, without mentioning that Doubleday had recently published two books that Reynolds himself had written. In the post–World War II years, Doubleday had been the single largest publisher of books in the world, putting out a long list and operating many bookstores and a successful book club. The senior editor, Kenneth McCormick, oversaw a large group of successful writers, including Leon Uris, Irving Stone, Allen Drury, Dwight Eisenhower, and Richard Nixon. McCormick and his small army of assistants would edit Haley's book, which they wanted to bring out soon.[5]

Haley was now connected to some of the most powerful people in American publishing. DeWitt Wallace and Charles Ferguson ran the most widely circulated magazine in the United States, Paul Reynolds was almost without peer among literary agents, and McCormick was one of the most influential and prolific editors in New York. The men saw each other socially and trusted one another professionally, and in 1963 they quickly brought Haley into their network.

Reynolds soon learned, however, that he would earn his fee for representing Haley. Malcolm informed Haley that his half of the advance should be made payable to Muhammad's Mosque No. 2, the NOI Chicago headquarters, and then wanted assurance that Reynolds would in fact pay out the Doubleday advance. Reynolds replied stiffly to Haley that Malcolm would not have to worry about collecting from him. Haley asked Reynolds for $500 of his advance before it came in from Doubleday. Reynolds sent the money but appended a note: "I can't always promise to be able to advance money at any time. I always tell authors that we're not bankers." Haley promised to deliver the book by September 1, 1963, less than three months away, because there was not "as much complex composition as another book might take." Reynolds replied that there was no need to rush, because Doubleday did not have time to publish the book in 1963.[6]

Haley immediately revealed a penchant for jumping ahead to another book before the one at hand was written. Just after signing the contract, he wrote to Reynolds, "It's my hope that quite early in 1964 I'm going to be able to hand over to you the first four chapters and remainder in outline of the novel that I nearly know by heart, 'The Lord and Little David.'" Reynolds gently advised him to slow down. "You're going to do a lot of books and I don't want you to kill yourself with work."[7] The admonition went unheeded. Two months later, having submitted nothing of the Malcolm X book, Haley wrote, "You mentioned that after this project, we would talk of others. I have it, Mr. Reynolds. I guarantee you a fine book, perfect for these times, its title to be 'Before This Anger.'" This idea was a slight variation on the one he had proposed for a book on Henning.[8]

Haley struggled at first to win Malcolm's confidence. In their early meetings, the NOI spokesman remained tight-lipped and noncommittal. Malcolm's wife, Betty, was also reserved and suspicious when she met the writer, but Haley charmed her when he admired a pie she had baked. "Hey, this is delicious," Haley, himself an experienced cook, said. "How on earth did you make it?" Betty soon decided Haley was wonderfully cosmopolitan: "I thought . . . this is a man of the world." Betty's biographer called Haley her "periscope to an urbane, secular scene." In the next few years, she and Haley often chatted amiably over the telephone, and their fondness for each other lasted for decades. Betty took care of several small children and took the unending telephone calls that came for Malcolm. Eventually she confided her frustrations with Malcolm to Haley. But she also mirrored Malcolm's growing affection for Haley. "I love Alex," she said years later.[9]

Once the autobiography was under way, in June 1963 Malcolm began coming to Haley's apartment in Greenwich Village late at night, arriving in his blue Oldsmobile. Their sessions went on for hours, with Haley typing notes. Haley thought the interviews got off to a poor start because the two men were "spooky" of each other. Malcolm still addressed Haley as "Sir," and his talk dwelt entirely on NOI philosophy and the evils of the white devil. He may have been reticent because he thought the FBI was bugging Haley's apartment. In the early interviews, Haley got little of a personal nature from Malcolm, and he feared he would have to tell the publisher that there was not going to be a book. He had to beg Malcolm for more interview time: "I badly need it. Justice to what the book can do for the Muslims needs it." To loosen Malcolm up, he had George Sims sit in on the interviews, because Sims seemed to relax Malcolm. Haley's son, Fella, was sometimes there, too, and the teenager soon announced he wanted to join the Nation of Islam.[10]

Haley noticed that Malcolm often doodled on napkins, writing sentences and phrases that revealed inner thoughts. For example, "[The white man] so quick to tell [the black man], 'Look what I have done for you!' No! Look what you have done *to* us." Another one: "[The] only persons [who] really changed history [were] those who changed men's thinking about themselves. Hitler as well as Jesus, Stalin as well as Buddha. . . . Hon. Elijah Muhammad." One scribble went, "Woman who cries all time is only because she knows she can get away with it," which prompted Haley to ask for Malcolm's views on women. "You can never fully trust any woman," he said, adding that his wife, Betty, was the only woman he ever met he could trust

75 percent of the time. He had seen too many men destroyed by their wives. But he scribbled, "I have a wife who understands, or even if she doesn't she at least pretends."[11]

Haley finally got access to Malcolm's personal life when he interrupted a rant against blacks who condemned Elijah Muhammad. "I wonder if you'd tell me something about your mother?" Malcolm's speech slowed down. "She was always standing over the stove, trying to stretch whatever we had to eat. We stayed so hungry that we were dizzy. I remember the color of dresses she used to wear—they were a kind of faded-out gray." Malcolm talked until dawn, and from the memories he recounted, Haley got material for the first two chapters of *The Autobiography of Malcolm X,* which for many readers would be the most compelling parts. At that point in American literature, there was little besides Richard Wright's novel *Native Son* that gave insight into the inner-city black experience. As the two men talked about Malcolm's time on the streets as a hustler, Malcolm became more introspective and self-critical. "The only thing I considered wrong," he said of those days, "was what I got caught doing wrong. I had a jungle mind, I was living in a jungle, and everything I did was done by instinct to survive."[12]

Manning Marable portrays Haley as an opportunistic, bourgeois, and politically conservative opposite to Malcolm, one who saw his collaboration with the NOI minister mainly as a chance at writing fame. In fact, as Haley accompanied Malcolm to college lectures, television appearances, and walks through Harlem over the next few months, the two men became friends. Haley listened to Malcolm discuss his intellectual interests in philology, and, like Paul Reynolds, Haley was impressed with Malcolm's intelligence and learning. Indeed, Malcolm was much more than the "fearsome black demagogue" Haley had promoted to the publishing world. Haley began to see that Malcolm's grievance about the demagogue epithet was justified. The two men's understanding of the world and the people in it were not so different. Haley found that Malcolm did not really consider all whites devils. Nor did Malcolm actually dismiss all middle-class blacks as Uncle Toms. He admired the photographer Gordon Parks, the actor Ossie Davis, and the psychologist Kenneth Clark as forthright supporters of all blacks; at the same time Malcolm disliked Thurgood Marshall, Carl Rowan, Jackie Robinson, and Roy Wilkins, who had all caustically dismissed the Nation of Islam. Malcolm liked the black journalists Louis Lomax, James Hicks, and Jimmy Booker, who took Malcolm seriously, and he admired the Christian sociologist C. Eric Lincoln. Malcolm soon made it clear that he also liked the bourgeois, Christian Alex Haley.[13]

Malcolm gradually revealed to Haley his sensitive nature. In the course of talking about his life as a hustler, Malcolm leaped from his chair in Haley's tiny apartment and demonstrated his prowess at the Lindy Hop, a dance popular in the 1940s, all the while "scat-singing" and snapping his fingers. He laughed freely and then scorned whites for not being able to do the same. He was touched when a Harlem couple named their baby after him, saying to Haley tearfully, "What do you know about *that?*" Walking around Harlem, Haley watched Malcolm avoid crowds at 125th Street and move among people living, literally, on side streets. To a wino, he said, "It's just what the white devil wants you to do, brother. He wants you to get drunk so he will have an excuse to put a club up beside your head." Haley thought Malcolm saw him as someone to whom he could express himself with candor, and "like any person who lived amid tension, he enjoyed being around someone, another man, with whom he could psychically relax."[14]

In 1963, while Haley conducted interviews with Malcolm, Malcolm never left the public spotlight. The speculation about his significance to American race relations never ceased. When Bull Connor, the Birmingham police chief, turned dogs on demonstrators, Malcolm said, "If anybody sets a dog on a black man, the black man should kill the dog—whether he is a four-legged dog or a two-legged dog." Asked to comment on Martin Luther King Jr.'s Birmingham

tactics, he said, "Real men don't put their children on the firing
line." After the demonstrations were over, *New York Times* reporter
Anthony Lewis quoted Malcolm telling a black audience in Washington, D.C., "You need somebody that is going to fight. You don't
need any kneeling in or crawling in." Lewis reported that the Kennedy administration told a group of white Birmingham businessmen,
"If they do not accept Dr. King's way they will get the Muslims'
way." To a Harlem audience Malcolm said, "The Rev. Martin Luther
King is an intelligent man. When he sees his method won't work,
he'll try something else." But in August, during the time of the historic March on Washington, Malcolm gave speeches in the nation's
capital damning "the farce on Washington" as a pointless demonstra-
tion controlled by the Kennedy administration.[15]

*   *   *

BY JUNE 1963 Haley was smitten with Juliette Collins, an airline
stewardess, and, like Nan and Jeanne Noble, pretty, demure, and
southern. He probably met Collins during his journalistic travels between 1960 and 1963. Reynolds gave a surprise engagement party for
Alex and Julie. Haley sent Reynolds a gushing note of appreciation:
"Julie is so impressed with sudden entry into a world where she meets
such important people. I likewise so much enjoy being your client, I
truly do, and . . . it's my full intent to make your investment of time
and interest in my development as an author prove to be variously
worthwhile." But Haley and Nan were still married, and when Haley
pressed his wife for a divorce, she did not cooperate. The record is not
clear as to when Haley and Julie married, though by early October
he was calling her his wife. Later, Nan and Fella said there were no
documents proving that Haley had obtained a divorce in Mexico, as
he claimed. By early 1964 Julie was pregnant, and at some point, she
and Haley were married legally.[16]

By September Reynolds was worried because he had not received
any chapters from Haley. "I think the situation is rather serious,"

he wrote to Haley. He and McCormick had expected to have an outline of the book by then. Haley told them that his conflict with Nan was keeping him from working on the book. "I realize you're having your difficulties and I suppose I seem to be unsympathetic," Reynolds replied, "but this book is very important to you for money and for your career and it's got to be licked." Thus Reynolds was relieved when Haley submitted two chapters, even if they were not in chronological order. In the first, entitled "The Farce on Washington," Malcolm alleged that the six most powerful black leaders at the March on Washington had taken $1.5 million from white men to prevent a radical turn in race relations. Doubleday's libel attorney worried that the allegation would invite suits from various directions, as had Malcolm's disparagement of Bull Connor. The Birmingham police chief had already won a $500,000 libel judgment against the *New York Times*.[17]

The first chapters were enough to worry Paul Reynolds about Malcolm's anti-Semitism, a bit of which the Yankee aristocrat seemed to share. "Our Miss Sherman," he wrote to Haley, referring to a person on his staff, "tells me he is always very anti-Jewish when he appears on television. I realize that he damns the whites, the negroes, the liberals, and everybody, and all of that is what's going to make it interesting to the reader, but the Jew is very sensitive and also of course very powerful in controlling newspapers, magazines and a good many book stores." Malcolm's across-the-board condemnation of Christians and Jews was where the trouble lay, Reynolds thought. "I realize he's got to damn them and of course it's his book, not yours," but he wished that the particular denunciations of Christians and Jews were no stronger than his damning of whites in general. Reynolds also suggested that Haley note in an introduction that Malcolm preferred for the sake of objectivity to have a non-Muslim help him with his book. "What I'm trying to say is for you to get in somewhere that you're not a Black Muslim. I'm just thinking of your future career."[18] Haley had another solution. "So I am going to encompass Malcolm's Jewish criticisms with the body 'white,' with no specifications. The section in which he, by implication, extolls the Jewish community—as a model for the Negro to study, and copy . . . will be retained as it is. Through careful handling, I feel that I can get this pattern past Malcolm X." But, in fact, a large number of anti-Semitic statements remained in the book.[19]

Haley and Reynolds were not the first to worry about the anti-Semitism of black nationalists. From Marcus Garvey to Elijah Muhammad to, later, H. Rap Brown of the Black Power movement, a number of black nationalists voiced special hostility toward Jews. Nor was Haley the first to attempt to expunge anti-Semitism from the published record of black nationalists. That had begun with W. E. B. Du Bois, who had studied in Berlin with anti-Semitic professors in the 1890s and brought home enmity that he integrated into *Souls of Black Folk*. Du Bois wrote that in the post–Civil War South "the Jew [was] the heir of the slave-baron. . . . Only a Yankee or a Jew could squeeze more blood from [the] debt cursed tenant." He denounced "shrewd and unscrupulous Jews" and "the enterprising Russian Jew," who by fraud had left blacks landless. Against such oppression, Du Bois advised that Negroes practice "the defence of deception and flattery, of cajoling and lying . . . the same defence which the Jews of the Middle Age used and which left its stamp on their character for centuries." In 1953, fifty years after *Souls of Black Folk* appeared, Du Bois substituted "immigrant" for references to Jews—very similar to the revision that Haley proposed.[20]

From the outset of the writing of *The Autobiography of Malcolm X,* Haley shaped the content of the book to maximize both its sensational value and its commercial success. He had the advice of mentors in making the manuscript accommodate political and commercial realities—and prejudices. Haley planned to append several essays to the autobiography in which he would interpret Malcolm's life from the point of view of a Christian, liberal black man. He would counter the Nation of Islam's anti-white positions, and then he would urge blacks toward Christianity, his answer to Malcolm X's message. Haley reported to his editors that Malcolm agreed to his appendices. "You write what I want to say," Malcolm concluded, "then you say whatever you want to." In Haley's mind, *The Autobiography of Malcolm X* was also the story of Alex Haley.[21]

Haley wrote Reynolds and McCormick long, excited letters, sometimes every day. The letters rejoiced over unwritten chapters. "Golly, what a book! I only wish that I could convey to you in one rush what a galvanic drama of the cartharsis of a man . . . is yet to unfold. It is such that even I do not fully appreciate its power until I get into the cumulative development of chapter by chapter." Haley was certain that "no one who reads it, including negroes, is going to put it down very quickly, or is going to 'pooh-pooh' it, or is going to fail to react to it." Another letter announced that "America's most dramatic, successful demagogue—a new breed, the black one, the *young*, black one—is onstage." By the time he wrote this, in the fall of 1963, Haley had heard Malcolm angrily reject the use of "demagogue" about himself, but Haley continued to use it to promote the sensational appeal of the book. The letters also contained minutiae about Haley's life. He signed one seven-page, single-spaced missive, "'Bye. I'm going to run across the street and get a bite." At the end of another letter, he reported, "Incidentally, I bought a car, that *runs*, a 1955 Dodge, for $80. Isn't that just wild!"[22]

Several times in the fall of 1963, Haley asked both Reynolds and Doubleday for more advance money. He needed it to fix his typewriter, to get his telephone turned back on, to go to Arizona to interview Elijah Muhammad, and to move from Greenwich Village to the town of Rome in upstate New York. George Sims's parents lived in Rome, which led Haley to move there at the same time Sims did. Haley's financial need made him tempted by the offer of an advance for a book on Sojourner Truth, to which Reynolds objected. "Signing contacts long before you can do the books is just a form of borrowing and you're paying the equivalent of a terribly high interest because you're not getting the best kind of contracts. Now you talk to your good wife and see if you can't pull in your horns and operate on this basis." That good advice went unheeded, and Reynolds sent more money anyway.[23]

By late 1963 Reynolds was worried that he would not be able to sell the serial rights for the book to a major magazine. Two magazine editors had already told Reynolds that the Malcolm X story was too explosive for them. "They also feel," he told Haley, that "they've perhaps over written about the problems of race relations." That year's Birmingham demonstrations, Medgar Evers's assassination, the March on Washington, and bombing of the Sixteenth Street Baptist Church in Birmingham placed racial issues foremost in the American consciousness. A fatigue about race concerns was setting in among whites.[24]

In late October Haley submitted two more chapters, these on Malcolm's early life. They contained scenes of angry encounters between his parents and between his mother, Louise Little, and Ku Klux Klansmen in Nebraska. When Malcolm's family moved to Lansing, Michigan, his father, Earl Little, came into conflict with both whites and Lansing's "complacent and misguided so-called 'middle-class' Negroes—the typical status-symbol-oriented, integration-seeking type of Negroes." White arsonists burned down their home. When Malcolm was six years old, Earl was run over by a streetcar and killed. Afterward Louise struggled to keep her eight children fed and clothed, but the family came under the control of welfare workers. Malcolm blamed the breakdown of his family and his mother's subsequent mental illness on the welfare system. He went through adolescence subject to the authority of white teachers and welfare agents, some of whom were kind and recognized his natural intelligence and leadership ability. But in middle school, when a white teacher asked about his career ambitions and Malcolm said he wanted to be a lawyer, the teacher responded that that was not a realistic goal "for a nigger." That response turned Malcolm against all authority figures in Michigan, and he went to live with his sister Ella in Boston. Had he not gone there, he concluded, "I'd probably still be a brainwashed black Christian."

Haley accepted Malcolm's story of his early life on its face. Malcolm was a young child when his Lansing home burned and his father died, and his accounts of his family's traumas were based on reports that came to him well after they occurred. Manning Marable wrote that investigators in Lansing suspected Earl Little had torched his own home for insurance money. Marable noted that local blacks believed that a white terrorist group had beaten Earl and left him on the streetcar tracks. Marable also believed that Malcolm exaggerated the extent of his criminal acts. Marable dismissed Haley as having been interested mostly in writing a "potboiler that would sell." Marable's evidence, on both Haley and Malcolm, is suggestive, not definitive, but it does point up the subjective, and sometimes fictional, nature of autobiography.[25]

Haley made up dialogue in relating Malcolm's relationship with one friend, the middle-class black girl called Laura. Haley's agent and editors disliked his creation, especially his use of black vernacular. Haley acknowledged that Malcolm had not liked it either. "He has a way of stroking his square chin," he explained to Reynolds and McCormick. "Er, can you take out the slang?" Malcolm had said to Haley. "I did talk that way then, but I don't now, and it's me now in the book." The vernacular was removed.[26]

* * *

THROUGHOUT 1963, Malcolm's growing national celebrity had escalated the suspicion and hostility toward him from other leaders in the Nation of Islam, including Elijah Muhammad, John Ali, and Ethel and Raymond Sharrief. Since at least 1962, Malcolm had been aware that Elijah had impregnated several secretaries who worked in the Chicago NOI headquarters. Such sexual immorality was an affront to NOI teachings about female purity and marital fidelity.

Malcolm was appalled but kept silent. His knowledge of the situation was discussed within the NOI, and, like his burgeoning national celebrity it was a threat to Elijah Muhammad. In September 1963 the *Amsterdam News* reporter James Booker wrote about a growing division in the NOI. Malcolm finally said to Haley, "Look, tell me the truth. You travel around. Have you heard anything?" Haley knew nothing at that point, but then he started to hear from C. Eric Lincoln, who had maintained close contact with people in the Nation, about rising hostility toward Malcolm.[27]

On December 1, 1963, Malcolm gave the first speech by an NOI leader since the Kennedy assassination. Muhammad had warned Malcolm not to criticize Kennedy, because the Messenger knew how popular the president was among blacks. The title of Malcolm's speech was "God's Judgment of White America," and in it, he called the president's assassination an instance of "the chickens coming home to roost" for a nation perpetuating violence in Vietnam. The remark defied Muhammad's order and provided a sensational example of Malcolm and the NOI's anti-American views. Malcolm's defiance proved to Muhammad's inner circle that he wanted to replace the Messenger. Muhammad suspended Malcolm from his position as minister.[28]

Haley was brought closer to the strife within the NOI when, in February 1964, *Playboy* assigned him to interview the boxer Cassius Clay. Haley asked Malcolm to help arrange the interview, a natural request after Malcolm had spent several days at Clay's Miami training camp and then more time giving the boxer a tour of Harlem. Clay was a member, or was soon to be a member, of the Nation. To Haley's surprise, Malcolm replied, "I think you better ask somebody else to do that." Elijah Muhammad, fearing that the boxer and Malcolm would align in a competing Muslim organization, soon announced that Clay needed a Muslim name and ordained him Muhammad Ali. Haley's interview focused mainly on Ali's boxing career; the fighter proudly discussed his psychological warfare against Sonny Liston. He dwelt on his calculated effort to become a celebrity. "People can't stand a blow-hard, but they'll always listen to him," he said. Ali spoke of his pride in being a Muslim but said little about Malcolm X. Haley believed, as did Malcolm, that Ali had betrayed Malcolm out of fear of Elijah Muhammad and his inner circle. "You just don't buck Mr. Muhammad and get away with it," Ali said. "I don't want to talk about [Malcolm] no more." Haley showed Malcolm the notes he had taken in the interview. Malcolm's hurt feelings were clear on his face and in his voice. Malcolm said he felt "like a blood big-brother to him. . . . He's a fine young man. Smart. He's just let himself be used, led astray."[29]

During the first days of 1964, Malcolm let Haley know that he, Malcolm, was in danger of being killed. Haley considered what that meant for the book. Malcolm had final approval of the manuscript. Who would give it if he was dead? Reynolds and McCormick worried that if Malcolm was assassinated the autobiography's sales would be reduced. In early February they pressed Haley for a new completion date. "I can have it all in by March 31," he replied. That was a ridiculously optimistic prediction: He had just received comments on what would be the sixth chapter of eighteen in the final version of the autobiography—with directions for a total rewrite. He was less than a third of the way through the book, but he began to produce chapters at a quicker pace, and in March 1964 he settled into a Manhattan hotel, where he said he would stay until he was finished.[30]

In February he explained to McCormick and Reynolds his plans for an afterword to the autobiography. "I plan to look at America and at the society which has produced the Black Muslims, [and] I plan to hit very hard, speaking from the point of view of the Negro who has tried to do all of the things that are held up as the pathway to enjoying the American Dream, and who (if not I personally, so many are) so often gets dissolusioned [sic] and disappointed." But rather than producing book copy, he sent long letters that described unwritten chapters and exulted over the power of the narrative. "We have here a book that, when it gets to the public, is going to run away from everything else." In late March, he wrote, "*Think* of this book's dramatic impact wherever books are read. Paul, *think* of the bidding for rights." He still had more than half of the book to write, but he promised that it would be finished in three weeks.[31]

Haley shaped *The Autobiography* into a powerful narrative. With his arrival in Boston as a teenager, Malcolm had become a prolific petty criminal. Malcolm "conked" his hair, "the emblem of his shame that he is black." He thought it was a sign of strength and status to scare whites. He became a procurer of drugs and prostitutes for white men, whose bad morals he later came to see as the source of all evil, including that done by blacks. Malcolm's misogyny was put on parade: white women were a status symbol to black men, and black men typically preferred them. White women were practical: they lusted after black men but had no intentions of having real relationships with them. But Malcolm himself had a lasting attachment to one white woman, whom he gave the pseudonym "Sophia." He had a long friendship with a Jewish man, "Hymie." Still, he held that whites could not see blacks as real people. Blacks functioned as "both servants and psychologists, aware that white people are so obsessed with their own importance that they will pay liberally, even dearly, for the impression of being catered to and entertained." In prison, Malcolm embarked on an impressive program of self-education. He read widely in the classics and in the new anthropology on the origins of man. While he was there, his brother told him about the Nation of Islam. Prison officials allowed him to write to Elijah Muhammad, because, Malcolm said, they knew the white man was the devil and felt guilt. The Nation of Islam brought him joy and self-justification. He embraced Elijah Muhammad's explanation that his imprisonment was the fault of the white devil and not the result of his own criminal behavior.

* * *

IN MARCH 1964 Malcolm faced up to the fact that he had no future in the NOI. He had begun discussing the Messenger's immorality with other NOI ministers, which his protégé Louis X (later Louis Farrakhan) reportedly passed on to the Chicago headquarters. On March 8, Malcolm went to M. S. Handler's home and told the reporter that he was leaving the NOI and creating a new organization, Muslim Mosque, Inc. Handler's story in the next day's *Times* reported that Malcolm was creating a black nationalist political party through which he intended to turn blacks from nonviolence to self-defense against white supremacy. "I remain a Muslim," Malcolm declared, "but the main emphasis of the new movement will be black nationalism as a political concept and form of social action against the oppressors." He said the NOI was "too narrowly sectarian and too inhibited" to advance blacks' cause and that he was prepared "to cooperate in local civil rights actions in the South and elsewhere and shall do so because every campaign for specific objectives can only heighten the political consciousness of the Negroes and intensify their identification against white society." Though he said he was not encouraging people to leave the NOI, he explained that Elijah Muhammad had kept him from participating in civil rights protests and that that was "going to be different now . . . I'm going to join in the fight wherever Negroes ask for my help." He especially intended to speak frequently on college campuses, because "white students are more attuned to the times than their parents and realize that something is fundamentally wrong in this country." He finally opened up about the hostility toward him in the NOI. "Envy blinds men and makes it impossible for them to think clearly. This is what happened."[32]

Once the break was made, Malcolm moved forward with his new approach. He met with civil rights activists and discussed efforts to desegregate schools in northern states. He gave a speech, "The Ballot or the Bullet," which displayed a much greater commitment on his part to voting rights than he had expressed before. In late March he went to Washington to observe the filibuster that southern senators were carrying out to thwart the omnibus civil rights bill that

President Lyndon Johnson and Vice President Hubert Humphrey were pushing. There in the gallery of the Senate, Malcolm met Martin Luther King Jr. for the first and only time. The two shook hands, looking for all the world like the image of a new, united black front.[33]

In hindsight, Malcolm's departure from the NOI marked a historic turn in the black freedom movement. Unburdened of the baggage of a secretive, corrupt sect, he could become the voice of a more militant approach toward white racist society. But he could also shed the anti-white racism that was central to the NOI. He had a huge, ready audience among young people, black and white, and among the dispossessed in American inner cities. He pointed black thought in the direction that would be manifest in the Black Power movement and other black liberation efforts in the coming years. Haley joined with a number of black admirers who believed that Malcolm's intelligence and eloquence would no longer be wasted in defense of a racist sect but applied to the cause of reforming American race relations. Malcolm's ability to promote assertions of black manhood surpassed that of Martin Luther King Jr., his admirers believed, and that was the next necessary step for lifting blacks in America.[34]

*   *   *

HALEY WAS CAUGHT unprepared for the rapid changes in Malcolm's life, but he made adjustments. Through Haley, Malcolm asked Doubleday to make his new organization the beneficiary of book royalties. In the event of his death, payments should go to his wife, Betty. He opened up to Haley about the internal workings of the NOI. Malcolm came close to tears as he said to Haley, "We had the *best* organization the black man's ever had—*niggers* ruined it!" It was the only time Haley ever heard Malcolm use the racial epithet.[35]

Malcolm's rejection of the Nation of Islam undermined Haley's narrative. Up to this point, Malcolm's story was about his descent into criminality, his re-education in prison, and his redemption under the tutelage of Elijah Muhammad. Now the Messenger was no longer his redeemer but a false teacher and a corrupt fraud. The abrupt revision of Malcolm's anti-white opinions prompted Paul Reynolds to advise Haley about rewriting the manuscript: "I think you're going to have to make it a little clearer that this is the past, when he was hating all whites."

Haley dreaded the thought of redoing Malcolm's character—and his book. He raised the problem with Malcolm, who had thought about it. "There are a lot of things I could say that went through my mind at times even then, things I saw and heard, but I threw them out of my mind," he said. He had decided against revising the book, saying, "I'm going to let it stand the way I've told it." If he did not see it immediately, Haley eventually realized that Malcolm's transformation put a sweeping curve in the book's narrative arc. The new turn would eventually account for much of its popularity. On March 26, Haley got a note from Malcolm that read, "There is a chance I may make a quick trip to several very important countries in Africa, including a pilgrimage to the Muslim Holy Cities of Mecca and Medina." Haley soon began to receive letters signed El-Hajj Malik El-Shabazz. His new name meant "Malcolm of the tribe of Shabazz has made the journey to Mecca."[36]

5

MARKED MAN

IN APRIL AND MAY 1964, MALCOLM VISITED CAIRO, Jeddah, Mecca, Khartoum, Nairobi, Lagos, Accra, and Algiers. He met many white Muslims, including one in Jedda who had given Malcolm his hotel suite, even though he had heard negative things about him from the American press. This man's generosity and openness prompted an epiphany: "It was when I first began to perceive that 'white man,' as was commonly used, means complexion only secondarily; primarily it described attitudes and actions. . . . But in the Muslim world, I had seen that men with white complexions were more genuinely brotherly than anyone had ever been." M. S. Handler reported that in Mecca Malcolm had "eaten from the same plate, drank from the same glass, slept on the same bed or rug, while praying to the same God" with Muslims "whose skin was the whitest of white, whose eyes were the bluest of blue." This had forced Malcolm to alter "my own thought-pattern, and to toss aside some of my previous conclusions."[1]

On May 21 a crowd of supporters at New York's Kennedy Airport greeted Malcolm, who had grown a beard on his trip, perhaps to emphasize the point that the journey had changed him. He and Betty, now pregnant with the couple's fourth child, picked up Haley and drove him to the Hotel Theresa in Harlem, where a large crowd of reporters and photographers was waiting. Haley and M. S. Handler sat together and listened in amazement to Malcolm's response to the question of whether he no longer thought all whites were evil. "*True,* Sir! My trip to Mecca has opened my eyes. I no longer subscribe to racism. I have adjusted my thinking to the point where I believe that whites are human beings as long as this is borne out by their humane attitude toward Negroes." Handler, taking notes furiously, muttered over and over, "Incredible, incredible." During a long question-and-answer period, Malcolm was supremely confident, often flashing a big smile to the room. "He had never been in better form," wrote Haley.[2]

Haley took a room at a hotel in the city in order to finish his interviews with Malcolm. They had little time alone. The room turned into a communications center for Malcolm to take calls from Africa and the Middle East, American and British newspapers and television, and his allies among American Muslims. Reporters and Muslim supporters often showed up, and Haley sometimes had to vacate the room for Malcolm to deal with sensitive matters.

Malcolm offered thoughts that he had earlier kept to himself. When he read a passage of the manuscript that described how he had intimidated his burglary ring by aiming a gun at his own head in a game of Russian roulette, he admitted to Haley that he "palmed the bullet." When Haley offered to change the manuscript, Malcolm decided to leave it as it was written. "Too many people would be so quick to say that's what I'm doing today, bluffing." Malcolm revealed guilt about how he had treated the middle-class black woman called Laura, who adored him despite his frequent callousness. "That was a smart girl, a *good* girl," he said. "She tried her best to make something out of me, and look what I started her into—dope and prostitution. I wrecked that girl." Malcolm objected to Haley's portrayal of his relationship with Elijah Muhammad as being like that between a father and son. When Haley reminded Malcolm of their earlier agreement not to change the already-written chapters, Malcolm replied, "Whose book is this?" He soon called Haley, apologized, and said that the chapters should stand as they were originally written. At this point, in mid-1964, Malcolm may have decided that he would have to trust Haley to finish the book on his own terms, because he already believed that he would not live to see its completion. The book continued to evolve. By June 1964 Haley had decided to scrap the three essay chapters in which Malcolm laid out his black nationalist views. The essays included Malcolm's harsh judgments about the March on Washington and his accusations of corruption among the main civil rights organizations. These sections came to be known as the "missing chapters" of the autobiography.[3]

Haley left out some events that were now embarrassing to Malcolm. In January 1961 Malcolm had met in Atlanta with Ku Klux Klan representatives. At that time FBI informants reported that Malcolm told the Klansmen that "his people wanted complete segregation from the white race." He also said that "the Jew is behind the integration movement, using the Negro as a tool." Later, at a Nation of Islam rally in Washington, D.C., Malcolm received American Nazi Party visitors and introduced their leader, George Lincoln Rockwell, to the audience. Perhaps these connections were so unsavory that he chose not to remember them. Haley had gained access to FBI sources through Alfred Balk and surely knew of the meetings with the Klan and the Nazis. But he also understood that nearly all Americans would have disapproved if they knew of it, and thus the knowledge would undermine Malcolm's critique of white America.[4]

The Autobiography of Malcolm X must then be understood as the *creation* of its subject's life, not a factual recounting of it. That can be said of all autobiographies. Malcolm, Haley, and his editors collaborated on an interesting narrative, but also one that would not repel readers.

Malcolm's life moved rapidly into new chapters. In June 1964 he created the Organization of Afro-American Unity, a name he borrowed from the Organization of African Unity, just created among postcolonial states in Africa. It was to be his vehicle for civil rights activism—at last an answer to critics who said he only talked and did not act. ("I'm going to join in the fight wherever Negroes ask for my help.") The new organization intended to send "armed guerrillas" to Mississippi and anywhere else white bigots threatened black people's lives.

Despite all the interruptions, Haley made progress on the book. In mid-May he assured McCormick that, with little more than half the book written, he was doing what was "needed for me to do to get this book headed for the presses at last, thence to the Best-Seller lists for, by golly, *I* predict, *months:* (I was born an optimist.)" On June 14 Haley assured McCormick that the final chapter would be in his hands by the end of the week. It was not.[5]

As Haley wrote feverishly, Malcolm sent him notes. His life was changing so quickly that he feared that today's views would soon be out of date. "So I would advise you to rush it on out as soon as possible," he wrote. Malcolm continued to receive threats from the NOI, and he confessed to Haley that he felt like a "marked man." In late June Haley wrote Malcolm a long letter begging him to be careful, to think of his children, his wife, and his sister Ella, all of whom loved him deeply. "Think of those followers ready to lay down their *lives* if you are harmed," Haley wrote. "Think of the *millions* of black people in America who respect and heed you. Think of the influence of your image and utterances among even *more millions* of white people, to make *them* see, many for the first time, the condition of the black people." Haley exhorted him, "Hell, think of *me!* . . . I never have had a close friend die." Was it not time, Haley asked, for Malcolm to undertake his hegira, referring to the prophet Muhammad's departure from Mecca in 622 CE, an exodus prompted by threats to his life from religious opponents? When Malcolm returned, his autobiography would be published, and it would give him "a greater voice as a single man than the entire Nation of Islam ever had collectively." Malcolm took his friend's advice. In early July he returned to Africa for what would be a four-month trip. For the most part, he was out of touch with Haley.[6]

*   *   *

HALEY'S WORK on the book mostly stopped then. Though far from finished with the autobiography, he turned to other writing projects out of financial need. Both Nan and Julie constantly required money. The Internal Revenue Service had billed him for unpaid taxes regularly since 1961, and the interest and penalties mounted constantly. He had spent $1,500 living at a Manhattan hotel as he worked on the book in the spring of 1964. His finances improved when Reynolds got a $20,000 advance on the serial rights for the autobiography from the *Saturday Evening Post*. Once that was shared with Doubleday and Malcolm, Haley still had far less money than he needed, but he believed that his financial difficulties were only a temporary situation, which would end when the autobiography made him wealthy. "It's sweltering here—but no matter," he told Reynolds from upstate New York in late June, "it won't be when, a year hence, I'll have myself some cool beach summer workplace."[7]

For Haley, the easiest way to address his financial woes was to get more publishing contracts. He now suggested to Reynolds a self-help book for white Americans: "If we could presume to divine white America's mass subconscious concerns, I think we would emerge with something approximating 'How to Co-Exist with Negroes.'" Whites would find in it "a non-challenging, palatable, at times even pleasant menu of things they hadn't known concerning Negroes. Many *little* things, that can make such difference to Negroes." Haley's hopeful assumption was that with the current racial tensions, whites were ready to be educated. Reynolds was dismissive. He could not see whites rushing to buy the book. Undaunted, Haley had an idea for a musical about black life, which he called "The Way." In 1961 Haley had gotten to know Lena Horne, who had starred in *Cabin in the Sky,* and Haley's musical bore some similarities to that film. Haley's musical would be set in a cosmetics factory run by a black executive who was surrounded by several stereotyped characters, including a hipster, a white racist, and a black racist. Alternating black and white choruses would sing "Camptown Races," with the black group performing spirituals in black dialect. Reynolds called the idea "very, very interesting."[8]

Without Reynolds's knowledge, Haley had proposed articles for *Life* and the *Saturday Evening Post.* When he found out, Reynolds warned Haley that he might hurt his relationship with *Reader's Digest,* which was still paying him a $300-a-month retainer. Reynolds wanted all queries to magazines to come to him first, even if Haley had a prior relationship with an editor. With regard to *Reader's Digest,* Reynolds wrote,"I always thought these regular monthly payments, even though they were small, were helpful. We are fairly close to the Digest. DeWitt Wallace [publisher of *Reader's Digest*] came to dinner at our house last Saturday evening." Haley replied that he believed he should dissolve the *Reader's Digest* arrangement. He had researched and written a lot of articles that the magazine did not, in the end, decide to publish. Charles Ferguson at the *Digest* was always complimentary of Haley's work, and Wallace noted how high Haley's stories rated on their reader-interest polls. But of every four articles he wrote, three were rejected somewhere in the editorial pipeline. Articles were returned with comments he did not understand. "A couple of re-writes were successful, but most weren't," Haley noted. "Each represented, at the least, a lost month of work."

Haley appreciated how much the *Digest* staff had helped him: "I enjoyed the Digest people, the camaraderie of the organization, the warmth of everyone, the niceness one wouldn't expect (such as Mr. Wallace and Mrs. Wallace sent a $100 check to Julie and me as a wedding present)." He enjoyed the perks of working for the *Digest:*

"The flying around the country first-class on Digest assignments, expenses paid, being wined and dined by subjects of pieces." But gossip going around New York had gotten back to him: "I attended one function where a friend introduced me to a personage, somewhat in his cups, who amiably chuckled, 'Oh, yes, you're the Reader's Digest fellow who flies around interviewing people and nothing ever happens.' That got to me."[9]

Haley had greater ambitions now. "Another factor, extraneous to the Digest, yet affecting the feeling that I have," he told Reynolds, was that "now I have tasted books." He reminded Reynolds of the inscription under Irving Wallace's portrait in the agent's office: "To Paul, who said 'Write books.'" The book he was thinking about was the one he now called "Before This Anger" about black-white relations in the South of the 1930s. He felt "the strength of my position as a Negro," one not given to violent protest, but who "can say powerful things of a nature that people will think about." In this spirit, Haley wrote an article for the *New York Times* on the stereotype of "Uncle Tom." A well-informed and sophisticated analysis, it explained how the image of Uncle Tom had become detached from Harriet Beecher Stowe's conception of her character.[10]

But his real specialty as a writer now lay in examining the black anger embodied in Malcolm. The summer of 1964 brought a release of some of that anger, even as the most far-reaching civil rights bill in American history was passed. As before, blacks' anger was fueled in part by violence against them, most notably that arising from the Mississippi Summer project, the effort of civil rights organizations to send hundreds of mostly white workers to the Magnolia State. Three of them—a young black man, James Chaney, and two whites, Michael Schwerner and Andrew Goodman—were murdered there. The summer also brought the first season of the 1960s' urban race riots, the most prominent of which occurred in Harlem in mid-July after a policeman shot and killed an unarmed fifteen-year-old black boy. Six days of looting shook New York City, and disorder soon spread to Rochester, Philadelphia, and several New Jersey cities. The 1964 riots seemed to confirm that black anger was rising. White opposition to the civil rights movement was also growing. In September the *New York Times* reported poll findings that most white New Yorkers believed the civil rights movement "had gone too far," that blacks wanted "everything on a silver platter." The *Times* concluded that a white "backlash" was underway.[11]

The *Times* asked Haley to do a piece on the aftermath of the Harlem riot. "They wanted a piece wherein Harlem's 'responsible' citizens would condemn the riots," he told Reynolds. He had asked many "such citizenry, who didn't condemn them as the *Times* desired." The *Times* turned down the article he submitted and assigned the piece to another writer, whose interviews in Harlem got the same undesirable answers.[12]

In August Haley met with McCormick and his young assistant Lisa Drew to talk about "Before This Anger." The book was similar to the project he had previously named "Henning, U.S.A." It would be about the South in the 1930s, when blacks and whites enjoyed friendly, peaceful relations. He discussed it in the context of the riots that had been dominating newspaper headlines the past few weeks, especially in New York. McCormick liked the idea because of the contrast with the present day. He took extensive notes at the meeting: "A book Southerners will read with appreciation. Told in terms of people . . . A book that exposes the warmth and love of the south." Doubleday offered a modest $5,000 advance, which hardly solved his financial problems, but it gave focus to what he would write next.[13]

Playboy assigned him to interview Martin Luther King Jr., which proved more difficult than any interview he had undertaken. King was reluctant to appear in a publication considered salacious and immoral. Even when he was persuaded that *Playboy* would reach an audience that could help his cause, his busy schedule made it extremely difficult to meet with Haley. During September 1964 Haley hung around Atlanta for a week before he got his first few minutes with King. Haley's approach was respectful and unchallenging. When asked about the Black Muslims, King suggested that the black man in Harlem embraced black nationalism because he had seen so little racial progress in his environment, whereas black southerners by 1964 believed that they were moving toward racial justice. King asked Haley off the record, "Well, what's Brother Malcolm saying about me these days?" King told others that when Malcolm "starts talking about all that's been done to us, I get a twinge of hate, of identification with him." When Haley next saw Malcolm, he asked Haley about his interview with King, "What did he say about me?"[14]

* * *

WHILE HALEY WAS IN ATLANTA pursuing King, the *Saturday Evening Post* ran excerpts of the autobiography under the title "I'm Talking to You, White Man." The magazine sent a photographer to Cairo to take color pictures of Malcolm, and the photography on both the cover and inside the magazine made the long excerpt almost as compelling visually as it was narratively. Though Malcolm had left the United States before the riots began in mid-July, he knew about them. "More and worse riots will erupt," Malcolm predicted. He accepted the reality of violence with near complacency. The followers of Elijah Muhammad would "consider it a first-rank honor to kill me," he said, adding that "any day, any night, I could die at the hands of some white devil racists." Malcolm insisted that he had rejected racism and was working to purge America and the world of it. "I dream that one day history will look upon me as having been one of the voices that perhaps helped to save America from a grave, even possibly fatal catastrophe." The *Post* carried a harsh editorial that read in part, "If Malcolm X were not a Negro, his autobiography would be little more than a journal of abnormal psychology, the story of a burglar, dope pusher, addict and jailbird—with a family history of insanity—who acquires messianic delusions and sets forth to preach an upside-down religion of 'brotherly' hatred." Malcolm, in the editors' view, preached hatred that "unquestionably . . . was behind some of the violence of the summer riots in the North." His followers, the Black Muslims, according to the editorial, represented a "sort of Negro Ku Klux Klan." Malcolm was incensed at the *Post's* characterization and furious that there was no recognition of how he had changed.[15]

He had not changed in every way. Malcolm sent word that he favored Barry Goldwater in the presidential race, because the Republican nominee "flatly tells the black man he's not for the black man." If Goldwater was elected, blacks would protest more aggressively, whereas if the "liberal fox" Lyndon Johnson won the White House, blacks would "keep on sitting around, begging and passive-resisting for another 100 years, waiting for 'time' and for 'good-will' to solve his problems."[16]

By the fall of 1964, Reynolds and McCormick were nervous because the autobiography was not finished. Haley blamed the delay on Malcolm's long absence and promised that it would finally be submitted by the end of January 1965. Then he took off in mid-October to begin research on "Before This Anger." George Haley was campaigning for the Kansas state senate as a Republican, and Alex went to Kansas City to write speeches for George and orchestrate last-minute politicking to secure him votes from overwhelmingly Democratic black voters. Haley's travel began just days after Julie gave birth to their daughter, Cynthia, his third child; he left mother and child in an upstate New York hospital. He was a proud father—from afar. He returned to his new family on Election Day, just in time to vote for Lyndon Johnson.

Contrary to what Haley had hoped, the hostility to Malcolm inside the Nation of Islam escalated in his absence. The sect took legal action to remove him from the house that it had provided him. Elijah Muhammad's representatives in New York publicly called Malcolm a "self-serving hypocrite consumed by a passion for personal power." Malcolm wrote from Mecca that he now rejected the Nation as a pseudoreligion and that he would not rest "until I have undone the harm I did to so many well-meaning, innocent Negroes who through my own evangelistic zeal" had embraced the Nation "even more fanatically and more blindly than I did."[17]

On November 24, 1964, on Malcolm's return from Africa and the Middle East, Haley met him at Kennedy Airport. There, in addition to supporters holding a banner that read "Welcome Home, Malcolm," were black plainclothes policemen taking photographs of everyone in the crowd to identify both Malcolm's followers and potential attackers. Malcolm and Haley met privately to talk about the Muslim leader's experiences abroad. "I was trying to internationalize our problem," he said, "to make the Africans feel their *kinship* with us Afro-Americans. I made them *think* about it, that they are our blood brothers, and we all came from the same foreparents." Malcolm now embodied the black nationalist desire for connection among all peoples of African heritage.[18]

Malcolm's life returned to the chaotic state it was in before he left. He was fighting the eviction from his house. People on Harlem streets were criticizing his new organization, the OAAU, for its failure to *do* anything. Armed men now suddenly appeared near him in public places, which forced Malcolm to travel with large contingents of bodyguards. During what little time he had to work with Haley on the book, Malcolm was not "his old assured self." He resented the fact that much of the media still treated him as a dangerous advocate of black violence and did not take seriously the threats on his life. He said, "No group in the United States is more able to carry out" a death threat than the Black Muslims. "I know because I taught them myself."[19]

For Christmas 1964 Haley bought "walking" dolls for Malcolm's two oldest daughters, Attallah and Qubilah. Malcolm was touched by the writer's thoughtfulness. "Well, what do you know about that!" he said, as he made the dolls walk. Then he confessed that he had never bought any of his children a present. "That's not good, I know it. I've always been too *busy*." Malcolm asked Haley to be the godfather of six-year-old Attallah. Haley nicknamed Attallah "Little Red" because of her strong resemblance to her father, "Big Red." He would become something of a father figure to Attallah after Malcolm died, even paying for her college education.[20]

In early January 1965, Malcolm picked Haley up at Kennedy Airport on the writer's return from George Haley's inauguration as a Kansas state senator. The two men sat in Malcolm's Oldsmobile in the airport parking lot. Tell George, Malcolm said, that "he and all the other moderate Negroes who are getting somewhere need to always remember that it was us extremists who made it possible." Malcolm was still frustrated that the media would not relinquish his "old 'hate' and 'violence' image." The main civil rights organizations dismissed him as too militant and the "so-called militants" as too moderate. "They won't let me turn the corner." Haley and Malcolm then turned to personal matters. Haley sent his regards to Betty, and the men discussed the imminent arrival of Malcolm's fifth child. "This one will be the boy," he said smiling. "If not, the *next* one!" It was the last time Haley saw his friend alive.

* * *

DURING THE EARLY DAYS of 1965, groups of Black Muslim men stalked Malcolm X in Los Angeles, Chicago, and New York. Malcolm spoke on a Chicago television show about the NOI's determination to kill him. Indeed, in Chicago, fifteen NOI men with guns were waiting for Malcolm at his hotel, but Chicago police warned them away. On February 14 Malcolm's home in Queens was firebombed. He and his family escaped without injury, but he was badly shaken. On February 18 Malcolm told an interviewer, "I'm a marked man." When Malcolm and Haley spoke on the telephone, Malcolm said, "Haley, my nerves are shot, my brain's tired." Malcolm wanted to visit Haley in upstate New York during the third weekend of the month to read the manuscript one more time. "Just a couple of days of peace and quiet, that's what I need."[21]

Even as the walls seemed to be closing in on Malcolm X, he continued to revise his views about race relations. In mid-January he declared publicly that "when you are dealing with humanity as a family there's no question of integration or intermarriage. It's just one human being marrying another human being." He worked to connect to the mainstream civil rights movement, traveling to Selma, Alabama, in late January to speak to activists in the midst of a voting-rights protest that would culminate in the massive march later that spring.[22]

In late January, still with no final manuscript, Paul Reynolds wrote to Haley, "I'm really getting a little worried over this, worried about it for you and your career." Again, Haley promised that the book would be finished in a few days. Then, as if to exasperate Reynolds on purpose, Haley sent him a treatment of his musical, "The Way." On Saturday, February 20, Malcolm called Haley to ask about the manuscript. Haley told him the final draft would go to Doubleday at the end of the following week, on or about February 26. Malcolm postponed his visit to Haley's home until after the weekend.[23]

On Sunday, February 21, Malcolm had just come to the podium of Harlem's Audubon Ballroom, where he often spoke, when a commotion distracted the audience and three gunmen rose and shot Malcolm many times with a shotgun and pistols. He died almost immediately. One of the assassins, Talmadge Hayer, was caught by the crowd at the scene. The other shooters escaped, but witnesses identified two of them as Norman 3X Butler and Thomas 15X Johnson, and they were apprehended. All three were convicted of the murder, but Butler and Johnson were innocent. Hayer later named four men from the Nation of Islam's Newark mosque who, he said, were involved in the shooting. Subsequent inquiry suggested that Hayer was telling the truth.

Haley told Reynolds he expected that they would soon hear from Betty Shabazz that she needed money. The book was Malcolm X's sole financial legacy to his widow and his four, soon to be five, daughters. "I'm just glad that it's ready for press now at a peak of interest for what will be international large sales, and paperback, and all. I'm just glad that it isn't a 'little' book, but one that can well really provide for his family as he would have wanted." In fact, the book was nowhere near ready for the press.[24]

For the week after Malcolm's assassination, New York City was in a state of turmoil. On Monday, February 22, the *New York Times* reported that the murder was "an example of the mounting pattern of violence in the Black Muslim movement," quoting a Malcolm loyalist as predicting "probable violence between Negro factions, and upon whites, in the wake of Malcolm's death." That day's editorial page carried the prediction that "this murder could easily touch off a war of vengeance of the kind [Malcolm X] himself fomented." The FBI heard many reports that "war was being declared between the NOI and Malcolm's followers." The next day, February 23, arsonists destroyed Mosque No. 7, Malcolm's original NOI temple. Hundreds of city police patrolled Harlem, on alert for a possible shooting war between the NOI and Malcolm's followers. Harlem residents were incensed because "the screaming headlines of many of our newspapers make it seem as if all of Harlem is an armed camp, ready to explode at any moment," when in fact few residents had responded violently.[25]

On Friday, February 26, Doubleday announced that it was canceling publication of *The Autobiography of Malcolm X.* Nelson Doubleday Jr., the owner, worried that a war between Black Muslims and Malcolm's followers could spill into the three Doubleday bookstores in Manhattan and others around the country. Ken McCormick objected strongly, but the owner prevailed. It was a unique event: Lisa Drew, McCormick's assistant at the time, said that up until then, no book had ever been canceled because of considerations originating outside the publishing house. Haley and Reynolds must have been shocked, but their responses went unrecorded.[26]

That day Haley stood in a long line at a Harlem funeral home to view Malcolm's body. "Under the glass lid, I glimpsed the delicate white shrouding over the chest and up like a hood about the face on which I tried to concentrate for as long as I could. All that I could think was that it was he, all right—Malcolm X. . . . Malcolm looked to me—just waxy and *dead*." At the funeral the following day, Haley heard the actor Ossie Davis eulogize Malcolm as "our manhood, our living black manhood! That was his meaning to our people."[27]

For mainstream opinion makers, the original, allegedly racist, and violent Malcolm was the one he had remained until his death. The *New York Times* editors wrote, "The life and death of Malcolm X provides a discordant but typical theme for the times in which we live." Malcolm, in the editors' view, had turned his "many true gifts to evil purpose. . . . His ruthless and fanatical belief in violence not only set him apart from the responsible leaders of the civil rights movement and the overwhelming majority of Negroes," but it marked him "for a violent end." Carl Rowan, the black newspaperman then heading the United States Information Agency, surpassed the *Times*'s harsh judgment, declaring, "Here was a Negro, who preached segregation and race hatred, killed by another Negro . . . that preaches segregation and race hatred, and neither of them representative of more than a tiny minority of the Negro population of America." Rowan was angry that newspapers in Africa were treating Malcolm as a civil rights martyr. Attendees at Malcolm's funeral hissed at the mention of Rowan's name.[28]

Haley's response to Malcolm's death seemed to lack emotion. Perhaps the long-standing threats had made the violent act, while shocking, also feel inevitable. The previous June, Haley had begged Malcolm to be careful, but when he returned from his hegira in November, he constantly put himself in harm's way. The night of the assassination, Haley wrote to Reynolds that he would have the manuscript by the following Friday. Haley was going to write an epilogue, "short, but I hope dramatic, about this man as I knew him, and actually I knew him pretty well." In fact, when he finished it, six months later, the epilogue was one-sixth of the book.[29]

*   *   *

IN MID-MARCH 1965 Paul Reynolds was having no success finding another publisher. He had hopes for Dell or the New American Library. "You understand, the public is less inclined to read a book about a man no longer alive," he told Haley. "Malcolm X is untried in the book field. He is no longer living, and it's a big guess how many people will rush to buy this book when it is brought out." It was harder now to sell the book because Doubleday's rejection made other publishers fear the controversy surrounding the life of Malcolm. Even so, Reynolds was determined still to get "a good royalty so that if this has a very large sale, you and Malcolm X's Estate will make a great deal of money, perhaps $100,000 or more. But I am no miracle worker and I think we ought to grab Dell if we can." Then both Dell and New American Library turned him down. McGraw-Hill thought the manuscript needed much editorial work. The Playboy Press editor said that he thought the writing was "little more than ordinary."[30]

A few weeks later Grove Press agreed to publish the book. Grove was the only publishing house that showed "any solid interest," one of Reynolds's associates admitted. Barney Rosset, Grove's publisher, had made history in American publishing when he brought to the American reader the works of Samuel Beckett, Pablo Neruda, Octavio Paz, and Harold Pinter—all winners of the Nobel Prize for literature—and many of the Beat writers, including William S. Burroughs, Allen Ginsberg, and Lawrence Ferlinghetti. Rosset's singular triumph was printing and then defending in court Henry Miller's *Tropic of Capricorn* against obscenity charges. Rosset had lived with controversy throughout his publishing career and was not afraid about any that might arise from *The Autobiography of Malcolm X*.[31]

Haley later claimed that he had sat down in the immediate aftermath of Malcolm's assassination and written the epilogue in two weeks. In fact, in May, after the deal was struck with Grove, it was still not written. "Grove Press is being very nice, and everybody is being very nice," Reynolds wrote to Haley on May 11, "but I think you are going to delay the book and delay sales and I really think you should stay up day and night until you get this done."[32]

Haley's delay in finishing the autobiography owed once again to his propensity to move on to the next project before the current one was finished. As always, he did so out of desperation for money. The IRS was making ever more serious threats about the consequences Haley would face if he did not pay some of the back taxes he owed. In May 1965 he met with theatrical producers in the hope of getting a commitment to put his black-themed musical "The Way" on stage. He proposed to Reynolds yet another book, a personal memoir, "The Malcolm X I Knew." Reynolds thought that was a bad idea, as was his proposal for a biography of the flamboyant and controversial lawyer Melvin Belli, with whom Haley was doing a *Playboy* interview. Finish the Malcolm book, Reynolds pleaded.[33]

In fact, the book was finished in time for him to have galleys by June 22. He added chapters on Malcolm's break with the NOI, his journeys to Africa and Mecca, and his sense of American society at the moment he died. Haley had achieved a nicely rounded narrative arc. The chapters in Africa and Saudi Arabia, while flat and without conflict, told of Malcolm's conversion to faith in universal humanity without racial distinction and his embrace of pan-Africanism, a belief that all black people were related and should share a pride in that heritage. Malcolm had come to advance a form of black nationalism that shed much of its anger and its anti-white hatred. Haley had originally intended an epilogue to be his critique of the anti-white, anti-Christian views of the Nation of Islam, but Malcolm's own rejection of the sect made such critique superfluous. In its final form the epilogue was far less an ideological corrective or critique than it was an account of Haley's work with Malcolm. Its length allowed Haley to extend the story of the relationship between the two men from its initial wariness to tolerance and finally to friendship and affection. It thus had an arc that paralleled the turn of Malcolm's narrative. Haley refrained from expressing admiration for, or friendship with, Malcolm, perhaps because Haley wanted to leave the impression of detachment. Even with Malcolm's transformation and his arrival at a philosophical view closer to Haley's own, the writer was restrained in his final assessment of Malcolm: "He was the most electric personality I have ever met, and I still can't quite conceive him dead."[34]

The Autobiography of Malcolm X was published in September 1965. It was reviewed widely, with universal praise from black newspapers and journals and mostly positive reviews elsewhere. There were excellent notices in leading newspapers. The *New York Times*'s Eliot Fremont-Smith called the book "brilliant, painful," and a "document of our time." In the *Washington Post,* the veteran civil rights activist Bayard Rustin expressed the view that one of the book's best features was its account of Malcolm's chaotic childhood, the beginning of the journey "of an American Negro in search of his identity and place in society." Malcolm had brought "hope and a measure of dignity to thousands of despairing ghetto Negroes." In the *Yale Review,* the southern writer Robert Penn Warren wrote that much of the book's value lay in Malcolm's telling whites and many blacks "what it means to be a Negro in America in this century, or at least what it so dramatically meant to one of unusual intelligence and powerful personality." Dissent came in the *New York Review of Books* from I. F. Stone, a radical journalist, who preferred a book of Malcolm's speeches to the *Autobiography,* because Malcolm's "most important message to his people," pan-Africanism, was muted in the *Autobiography*—"perhaps because Alex Haley, its writer, is politically conventional."[35]

Starting in 1967 the book sold at the rate of seventy-five thousand copies per month, for a total of more than two million by 1969.

A 1969 survey of college bookstores reported that *The Autobiography of Malcolm X* was on the list of the ten most-read books on six of the eight campuses (four from the Ivy League) reporting, its popularity surpassed only by that of Eldridge Cleaver's memoir, *Soul on Ice*.[36] Asked to explain the book's popularity, a man in Harlem said that Malcolm had given blacks "a sense of history they had never known before, a sense of pride and destiny. And the key point is that he spoke from the world of the streets." *Time* magazine and the *New York Times* named *The Autobiography of Malcolm X* among the ten most important books of the 1960s.[37]

Over time, some readers became skeptical of the dramatic turn in Malcolm's racial attitudes. In his 2011 biography of Malcolm, Manning Marable attributed the transformation, as related in the autobiography, to Haley's desire to undermine the potential influence of black nationalism. Haley's rendering of Malcolm as a liberal reformer and integrationist, Marable wrote, undercut the militancy and radicalism for which Marable thought he really stood. Marable said that the autobiography "does not read like a manifesto for black insurrection" but like the traditional American autobiography of self-education and self-help. Marable blamed Haley for this interpretation. Marable himself would be subject to the same accusation—that he had minimized Malcolm's commitment to revolutionary black nationalism. Marable's accusers made no mention of Haley's having similarly diminished the revolutionary content of Malcolm's message. The intense hostility to Marable, who died three days before his book came out, suggested that the great devotion to Malcolm that existed among scholars and activists who discussed "Malcolm X studies" as a distinct discipline, based on the autobiography and collections of his speeches.[38]

The Autobiography of Malcolm X, in fact, contained sufficient elasticity of meaning to gain a broad and disparate readership. To many, Malcolm's transformation was a comforting rejection of racial and religious intolerance. He seemed to have been on the verge of becoming a major international race reformer, one who was killed by Black Muslims before he could realize his great potential for good; he was thus a tragic hero. To other readers, *The Autobiography of Malcolm X* was a statement of black anger and a rationale for an aggressive black response to the historic mistreatment of African Americans. Todd Burroughs, an academic advocate of black nationalism, later credited the autobiography with having "intellectually birthed so many of us in the first place." In the years after 1965, when black anger was given voice much more freely, Malcolm's story would be valued widely for the aggressive, anti-white message of the early chapters. In 1992, with the appearance of Spike Lee's film on Malcolm, 84 percent of blacks between the ages of fifteen and twenty-four viewed Malcolm as a "hero for black Americans today." Barack Obama, who read the autobiography as a teenager struggling with his racial identity, took from it the message that it was "important for African-Americans to assert their manhood, their worth. . . . That affirmation that I am a man, I am worth something . . . Malcolm X probably captured that better than anybody."[39]

In due course, the book was recognized as one of the greatest of American autobiographies. It remains on required-reading lists in high schools and colleges. In 1997 *The Norton Anthology of African American Literature* included a long excerpt from the book and noted that it "remains a classic of American autobiography." In a 2010 book dedicated to scholarly appreciation of Malcolm's significance, the literary critic Robert E. Terrill wrote that *The Autobiography of Malcolm X* was "the fundamental text at the center of all studies of Malcolm," a "literary masterpiece" that showed his own transformation and, "through his eyes, the world in which and against which he wrought those changes."[40]

The Autobiography of Malcolm X conformed to the genre patterns established two centuries earlier in Benjamin Franklin's autobiography in the way that it moved, as the literary scholar Carol Ohmann wrote, from "inexperience to sophistication, from ignorance to enlightenment, from obscurity to worldly prominence." Like Franklin, Malcolm projected himself as a rational man committed to understanding and mastering society. As with many other American autobiographies—those of Andrew Carnegie and Booker T. Washington are examples—Malcolm embraced the Franklin virtues: cleanliness, frugality, morality, and hard work. But *The Autobiography of Malcolm X* was also distinctly African American in the way that it conformed to patterns established by previous memoirs and autobiographies by black writers, works that Robert B. Stepto has referred to collectively as the "narrative of ascent."[41]

In its re-creation of one life, *The Autobiography of Malcolm X* was not objective or definitive. No less an authority than W. E. B. Du Bois admitted in his third and last autobiography that such was impossible: "Autobiographies do not form indisputable authorities. They are always incomplete, and often unreliable. Eager as I am to put down the truth, there are difficulties; memory fails especially in small details, so that it becomes finally but a theory of my life, with much forgotten and misconceived, with valuable testimony but often less than absolutely true, despite my intention to be frank and fair."[42]

Unlike other autobiographies, *Malcolm X* takes the reader through to the end of its subject's life, although it is not Malcolm but Alex Haley who escorts readers to Malcolm's death. In the body of the book, Haley skillfully keeps the focus on Malcolm's life and death, but the epilogue is almost as much the story of Haley as of Malcolm—the story of the most important part of Haley's writing life. In that sense, *The Autobiography of Malcolm X* is also Haley's act of self-invention.

6

BEFORE THIS ANGER

I N 1964 AND 1965, BEFORE HE COMPLETED *THE AU-tobiography of Malcolm X,* Haley took three trips that shaped his next project, "Before This Anger." The contract he had signed with Doubleday in August 1964 remained in force after the publisher canceled *Malcolm X.* In early 1964 Haley went to London to do a *Playboy* interview with the actress Julie Christie, and when the interview was canceled, he visited the British Museum. There, he saw the Rosetta Stone, the second-century BCE artifact that displayed a message in three ancient languages, which enabled a French scholar to translate Egyptian hieroglyphs. Haley was excited by how the Rosetta Stone had unlocked "a door into the history of man." He felt vaguely that it had personal significance, which finally dawned on him: he wanted to find the meaning of the words of his African ancestor.

When he went to Kansas City in October 1964 to help with his brother George's campaign, he visited with his cousin Georgia Anderson, the last survivor among the women on Cynthia's front porch. Georgia was thrilled to discuss Haley's plans to write the family history. "Our history needs to be writ," she said. "We can't speck white folks to write our history for us. They's too busy writin' 'bout theyselves." She told him to get on with the work. "Yo' sweet grandma an' all of 'em—dey up dere watchin' you." Haley returned for George's swearing-in ceremony, at which Georgia said to Alex and his brothers, "Y'all chillen jes' keep on. Go *fowud!* Go *fowud,* boys!"[1]

Then, on a Saturday in 1965, Haley went to the National Archives in Washington, D.C., and looked at census records from Alamance County, North Carolina, for the years just after the Civil War. In the story told on the front porch, Alamance was the place where his great-grandfather Tom Murray lived before moving to Henning. He looked at frame after frame of microfilm of the 1870 census, and he was at the point of frustration when he found the names Tom and Irene Murray. Then he found a young child, Elizabeth. This was his Aunt Liz. Cynthia was not listed, he realized, because she was not yet born. Thrilled with his discovery, he returned for more research at the archives, the Library of Congress, and the Daughters of the American Revolution Library.[2]

These discoveries, coupled with Cousin Georgia's exhortations, led Haley to change "Before This Anger" from a portrait of the 1930s South to the story of his family. He wanted to start with the original African taken into slavery. "His name no one seems ever to have heard," he told Reynolds. Haley soon began calling him the Mandingo and reported that he "sired a number of children on the several plantations to which he was sold." One of those children, the last one, Haley believed, told the Mandingo's story to Chicken George, his great-great grandfather, who handed it down to Tom Murray. Tom told it to Cynthia and Liz, who repeated it to little Palmer Haley.

Alex began to think of his family's experience as representative of all African American families. "In America, I think, there has not been such a book," he told Reynolds. "'Rooting' a Negro family, all the way back," was "part and parcel of the American saga." He would recount the story "without rancor, which I do not feel." The triumphal moment of the story would be George Haley's political success. The book would be one that "America, the world *needs* to read," he believed, and "I shall write it with love." But he had much research to do first, and he pleaded for Reynolds to be patient. "All will be justified within this year. You watch!" Haley was promising the completed book by the end of 1965.[3]

Haley knew little about the experience of slaves in the South. Most of his impressions of slavery were from the novels *Uncle Tom's Cabin* and *Gone with the Wind* and the movie adapted from the latter. His grandmother had reproved his mother for dismissing all discussion of slavery, and Haley realized by the 1960s that he was like Bertha—he had no "interest in slaves."[4] The history of American slavery was in the midst of a far-reaching revision in the 1960s, largely influenced by the civil rights movement. Younger historians rejected the view, promoted since the late nineteenth century, that slavery was a benign institution populated by happy slaves and kindly masters. Scholars began to offer a harsher view, but the interpretation that captured the most attention in the 1960s was that of Stanley Elkins, which drew an analogy between American slaves' behavior and the way Jews in Nazi concentration camps cowered before their oppressors' authority. Elkins suggested that, to survive their ordeal, slaves assumed the pose of "Sambo," who was "docile but irresponsible, loyal but lazy, humble but chronically given to lying and stealing." George Sims, helping Haley research "Before This Anger," found a collection of two thousand slave interviews recorded by the Works Progress Administration in the 1930s. To Haley, the interviews duplicated the "stories and phrasings I had heard as a boy on the front porch in Henning."[5]

In October 1965 Haley published an article entitled "My Search for Roots" in the *Philadelphia Sunday Bulletin*. "I have travelled thousands of miles to see and question our family's oldest members. . . . Their narratives often were emotional experiences. Sometimes I had to take notes through tears." He discussed the fact of white paternity in many black families. His paternal great-grandparent, a Confederate colonel named James Jackson, presided over an Alabama plantation. Haley revealed that he had already established the time—1766—that his ancestor had been brought on a slave ship to America. He intended to travel to the "slave coast" of Africa and then "return here, symbolically, by ship." Haley reported happily that as he did genealogical research on his family, he encountered many other blacks doing the same thing.[6]

If Haley was getting well versed in American slavery, he knew almost nothing about Africa. Predominant in the minds of most Americans were images of Africans swinging on vines—acting very much like the apes with whom they shared the jungle. Edgar Rice Burroughs's Tarzan novels, and the many movies made from them, depicted Africans as dumb and superstitious, teased by white Europeans who called them "boy." For Haley this was an uncomfortable view of his heritage, certainly as compared with whites' pride in their European ancestry. He had no idea how the slave trade worked. Africans had not "simply walked into slave ships." He knew nothing of the passage across the Atlantic. "What must it have been like for those Africans, naked, chained, terrified, in unquestionably small wooden ships, in particular when they got into rough seas[?]"[7]

At the end of World War II, no American university had yet treated the history of Africa as more than a study of European exploration and exploitation. Some academics thought that Africa was not a legitimate historical subject because there were few written documents other than those created by European colonial regimes. What little interest there was in Africa in the United States was shaped by American concerns. In 1941 the anthropologist Melville Herskovits at Northwestern University published *The Myth of the Negro Past*, in which he argued that there were many African cultural practices that survived in the lives of American blacks. But Herskovits came under attack from E. Franklin Frazier, an influential black sociologist, who suspected that the emphasis on African cultural survivals was an attempt to support innate, persistent biological and cultural differences between blacks and whites. Haley surmised that most scholars believed that "there was no legacy, the break had been absolute." But he began doing research anyway, "digging out actual facts of African cultural life."[8]

Interest in the study of Africa grew in the 1950s, spurred by the independence movement that spread across the continent. Thirty new African nations were chartered in the decade after 1952, and their creations were continuously reported in the West. Working with Malcolm had educated Haley about African political events. Herskovits developed the first academic program for the study of African history, assembled at Northwestern a large collection of African artifacts and historical material, and in 1957 started the African Studies Association. But Haley learned from his reading about Africa in 1965 and 1966 that he probably would not find what he was seeking about his ancestors in traditional, written sources. Having discovered most of what he knew from the stories his grandmother told, he believed that he would need oral sources.

As it happened, a scholar had just emerged whose work provided a strong rationale for using oral sources. In 1961 Jan Vansina, a Belgian anthropologist who had done extensive work in Central Africa, moved to the University of Wisconsin at the same time he published a seminal book, *The Oral Tradition*. This work considered the nature of oral evidence as an historical source and justified its collection and its use in history. Vansina wrote that the historian "using oral traditions finds himself on exactly the same level as historians using any other kind of historical source material. No doubt he will arrive at a lower degree of probability than would otherwise be obtained, but that does not rule out the fact that what he is doing is valid, and that it is history."[9]

*   *   *

ALMOST AS SOON as *The Autobiography of Malcolm X* was in bookstores, Haley began promoting the development of a film based on it. Most of the celebrities he had known in San Francisco and New York worked in the movie industry. One could earn fame as a best-selling author, but great heights of celebrity were achieved on the big screen. He also wanted to sell the movie rights for the money it would bring in. The actor James Earl Jones expressed an interest in playing Malcolm on both stage and screen, and the film producer and director Elia Kazan wanted to bring Malcolm's story to the New York stage. Marvin Worth, an agent for musicians, declared his interest in producing a film. James Baldwin was engaged to write both a play and a film script. When Haley told Paul Reynolds of the exciting prospects, Reynolds warned him that film and theater people often did not follow through with their plans. As he typically was, Reynolds was right.[10]

By June 1966 the autobiography had sold fourteen thousand copies in hardback, hardly the numbers of a best seller. Appreciation of the book had grown, however, owing to the veneration of Malcolm that spread after his death. The Black Power movement had exploded in the South in May and June as the Student Nonviolent Coordinating Committee ejected its white members and denounced nonviolence. The memory of Malcolm's anger against whites and his projection of black manhood spurred the growth of black nationalism, especially among younger civil rights activists who had become frustrated with what they viewed as the slow pace of change. Nonetheless, for the moment, *The Autobiography of Malcolm X* did not solve Alex Haley's financial problems.[11]

Haley's magazine work diminished as he devoted more time to "Before This Anger." He did have a memorable experience interviewing the American Nazi Party leader George Lincoln Rockwell for *Playboy.* Haley was now paid $1,500 (about $11,000 in 2015 dollars) for doing an interview. Rockwell was an American eccentric, a career military officer until his fascist politics got him dismissed from the army. When Haley contacted him by phone about an interview, Rockwell asked if he was a Jew. Haley said no and chose not to mention that he was black. Meeting Haley in person, Rockwell received the writer but armed himself, placing a pearl-handled revolver on his chair. Haley's first question was why Rockwell needed the gun when there were armed bodyguards all around. Rockwell answered that he received thousands of threats against his life. (Indeed, a member of his own organization would assassinate him the following year. Haley would later note that three of his early *Playboy* interview subjects were assassinated.) Rockwell declared, "It's nothing personal, but I want you to understand that I don't mix with your kind, and we call your race 'niggers.'" Haley answered that he had been called "nigger" many times, but "this is the first time I'm being *paid* for it. So you go right ahead." He followed that with, "What have you got against us 'niggers?'" Nothing, Rockwell answered; he just thought blacks would be happier where they came from, and "white people in America simply aren't going to allow you to mix totally with them." Haley noted that the civil rights movement was concerned with equal rights, not miscegenation. Rockwell shot back, "Race mixing is what it boils down to in practice; and the harder you people push for that, the madder white people are going to get." The interview continued in the style of a debate, with Rockwell expending much effort in denying the Holocaust.[12]

Later in 1966 Haley interviewed Sammy Davis Jr., the singer, dancer, and actor he had met in San Francisco in the late 1950s and with whom he had renewed his acquaintance at London's Playboy Club in 1964. The interview proved to be one of Haley's most enlightening efforts in what it revealed about the struggles of a black celebrity. Whereas Miles Davis had confidently expressed anger over racial indignities, Sammy Davis revealed to Haley the vulnerability he had felt continuously, beginning with his childhood days of performing in vaudeville with his father. Davis was often hungry, never went to school, suffered racist abuse in the army, and endured constant humiliations as a touring entertainer. He tried to counter prejudice with his performances. His great talent was recognized during his nightclub appearances in the early 1950s, and he was propelled to national fame as both a singer and actor. But he always went on stage conscious of race, anticipating "what people out there may be feeling against me emotionally" and intending to "rob them of what they're sitting there thinking: *Negro.*" The pressure of success led him to extravagant living and gambling at the same time that he became the object of abuse for partying with the white actress Ava Gardner and dating Kim Novak, a beautiful white starlet. The black press attacked him for insufficient "race consciousness" and the white press for breaking the race-sex taboo. By 1966 Davis had overcome a wealth of abuse and was doing well financially and personally—with a Swedish actress, May Britt, as his wife—but he never felt secure. "Things are really swinging for me now, but I can't help thinking that I might wake up some morning and find myself out of vogue, kaput." He'd had a recent experience when he was gripped with fear and thought to himself, "I'm going to die, because things are going too well."[13]

* * *

IN AUGUST 1966 Haley told Paul Reynolds that his marriage was failing but that he and Julie were trying to reconcile. "She always felt left out because attention was always on Alex," observed a man who knew Julie at the time. Marital problems worsened Haley's financial strain. Julie demanded money, though there is no indication that her demands were anything but reasonable, given that she was tending to two-year-old Cynthia. Traveling frequently to locations that he kept secret and living in hotels cost money that Haley did not have. He now wanted to move the family, intact, to California for a new start in the marriage.[14]

Haley's tax problems were mounting. The IRS was hounding him with "cold adamance and actually humanly devastating collections," he said, and was trying to obtain 100 percent of his income. In October 1966 Haley received a bill from the IRS for $4,577 for back taxes from 1963. (In 2015 dollars, that was about $32,800.) Haley told Reynolds that he was spending a lot of time fending off creditors. He owed Diners Club for accumulated travel expenses. Could Reynolds lend him $5,000, most of which would go to the IRS? "I have owed them *so* long," Haley said. Reynolds worked with lawyers on Haley's IRS problems and lent him the money.[15]

Haley complained that Doubleday should provide a larger advance. He had accepted a $5,000 advance in 1964, and in the ensuing years, he saw Doubleday give advances to other writers that were a hundred times larger. In the late 1960s publishers began paying much higher advances in general for books they believed would find large audiences. He felt that as a result of the critical acclaim for *The Autobiography of Malcolm X* he should receive more money. "I write now of *my family*. . . . I know I will make my family name, Haley, famed far beyond Malcolm X." He knew "what I could have as a book, if I could go all out" and travel to Africa and other places to do research. "I make you a prediction, friend. I won't come right out and call the name of the Prize. I just say to you: you just *watch* what we are going to win. Because just ain't never *been* a book like this one."[16]

To address his financial crisis in 1966, Haley signed on with the Colston Leigh agency, an established speakers' bureau that represented many celebrities. Haley was steadily gaining fame as Malcolm X's co-author. That fall he gave a lecture at Hamilton College titled "The Story Behind the Story of Malcolm X" for $300 (about $2,200 in 2015 dollars), and at the World Press Institute he delivered a talk titled "What the Negro Must Do for Himself," for $400. In 1967 lectures became his main source of income.[17]

Also in the fall of 1966, Haley attended a garden party at the Westchester County home of DeWitt and Lila Wallace. Haley explained to

Lila Wallace his family history project, and the next day she convened a meeting of editors at *Reader's Digest* to hear more about the forthcoming book. Haley mesmerized the editors for three hours. At the end of the meeting, the *Digest* offered him an advance of $12,000, most of it to cover travel while he finished the book. The magazine received serial rights for "Before This Anger." After having rejected the *Digest*'s support in 1964, he gladly returned to the fold.

Haley was determined to get to Africa to uncover the African part of his family story. He began going to the United Nations in Manhattan to look for Africans who might help him translate the words he had heard as a child in Henning. He stopped many Africans and repeated the words he had heard on the porch in Henning. After two weeks, he had stopped dozens of Africans, "each and every one of whom took a quick listen to me and then took off." They dismissed him as some kind of American eccentric.[18]

Then, in September 1966, while participating in a seminar at Utica College, Haley described to a faculty member his attempt to get the African words translated. The professor told him that there was a student from the Gambia at nearby Hamilton College. On October 11, 1966, when Haley gave one of his first public lectures at Hamilton, he insisted on meeting the student, Ebou Manga. Haley later described him as short and very dark-skinned with short-cropped hair and "clear, frank" eyes. Manga was a solemn young man, a Muslim from the Wolof tribe, who "considers at length before he speaks." In this meeting and another a few weeks later, Manga told Haley that Mandinka was not his native language but that he understood it. In Mandinka, he said, the word he heard as "Bolongo" meant "river" and "Kamby" was the Gambia River. He then translated all the other words that Haley remembered. Along the way, Manga told Haley something that excited him: "We have in The Gambia what they call 'traditional historians,' . . . oral historians. Senegal is trying to get all these historians to make a collective history." Manga told him about "village books" written in Arabic and kept in each Gambian village that recorded its history. There is no evidence that, before his encounterters with Ebou Manga, Haley had focused on the Gambia as the home of his African ancestor. His previous mention of his ancestor's place of origin, made in the *Philadelphia Bulletin,* had been "the slave coast." But the slave coast encompassed thousands of miles in West Africa.[19]

In November 1966 Haley went to Ireland to research his father's roots. He traveled to the village of Carrickmacross in County Monaghan, fifty-five miles north of Dublin, to find relatives of his paternal great-grandfather James Jackson. Haley's research had already established that a James Jackson had left that part of Ireland and arrived in Philadelphia in 1799. He inquired at both the Catholic and Protestant parishes. The Irish were cordial to Haley and far more concerned with his religious affiliation than his race. A local woman was a Jackson descendant, but she thought Haley's ancestor came from a different line and suggested that he visit genealogical libraries in London. Haley went but made no discoveries there. Then he went to the Gambia High Commission offices in London to follow up on the information from Ebou Manga. Haley was in search of the African ancestor he now called "the Mandingo," who he believed was put on a slave ship in 1766. In Virginia Haley had found a deed transferring "one Negro man slave named Toby"—the white man's name the African had always objected to—from John Waller of Spotsylvania County to his brother William in 1768. With that information, Haley deduced that the Mandingo had crossed the Atlantic in 1766. At the commission offices, he was led to believe that in Bathurst (now Banjul), the largest city and the capital of the Gambia, he could find the name of the ship that had brought his African ancestor to America.[20]

* * *

BY JANUARY 1967 Ken McCormick was getting worried about "Before This Anger," which he wanted to publish in 1968. The book had now been under contract for two and a half years, and

McCormick wanted to see copy. Reynolds told him that he thought the book would be finished by the end of 1967. Haley told Reynolds, "It's my particular style (maybe I'm just not *like* other authors in this way) to spend 75% of my time gathering my material, and combing and cross-indexing it, until I feel the book is as I want it, in my *head*, and *then* I write, and very fast." Haley remembered, erroneously, that he had turned in a chapter of *Malcolm X* about every two weeks. "Before This Anger" was not "going to get written, under my circumstances at present. It won't get written until I can get enough money, at one time, to pay off sundry debt harassments [*sic*], . . . to be able to do the sustained *concentrating* on this book."[21]

In early 1967 Haley's money problems seemed to be getting the better of him. The IRS had found him negligent in paying his taxes in 1960, and it appears that from then on, his file was tagged for investigation for nonpayment. The fact was that after he left the Coast Guard, he did not earn enough to pay what he owed. In February 1967 Reynolds received an IRS order for the garnishment of Haley's royalties for payment of back taxes, which Reynolds said he intended to ignore. He would pay to Haley what he had coming for *Malcolm X*. But Reynolds then found out that Haley had been signing additional book contracts, and he demanded to know the details. Haley had signed one with Grove Press for a biography of Melvin Belli, although it is not clear that he told Reynolds about this. Haley had also contracted with Viking Press for a children's book. Reynolds worried about all these commitments and warned Haley against it—in an elliptical fashion. "I know your desperate problems. But one has to be candid in these matters and tell what has happened or one gets in real trouble when one discovers these things."[22]

Haley was unrepentant. Under his current pressure, "I will entertain any honorable way to relieve it, at least that I interpret as honorable." He again complained about the Doubleday contract for "Before This Anger," which carried an advance of only $5,000 in August 1964 ($38,000 in 2015). That money was long gone. "Anytime a publisher advances $5,000, he cares but scantly for the book," Haley said. The only other potential revenue sources were the paperback rights, and Doubleday was dragging its feet on selling those. "I will tell you something else they are not," Haley wrote, "and that's investing concern in a writer" destined to be in great demand. If Doubleday did not sell the paperback rights, then he would stop working on "Before This Anger" and start getting magazine assignments. "I will resume work on the book when I get—enough—working money. . . . I just happen to be that necessary evil, the writer. Nobody is going to get this book *until* I write it. And the book that is here, the Olympian chronicle, *my* family, *my* forebears, I am not going to half-write."[23]

Reynolds replied that the Doubleday contract had been signed long before Haley was well known, and at a time when publishers were not paying the large advances that writers were now getting. "Let's grant it was a mistake—my mistake if you want to," but "when a publisher has a firm contract at one price it's awful hard to make him pay more money. From his point of view, why should he?" Reynolds presented three possible solutions. They could get a big paperback contract, they could buy Doubleday out, or they could abandon "Before This Anger" and come up with a new, more lucrative, book idea. Reynolds then learned that Haley had signed a contract with William Morrow and Company for $12,500 to publish a collection of his interviews with celebrities. A Morrow editor had told another agent in Reynolds's firm that Haley had sought the contract to get the money to finish "Before This Anger." The writer was also working with James Baldwin on a script for a play about Malcolm X. Reynolds pleaded with Haley not to commit to anything else: "If you can say no to the small things and sort of keep in hiding, I think both of these books can be done this year, and this will come pretty near to solving your troubles." Haley then told Reynolds he had also been talking to Elia Kazan about a film version of "Before This Anger," for which Haley would write the screenplay. Reynolds answered that few nonfiction books were turned into movies, but because "Before

This Anger" was uplifting, "it may make a picture." Reynolds was desperate for Haley to keep first things first. "When can you promise me the first 10,000 words?" Not a word of the book had been written at this point, in the spring of 1967. Reynolds soon had an offer of $15,000 from Dell Publishing for the paperback rights to "Before This Anger."[24]

*   *   *

IN MARCH 1967 Haley organized his first trip to Africa. George Sims gave him a list of African historians, and he was most impressed with the qualifications of Jan Vansina. Haley wrote to him, but the professor was doing fieldwork in the Congo, and the letter was delayed in reaching him. With the new focus on the Gambia that Ebou Manga had provided, Haley read up on the country in John Gunther's *Inside Africa*. The Gambia had just won its independence from Britain in 1965. A tiny country geographically, a thin snake following the path of the Gambia River on both banks, it had a population of about three hundred thousand, most of whom were Muslim, and less than three hundred of whom were white. Few were literate, but there was a small black professional and civil-servant class. The country was dependent on a single crop—peanuts.[25]

Ebou Manga agreed to help Haley. His father, Alhaji Manga, a pharmacist who worked for the Gambian government, provided Haley with a list of Gambians who could assist in tracing his ancestor. On March 16 Haley wrote letters to the thirteen contacts. He described his book to an official in the office of the Gambia's prime minister, explaining that *Reader's Digest,* read by 24 million people in thirteen countries around the world, was going to condense the work. He added, "Recently America's greatest cinema director [Kazan] has announced plans to film from the book a major motion picture. A sizeable portion will be filmed in The Gambia, employing many Gambians as actors. I think it's safe to predict that by 1969, The Gambia will enjoy world recognition—and tourism."[26]

Haley paid for Ebou to travel ahead of him and set up meetings with people in the Gambia who could help. Ebou formed what came to be called the Haley Committee, providing its members with information he had gotten from Haley as well as an idea of what Haley wanted to find. On April 9 Ebou and his father brought the Haley Committee together at the bar of the Atlantic Hotel in Bathurst. Haley met with six men, including the minister of local affairs and the secretary of the Gambia Workers Union. Ebou identified each man's ethnicity; there were four different groups represented—Jola, Serahule, Fula, and Serere—but no Mandingo. One of the men lectured Haley: "You Negro Americans feel that you have been depersonalized. Well, so have we." Haley in turn disapproved of what he saw as the Africans' posturing. "They acted more British than do the British," a shame, he thought, "when the African, being African, is such an utterly charming person." He lamented "how much very vital time and psychic energy the Africans with any kind of position whatever waste acting like what they are not." It was like how "many Negroes in America try to ape sundry white people." He sounded a lot like his friend Malcolm X.[27]

In the lobby of the hotel, a member of the committee happened to see Alhaji Alieu Ebrima Cham Joof, a trade unionist, journalist, and radio broadcaster who had been a leader in the Gambian nationalist movement. Haley was introduced to Cham Joof, who was interested in Haley's purpose for visiting. Cham Joof in turn introduced Haley to M. E. Jallow, K. O. Jannch, and A. B. Sallah, all of them Cham Joof's colleagues in Gambian nationalism and trade unionism. These four men offered to help with Haley's research and proved to be the most active in finding his ancestor. Haley told them that his forefather's name was Kin-tay and that he believed he was taken from the Gambia in the late 1760s. He gave the committee pictures of his family. The Gambians thought that the name was significant because, they said, "our oldest villages tend to be named for those families which founded" them. They examined a map on which were marked two villages, Kinte-Kundeh and Kinte-Kundeh-Janneh-Ya. They explained about griots, to whom Ebou Manga had alluded in his first meeting with Haley. Griots functioned as oral historians; they told stories over and over about the history of villages, clans, and empires. What Haley needed was a griot of the Kinte clan, and the committee promised to see if they could find such a person. After five days Haley returned to the United States.[28]

*   *   *

HALEY IMMEDIATELY WROTE to Reynolds. "I am about to produce the single *biggest* book success of 1968. You watch! Can you imagine that in Africa, they were able to determine for me even the very *village* from which my 1760's forbear [sic] was taken! And the history of that *village* can authentically be taken back to about 1600! Ain't *never* been a book like this! We're going to go hang a Pulitzer Prize copy on that Reynolds office hallway wall!" He had a letter from Jan Vansina, whose advice was similar to that of the Gambian men: look for a clan name, and if one was found, it probably still existed. Then a letter arrived from Cham Joof saying that a griot had been found. Haley should return and be prepared to travel up the Gambia River. Haley needed money to go back. In the second half of April, he delivered six lectures for Colston Leigh in ten days and made $3,200 ($22,300 in 2015).[29]

He and George Sims arrived in Bathurst on May 13 and met with the Haley Committee. A. B. Sallah had an employee named Demba Kinte, who came from the village of Juffure and had discovered Kebba Kanga Fofana, identified as the griot of the Kinte clan. Cham Joof and Sallah had met with Fofana, the seventy-two-year-old whom they described as shy and reticent but from whom they had elicited the needed information. Sallah told Haley that often the easiest way to establish a family connection was to examine facial features. His employee Demba Kinte resembled the photograph of Chicken George that Haley had given the Gambians. After talking

with Fofana, Cham Joof and Sallah had calculated that a Kinte ancestor called Kunta could logically have disappeared in the 1760s.
"You see, Mr. Haley," Cham Joof said, "Kunta Kinte seems to be
our man." To go to the griot, Haley engaged a small steamboat that
would transport a photographer; a radio producer; three musicians
necessary for eliciting a performance from the griot; and Cham Joof,
Jallow, Sims, and Haley. On May 17 the party sailed. Another party
from the Haley committee traveled overland in a Land Rover.[30]

Thirty kilometers upriver, they came to tiny James Island, site
of the oldest British fort in West Africa, where captured slaves were
collected for shipment across the Atlantic. Haley explored a dungeon
where slaves had been chained. They moved to the river's north bank
to a village called Albreda, where they were greeted by people from
Juffure. "Asalakium Salaam," they said to Haley. "The first thing
that hit me was the intensity of their stares," he later wrote. "Their
eyes just raked me." They walked a kilometer to Juffure, a collection
of mud houses with thatched roofs, home to seventy adults. Suddenly
the crowd parted and three old men approached. The one in the center, the oldest, wore a white robe and a white pillbox hat, and Haley
knew instantly that this was the man he had come to see. The man
was Kebba Kanga Fofana, the griot. He looked at Haley and spoke
in a formal, reserved tone. Through an interpreter, he said, "You resemble the Kintes, especially the one called Mali Kinte, except that
your light color is different." Fofana pointed to a man in the group
who was the son of Mali Kinte.[31]

Then Haley asked the interpreter to tell the people that he had
come there "to find out who I am" and to learn of his ancestor Kinte.
He passed around pictures of the Palmer and Haley family members
in America. Then Fofana said, "Everybody should try to know where
he came from—yourself, your father, your grandfather, your great-
grandfather, your great-grand ancestors, all should want to know
where they came from." Fofana said that they heard through the ages
that they had many relatives "in the white man's country." Then,

as Haley recounted it, Fofana sat down and began to speak differently, as if he were reading from a scroll. His torso bent forward and the veins in his neck bulged. Haley later recorded in his notes that Fofana said that their forefathers had come from Mali, where they "conquered fire," which meant they were blacksmiths.

Fofana recited many generations of the Kintes' history. The family grew larger over the generations and was forced to spread to new areas and build new villages. In Juffure, Omoro Kinte had married Binta Kebbe, and they had four sons: Kunta, Lamin, Suwadu, and Madi.

Fofana descended from Lamin. The sons of Omoro suffered tragedy: one drowned and one died of sickness, and Kunta Kinte suffered a particularly tragic end.

> About the time when the king's soldier's came,
> He went away from his village
> To get wood from the bush,
> And he was never seen again.

Haley later said he heard no more because what Fofana said "meshed perfectly with what I'd heard on the front porch in Henning." Haley asked the interpreters to explain to Fofana and the villagers that this was the story he had heard in America. Then the people formed a circle around him and, moving counterclockwise, began chanting softly, then loudly, and then softly again. Then, one after another, the mothers of the village stepped into the circle, thrust a baby into Haley's arms for a long moment, and then snatched it back. This was a ritual, an anthropologist later explained to him, in which the women said, in effect, "Through this flesh which is us, we are you and you are us." The photographer took pictures of Haley and his relatives, and then they all went to the village's tiny mosque. The main message of the villager's prayer that day was, "Praise be to Allah for one who has been long lost from us, whom Allah has returned."

Haley returned to Bathurst overland, passing through the village called Kinte-Kundeh-Janneh-Ya. Villagers lined up to see Haley, now standing up in a Land Rover, and all of them were chanting something that he did not at first understand. Elders in white robes, maidens and mothers, naked children, all looked up at Haley, waving their arms and crying out together in English, "Meester Kinte! Meester Kinte!" He later said, "A sob hit me at about ankle level and just rolled up. . . . I began just shrieking, crying as I have never cried before or since in my life."

Alex Haley would often say that this day in Juffure and Kinte Kundah Janneh-Ya was the "peak experience" of his life. His account of that day would be the main pivot in the book he would write, but it would also be a story that raised many doubts about whether it happened the way he told it.

Alex Haley heard his family stories as a child on the front porch of this house. He was buried in front of it in 1992.

Courtesy of Christy Hunter Photography, Munford, Tennessee

Bertha Palmer Haley, the indulged only child of the well-to-do Will Palmer, died when her first child, Alex, was only ten years old.

Courtesy of the Anne Romaine Collection, University of Tennessee Knoxville Libraries

Alex Haley joined the United States Coast Guard at age eighteen in 1939 and developed a successful career as a writer over the next twenty years.

Courtesy of the United States Coast Guard

The exciting life of George Lea, "Chicken George," captured the imagination of his great-great-grandson Alex Haley.

Courtesy of the Anne Romaine Collection, University of Tennessee Knoxville Libraries

Despite some tense times early in their collaboration, Malcolm X and Haley became good friends.
Courtesy of the Library of Congress

The Autobiography of
Malcolm X, *published in
1965 by Grove Press, had
modest sales in its first two
years before becoming a
runaway best seller in the
late 1960s.*

THE AUTOBIOGRAPHY OF
MALCOLM X

ROOTS
The Saga of an American Family
ALEX
HALEY

Roots *was an instant
best seller even before the
television miniseries was
shown, and after that
bookstores had difficulty
keeping it in stock.*

When wide national and international fame came to him, Alex Haley often gave commencement addresses and received many honorary degrees.

Courtesy of the Photographic Department, University of Tennessee Knoxville

Alex Haley became a national celebrity in 1977 and for the remainder of his life was frequently seen on television programs like Hee-Haw, *as shown here with Minnie Pearl and Archie Campbell, stars of the* Grand Ole Opry.

Courtesy of the State of Tennessee

Alex Haley enjoyed life on his farm near Knoxville when he moved there in the 1980s.
Courtesy of the Photographic Department, University of Tennessee Knoxville

The week after Roots *aired,* Time *magazine put the phenomenon on its cover and assessed its meaning.*

On the twenty-fifth anniversary of the Roots *miniseries in 2002, Warner Brother reissued the series on DVD.*

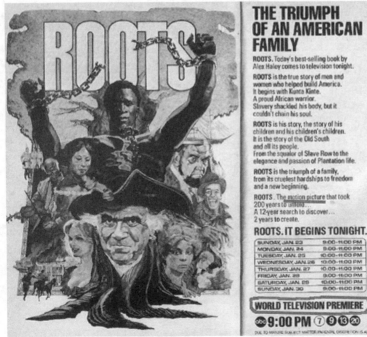

In its ad for the Roots *miniseries, ABC emphasized its historic significance and its interracial cast.*

7

THE AMERICAN GRIOT

ON HIS RETURN FROM AFRICA IN LATE MAY, HALEY reported to Paul Reynolds that he could now trace his family back nine generations, to 1705. He was even more ecstatic about the book's prospects. He thought it would have a reception comparable to that of Truman Capote's *In Cold Blood*, which was in its author's description a "nonfiction novel" about the murders of a Kansas family and had sold 325,000 copies in 1966. Capote acknowledged that he had imagined parts of the book, and he insisted that his departure from facts improved it. Reynolds raised the matter on his mind. "When will I be able to see the first 100 pages?" Almost three years had passed since the book contract was signed, and the book was a year and a half past the promised delivery date. Haley replied, "Don't you worry, friend: I push me harder than any six other people ever could." In July Reynolds wrote: "How much have you got on paper? I long, oh I long to read the first 50 pages as soon as possible." In August Haley told Reynolds he was "working beautifully" on the book. "I get goose pimples. It's going to be *so* great!" He promised to deliver the finished manuscript in December 1967. Still having seen nothing in September, Reynolds pleaded with Haley: "I think the time has come to completely stop all research work and write the book."[1]

Haley had returned from Africa with a determination to discover the ship that had brought Kunta Kinte to America. In the summer of 1967, he spent six weeks looking in shipping records at Lloyd's of London in search of the right ship. He got frustrated at not finding it and angry that participants in the slave trade regarded their work "simply as another major industry, rather like the buying, selling, and shipping of livestock today." Then, while looking over the 1,023rd sheet of slave-ship records, he found a listing of about thirty ships that had entered and exited the Gambia River. Well down the page, he saw an entry for the *Lord Ligonier,* captained by Thomas Davies, which on July 5, 1767, set sail for Annapolis, Maryland, with 140 slaves.[2]

Haley believed that this was the discovery that tied the information he had gained at Juffure about the capture of Kunta Kinte to his ancestor's arrival in America. He immediately flew to Washington, and at the Library of Congress he examined a book he had seen earlier, concerning ships arriving at Annapolis. This book confirmed that the *Lord Ligonier* had arrived in Annapolis on September 29, 1767. He then looked at a Maryland newspaper for the time and saw an advertisement: "JUST IMPORTED, In the ship of *Lord Ligonier,* Capt. Davies, from the River Gambia . . . A Cargo of CHOICE HEALTHY SLAVES." The ad mentioned ninety-eight slaves for sale, which meant that 30 percent of the original 140 Africans on board had perished. Haley then raced to Annapolis, where he worked at the Hall of Records at St. John's College. On September 29, 1967, exactly two hundred years after Kunta Kinte had presumably arrived there, Haley stood on a dock and looked at the Atlantic Ocean.[3]

In October 1967 Haley went to Madison, Wisconsin, to meet with Jan Vansina at last. It is not clear whether he revealed to Vansina that he had already translated the African words handed down in his family. Vansina confirmed the translation that Ebou Manga had offered a year earlier. He consulted with his fellow Africanist at Wisconsin, Philip Curtin, who came to the same conclusion about the Mandinka words and the likelihood of Haley's ancestor descending from the Kinte clan in the Gambia River region.[4]

Haley was slow to begin the writing of his book. He loved to do research and intended to insert as much historical authenticity as possible into "Before This Anger." He and George Sims studied anthropological works on West African life. Sims, who did not type, took notes in longhand, often on library order slips. Haley then typed them or gave them to a typist. He accumulated thousands of pages of notes typed on strips of paper and stapled onto full sheets. Periodically, he rearranged, purged, and added to his notes and then retyped them. Sometimes the source of the information was lost from one copy of notes to the next. Haley always told his agent and editors that the writing was going well, even as he delayed sending them the manuscript, but he struggled to get words on paper during the first five years of the project. He drafted "Before This Anger" in longhand on legal pads, relying on his memory of his mountain of notes. The first draft was a compendium of anthropological information on African life. The text was disjointed, overly detailed, and clumsy, as first drafts often are. He said privately that he was only an adequate writer; his talent lay in storytelling, which he did best orally. But after the book was finished, he would tell a somewhat different story. He said in 1976 to an interviewer from *Publishers Weekly* that there was "nothing I'd rather do" than write, "except perhaps be a surgeon." Both writing and surgery were "delicate, careful work, and I act like a surgeon." When he was writing, he said, he practiced a surgeon's hygiene. "I take six showers a day, and wash my hands maybe 20 times." But he also acted like a musician. "When it's going well, I find myself tapping my foot in rhythm with the keys, as if there's a cadence going." He wrote first drafts at night, when he was tired, "and then do the surgical work in the morning when I'm sharp."[5]

One way to avoid writing was to do more research. Haley examined hearings in the British House of Commons on the slave trade. He traveled to Wilberforce, England, to study artifacts from the slave trade and British abolitionism. In trying to understand the perils of the Middle Passage, he studied the habits of sharks that trailed trans-Atlantic ships. He searched the Virginia State Archives for family records of "Massa Waller," who had purchased the African. He traveled to Spotsylvania County, Virginia, and wandered on paths he believed Kunta Kinte had also walked. He did the same in Caswell County, North Carolina, where Chicken George had lived. In early 1968 Haley went to Scotland to research cockfighting, Chicken George's vocation. He spent months researching blacksmithing, Tom Murray's trade.[6]

After his six months of research in the Gambia, London, and Washington, Haley spent two months in Haut de Cagnes, France, a village near Nice, to write "Before This Anger." He sublet an apartment from the actor James Earl Jones, whom he had gotten to know when the actor sought him out in the hope of playing Malcolm on the stage and screen. In France he also met with James Baldwin, who was writing the script, based on Malcolm X's autobiography, to be made into a play directed by Elia Kazan. Haley was worried that Louis Lomax already had a deal with Twentieth-Century Fox for a movie about Malcolm's life. Kazan abandoned the idea of a play because he had heard that Columbia Pictures was going to make a film about Malcolm X. In March 1968 Vincent Canby reported in the *New York Times* that there were two Malcolm X films in production.[7]

At the end of 1967, Haley wrote to Ken McCormick and Lisa Drew, who were now assuming most of the responsibility for Haley's work, about "Before This Anger." He was on his way home from France with, "hopefully," a full draft. Yet he had written little of the book. Years later, he admitted that "many times" he told Drew that the writing of the book was much further along than it was, because he thought it would "help her feel better while I finished." In 1977, when Haley himself was the subject of a *Playboy* interview, he told of how he had placed 750 pages of typed manuscript on Drew's desk. He had polished the first twenty pages and the last few and then tucked more than 700 pages of typed notes in between. "She began to read the first page, then the second and the third, and she began to smile, wider and wider. But when she kept on turning pages, I started talking and kept talking, faster and faster, asking so many questions that she finally began skimming and then riffling around page 15. Then, as I knew she would from long acquaintance, she turned to the last page and read it carefully. I'd really poured it on at the end, and when she looked up, it was with moist eyes and a tremulous smile." Drew was happy when he left, and he was, too, because Doubleday had decided to give him more advance money.[8]

All the travel in 1967 had left Haley in dire financial straits, and he hoped that the solution to his problem would be to sell the movie rights to "Before This Anger." In 1968 Barnaby Conrad introduced him to Louis Blau, a Hollywood lawyer and agent who had represented Conrad and such stars as John Wayne. Blau was not familiar with Haley's work, but Blau's son, a student at Hollywood High School, told him that *The Autobiography of Malcolm X* was his favorite book. Blau listened for three hours as Haley spun out his family story. He and Haley then met with Columbia Pictures executives, who optioned the movie rights for $50,000. Haley's half of that represented the biggest payday he had ever had.[9]

Starting in 1967, Haley's lecture schedule grew heavier each year, and the momentum was due mostly to the growing influence of *The Autobiography of Malcolm X*. He had witnessed Malcolm at the college lectern, and he appreciated the power that one could exert there. Performing well gave Haley a rush of excitement, and lecturing appealed to his desire to influence young blacks' thinking about their past and whites' thinking about blacks. He seemed to be born to the lecture stage. The Harvard professor Richard Marius, himself a Tennessean and a noted storyteller, wrote that Haley "ambled to the platform always with an air of becoming modesty. He faced his audience with a genial reserve, and he spoke in a conversational baritone, reeling off stories of his childhood, of women rocking on a front porch, the sound of their rockers going 'thump-thump' as they mused over the oral history of their ancestors." Haley's lectures were like the public appearances of Frederick Douglass and other escaped slaves who spoke of the horrors of slavery to sympathetic audiences in the antebellum North and in England.[10]

Haley delivered twenty lectures in 1967, most of them for $500 each, of which the Colston Leigh Agency took 35 percent for booking the lectures and arranging his travel. In 1968 he gave forty-one lectures, in 1969 fifty-six, and in 1970 fifty-nine. About 90 percent of the lectures were to college audiences. Fees for lectures were rising rapidly in the late 1960s. By 1969 Haley was earning an average of $800 per lecture, and in 1970 most lectures were done for $1,000 (about $6,000 in 2015). He continued to give talks with titles such as "What the Negro Must Do for Himself" and "The Story Behind the Story of Malcolm X," but his most popular lecture was "Saga of a People," based on "Before This Anger." Haley gave this lecture over and over, more than a thousand times. "*Roots* was spread all over before it was published," he said. He estimated he had talked to more than a million people about the book. At each lecture, he promised that the book would be finished in six months' time. Soon Doubleday began to get hundreds of letters from people who had been in Haley's audiences and wanted to know where that book was. He later said: "I never really thought I was saying what was not accurate; I really felt I'd be finished with it in six months."[11]

On the lecture trail, Haley encountered people who helped him advance his research. After the lecture, listeners sometimes handed him notes with research leads. At Simpson College in Iowa, he was approached after his lecture by the college's dean, Waller Wiser, who explained that he was descended from the Waller family of Virginia, who had owned Kunta Kinte. Wiser explained that his wife was an excellent genealogist and knew his family's history well. Haley went home with Wiser that night, soon returned to give a commencement address and receive his first honorary doctorate from the college, and continued to gather information on the Wallers.[12]

The Black Power movement advanced Haley's career as a campus lecturer. In 1968 student revolts took place on campuses across the United States, initially in protest against the Vietnam War. Black students used the turmoil to advance Black Power. When Students for a Democratic Society occupied buildings at Columbia University in the spring of 1968, black members ejected white students, invited people from Harlem to campus, and demanded that Columbia change its name to "Malcolm X University." The winter and spring of 1969 brought Black Power protests in which African American students occupied buildings on campuses across the country. They demanded that colleges enroll more black students and hire more black faculty, create centers for black culture, and include in their curricula more study of African culture and African American history. These demands reflected the rising Black Studies movement, begun in 1967 at San Francisco State University, which promoted Black Power and all forms of black nationalism. The editor of the journal *Black Scholar* declared in 1969 that "a black-studies program which is not revolutionary and nationalistic is, accordingly, quite profoundly irrelevant." Black Power accelerated the need for black speakers on college campuses. In 1968 a *New York Times* writer concluded that "the most popular form of anti-establishmentarianism, the big *shtick* on campus today, is Black Power," which came "in several shades of militance but a single scorching degree of intensity." Black Power advocates Stokely Carmichael and H. Rap Brown were on the lecture circuit, as was the sardonic critic of white society, Dick Gregory.[13]

Haley offered a softer and more palatable expression of black nationalism. If Carmichael and Brown gave voice to the black anger against whites, Haley expressed pride in the black family and the connection to Africa and African peoples that had always been central to the ideology. His posture was compatible with the emerging Black Is Beautiful movement, which encouraged wearing dashikis and "natural" hair, the style soon called "the Afro." The story he told was not just about his family; it was "the saga of a people. Every black person shares this ancestral story of capture, slavery and obliteration." In 1969 he spoke at a conference of black students from all over New England, titled "Black Power: Milestone Toward Unity." Workshops at the conference included "Bridging the Black Generation Gap" and "Relationship Between the Black Man and His Black Woman." Haley's talk on his search for his family's roots provided cultural and historical balance to the intensely political nature of the remainder of the conference. He later spoke at the University of Connecticut. "Alex Haley tells a story that brings audiences to their feet around the country, and it's not a political story," the local newspaper reported. The 250 listeners gave shouts of "Right on!" during the standing ovation after he spoke.[14]

Newspaper coverage brought more attention to Haley. In 1969 UPI ran a story headlined, "Negro Finds Tracing Ancestry No Easy Task." The *Cleveland Plain Dealer* reported that Haley had riveted the audience at a local college. "He's probably the only one of the 25 million black Americans who ever will find out who his great-great-great-great-great-grandfather was. . . . This systematic destruction of families during the slave days killed the sense of tradition and history among America's Negroes." In 1972 the *Wall Street Journal* noted that Haley's message came at a time "when blacks, particularly students, are seeking to forge a sense of solidarity based on a documentable heritage." College professors and administrators noted that the interest in black genealogy coincided "with a decline in campus militancy and a rise in the introspection among students." It represented "a rechanneling of the impetus—sparked by the Black Power movement of the 1960s—to reaffirm the positive aspects of black culture."[15]

Haley knew the lectures were building a huge audience for the book. In early 1971 he encouraged Reynolds and McCormick to attend a lecture at New York University. By now, seven years after Haley had signed the original contract, each man's patience with the writer had almost run out. Haley wanted them to "gain some visual and aural appreciation of the way that by now literal[ly] hundreds of thousands of people (in audiences for three years) across the country [are] awaiting this book." McCormick found that Haley's lecture "absolutely hypnotized" the audience, himself included.[16]

*   *   *

HALEY'S "SAGA OF A PEOPLE" LECTURE, which comprised about sixty typed pages and took him two hours to deliver, has been preserved from an audio recording. It appears to be from a relatively late version of the lecture, given after he had perfected his delivery over hundreds of occasions. The transcription has no paragraphing and thus leaves the impression of a stream-of-consciousness recitation, when in fact there is a clear structure. The lecture was the first draft of what would become *Roots*. Haley began with his childhood and the scene on Cynthia's front porch in Henning, when the old ladies told, retold, and acted out the family history. One of the ladies would start talking about something that had happened in her girlhood, and "she would kind of turn around rather abruptly and thrust her finger down [at] me and exclaim something like, 'I wasn't any bigger than young'n here.'" He told of the capture of the African and the brutal punishment his rebellion brought from his white masters. Slaveowners' denial of his African name was "the first step in the psychic dehumanization of an individual or collectively of a people." Haley recited the Mandinka words that the African handed down, Haley's Rosetta Stone for unlocking his past. Ten pages into the text, Haley returned to his own life, recounting it with self-deprecation and good humor. Enlistment in the service, he now thought, "was to play its role in this book," because it was "meant to be" that he would get out in the world and have an opportunity to become a writer, starting with composing letters for his fellow sailors.[17]

After that, Haley embroidered his account to improve the story. He said that he just happened to be walking past the National Archives when something provoked him at the spur of the moment to go in. In fact, he already had a contract to write the book about his family, and doing genealogical research was an obvious step to take in its writing. "It gives me the quivers to reflect upon how easily, in fact, I might have walked on out of The National Archives and . . . and if I had, I'm sure I would have never, ever have given it another thought." He attributed his translations of the African words, his "Rosetta Stone" moment, to Jan Vansina, when in fact he had gotten the translation from Ebou Manga. He met Vansina in person only after he had made two trips to Africa, including the important experience in Juffure. Perhaps Haley wanted the imprimatur of Vansina's academic standing to validate his research.[18]

Haley recounted at length his "peak experience" of May 17, 1967, in Juffure. He told the story in much the same way he recorded it in his notes after the events, with both versions including his intense emotional reaction. The day's events did not take place in quite the way he described them, however. A transcript of Kebba Kanga Fofana's interaction with Haley and the translators contains none of the fluid oration that Haley later set down as his narrative. Prior to his meeting with Haley, the griot had been informed of Haley's beliefs about the name of his ancestor and the date of Kunta Kinte's capture. The griot may have accommodated his narrative to the facts that Haley had provided his Gambian sponsors. Haley may have been overcome with emotion from what the entire scene represented, but the emotion probably did not result from any surprises. Having narrated his peak experience, Haley then told of flying home to New York, meeting with publishers, and "finally [telling] them that I felt I had to write a book." Of course, by the first occasion on which he delivered this lecture, in 1968, his book had been under contract for four years.[19]

Excellent storyteller that he was, Haley observed his listeners closely. "You watch your audience," he explained later, "and see what the audience is responding to most." Haley took out some elements and added others as he told the story over and over. In its early versions he talked about going to Ireland in search of his Jackson ancestors. The Irish did not seem to think it odd that an American black man was looking for an Irish ancestor. But "when they found out I was Protestant, they ran me out of town." This was funny but probably not true; he did not mention it in accounts he wrote just after the visit. Over time, as his story became an exclusively African and black narrative, he deleted the passage about Ireland.[20]

By the time he finished the book, the "Saga of a People" lecture had become Haley's version of the truth, even if he knew he had been unfaithful to it in some places. The lecture version is almost identical to the final chapters of the book he was writing. When confronted twenty years later with the inconsistencies in his story, Haley would say that none of them were "an effort to slick over something" but just part of "the quest for the symbolic history of a people."[21]

*   *   *

IN AUGUST 1969 Haley told Reynolds that he and Julie were going to divorce. "She's doing all the mud-slinging she can, and one of my best defenses is that she not know where I am." He warned Reynolds that Julie might call him asking for Haley's whereabouts, which should not be revealed. She had taken to calling Haley at 3 a.m. and haranguing him for two hours. The break was finalized in June 1971. Haley was now supporting two ex-wives and his daughter Cynthia, only seven years old that year. Much of his lecture income was paid to Nan. By then *The Autobiography of Malcolm X* was a best seller, but the royalties for the mass-market paperback were small, and they were split with Betty Shabazz. He supplemented his income starting in 1968 by teaching at Hamilton College, where he had met Ebou Manga. "I was flattered like hell to go up there and actually be faculty," he later said. Haley's classes at Hamilton did not cover any subject in the college catalogue, and he did not hold class on a regular teaching schedule; what he taught was "really more a class in Alex Haley." Hamilton needed him "for racial reasons," seeing in him someone who could "represent black myths." Students who needed good grades came to him. If he felt sympathy for the student, Haley gave him an A minus. Inevitably, criticism arose as word of his liberality with students got around. The next year he was made a "writer in residence."[22]

Haley did not get much writing done at Hamilton, and in 1969 it began to catch up with him. In March he faced the anger of Hillel Black, president of William Morrow, for his failure to deliver a book of interviews contracted with Morrow in 1967. Reynolds tried to calm Black by sharing his own frustration: "He's never completed his book to Doubleday," and, indeed, Reynolds himself had not "seen a word of it." Three years later, in 1972, Haley still had not written any of the book for Morrow, and Black demanded return of the $12,500 advance. Haley no longer had the money, and he passed responsibility for appeasing Black on to Reynolds. Reynolds's frustration about not having seen any of "Before This Anger" caused Haley in late July 1969 to turn in what he had written. Though pleased to get something, Reynolds did not like what he saw. "You are going to need a great deal of condensation. . . . I would like a long, big book, 150,000 to 200,000 words, but not a million or million-and-a-half words." Haley sent the text to Lisa Drew, who also thought it was poorly written. At this point Haley again turned to Murray Fisher, who took Haley's swollen text, deleted a high percentage of the verbiage, and remade it into a coherent and readable narrative. In a surviving file named "Fisher-edited copy," page after page of Haley's text is covered with red editing marks. Reynolds read this copy and told Haley he was "off to a fine start." Based on these chapters about the African origins of Haley's family, Reynolds raised the question of whether the book was fact or fiction. "These pages are pretty fictionalized for the *Digest* magazine," he observed, thinking of the serialization of the book. But he thought the manuscript would be fine for the *Reader's Digest* Book Club, which published much fiction. Reynolds's comments suggest that people in the publishing business accepted a liberal definition of historical truth. Others, it would turn out, had a much narrower criterion.[23]

Then progress on the book seemed to stop. Again, other projects diverted Haley. In the summer of 1970, he wrote a play he called "Booker," the idea for which came to him in a dream. The play was another autobiographical exercise, about a man from Henning who migrates to the North and faces a jarring change of scene in a northern ghetto. "I realized I knew that play, in large part because I grew up in it," he told Reynolds. "I simply could not refuse that play's urgency to be born." Haley told McCormick about the play, at the same time promising that he would have "Before This Anger" completed by the end of 1970. McCormick wrote to Reynolds, "This I will believe when I see it." In late 1970 Haley confessed to Reynolds that with the help of an agent who had left Reynolds and knew of Haley's financial problems, he had signed a contract to write a biography of Melvin Belli. "I simply was broke, *in a mess,* and trying anything that looked potential[ly] as a salvation."[24]

By 1971 Reynolds had lost his good humor about Haley's money problems and his inability to finish "Before This Anger," now almost six years late. He reminded Haley that book contracts made in desperate pursuit of an immediate payday had compromised his long-term value as a writer: "Due to need of money you have got a not too desirable contract with Doubleday and a miserable commitment with Dell for the paperback." But by 1971 the sales of *The Autobiography of Malcolm X* had cemented Haley's reputation as a best-selling author. Haley wrote to Reynolds that high schools and colleges were desperate for any works on black history, and most of the readers were white students. Reynolds already knew that Haley's stock had gone up. "A good idea for a book by Alex Haley put up for auction could bring an enormous sum of money," he acknowledged. But he was adamant that Haley should not write the Belli book, which he thought would be viewed as a puff biography.[25]

* * *

HALEY'S FINANCIAL and marital woes, combined with the slow pace of his writing, made the summer of 1971 a low point in his life. He turned toward the sea to get away from his ex-wives, the IRS, and the editors at Doubleday. He liked to say that he had learned to write on ships and did his best work on the high seas. In March 1971 he spent eleven days on the *African Star,* a freighter he boarded in Liberia for the Atlantic crossing. He later recounted how at night he stripped to his underwear and lay on a rough board in the cargo hold to get a sense of how the captive Kunta Kinte might have felt. But the feelings that this experience engendered further depressed Haley, because he could not fully imagine the suffering of someone chained in the belly of a ship. He stood on the dark deck one night and realized there was an answer to his problems. "Simply step through rail and drop into the sea. It was almost a euphoric feeling. . . . No more debts, no more deadlines, no more agonizing over slavery, no more nothing." He later said that what prevented his jumping were the voices of the generations of women in his family telling him not to do it.[26]

Starting in May 1971 he took a Norwegian freighter on a three-month trip around South America. He reported that he got much writing done, although he left the ship for several days to go New York to finalize his divorce from Julie. In July 1972 Haley found a berth on a wooden ship, *The Eagle,* which sailed from Connecticut to Sweden, so that he might know the feeling of sailing on a ship like the one in which Kunta Kinte crossed the Atlantic. In December he left San Francisco for a fifty-five-day trip on the SS *President Polk,*

a freighter bound for Taiwan. Haley relayed his shipboard schedule to a reporter friend in Chicago: "The first day goes to catch-up
sleeping. The second day, suicidal impulses attend comprehending
really how far behind in work I am. The third day, sorting it all into
priorities, I start digging in. Well out by then, somewhere on the
ocean commences the pure euphoria of writing for a disciplined 12
hours daily—resulting in a quantity of pages of draft copy seemingly
impossible for me to achieve otherwise. Interspersed are ample naps,
along with eating too much thrice daily . . . and the wee hours usually see meditative, introspective meanderings about the decks."[27]

In 1972 Haley sought greater media attention for his book. In
early May he made what would prove to be an effective change in
the title, when he began referring to the work as "Roots." In April
Haley had appeared on the television quiz show *To Tell the Truth*,
on which he was the figure he and two impostors claimed to be. He
identified "Alex Haley" this way: "Actually my story is much more
than the story of one family. In effect, I have charted the history of
every black American. I say this because every one of us is directly
descended from some African who was taken from his homeland,
dragged to America, chained in the hold of a ship, and callously
sold as a slave." Later that year he appeared on David Frost's late-
night talk show and spoke with what the *Christian Science Monitor*
reported was "a cool neutrality that adds to the excitement" of his
writing project. In July 1972 Haley published his first article about
the book since 1965. In "My Furthest-Back Person—The African,"
which appeared in the *New York Times Magazine,* he gave an emotional rejection of his own mixed racial identity, one that departed
from the earlier equanimity, even pride, about his Irish ancestry. Arriving in Juffure, he wrote, he had been surrounded by the villagers.
"It hit me like a gale wind: every one of them, the whole crowd, was
jet black. An enormous sense of guilt swept me—a sense of being
some kind of hybrid . . . a sense of being impure among the pure. It
was an awful sensation."[28]

In August 1972 Paul Reynolds read a further-revised 408 pages of "Roots," the part called "The African Heritage." Reynolds thought the pages were "beautifully written" and added that if Haley wanted to become a novelist, "you would be a very successful one." But Reynolds said he was "a little appalled at the length this book is going to be." The book might have to be published in two or three volumes, because one book containing the entire text would require a price so high it would hurt sales. (Later in 1972 Haley reported that the 952 pages of the book had all been written the previous summer.) But in the spring of 1973, Doubleday made clear that it was publishing only a single volume.[29]

Haley taught black history at the University of California at Berkeley in the spring of 1973; there, he wrote the Middle Passage section of "Roots." He also spent time in Los Angeles working with Fisher on the book. He liked California for the old friends there. Through Lou Blau, he now knew more people in Hollywood. By this time he was turning his ambitions to film and television, though he still talked about books that he would write after "Roots." The money in Hollywood was better than in publishing, and his role in the creation of entertainment for television was less laborious than writing for print. He wrote the script for a 1973 film, *Super Fly T.N.T.*, the sequel to the successful blaxploitation film *Super Fly*, starring Ron O'Neal as a Harlem cocaine dealer. O'Neal starred in and directed *Super Fly T.N.T.*, which was a commercial and artistic failure.[30]

In May 1973 Haley told Reynolds that he planned to take out a loan for a year's projected expenses so that he could stop lecturing and spend long periods of time writing aboard freighters. Reynolds thought that was a good idea, because he was "beginning to get a backlash" from those—no doubt at Doubleday—demanding to know, "Where is the book?" It is not clear whether Haley got the bank loan, but he certainly did not abandon the lecture circuit. He gave thirty-seven lectures in the next year. But rather than spend another summer on a merchant ship, he rented a house in Negril, a village on Jamaica's western coast. He loved the setting and the climate. There were few telephones, and the mail was slow. He worked there for much of the next two years.[31]

In 1973 the IRS put a lien on Haley's bank account. He had deposited $800 and written checks for twenty-two bills, every one of which bounced because the IRS had confiscated his funds. "That kind of thing would plunge you into an abyss and for that moment, [I thought], you dumb son of a bitch, what in the world are you doing?" Julie had been put in a psychiatric hospital, and he needed money to look after Cindy, now nine years old.[32]

Help came from Hollywood. In 1974 Columbia Pictures canceled its 1968 contract for film rights to "Roots" because of the studio's financial problems. Lou Blau then negotiated with Warner Bros. for film rights to "Roots," but nothing came of that. David Wolper, a producer of documentaries, had heard of Haley's book in 1969 from the actress Ruby Dee, wife of Ossie Davis. Dee and Davis had known Haley through Malcolm X, and at black arts events in New York, they heard him talk about his family research. From the moment Wolper heard of "Roots," he wanted to produce it. In 1974 Wolper heard that Warner had relinquished the rights, contacted Blau, and negotiated a contract for a television series. He paid Haley a $50,000 option on the $250,000 full fee for rights when the book was finished.[33]

With Hollywood money starting to flow, Haley bought a house in Jamaica. At Blau's suggestion he set up the Kinte Corporation, a tax shelter. He and his brother George were planning to produce a line of dolls and other memorabilia that capitalized on the new interest in the African past. They had already created a foundation to gather material for a genealogical library. Leonard Jeffries, chair of the Black Studies Department at the City University of New York, did much of the work for this project. The Haleys received a grant from the Carnegie Corporation for almost a half-million dollars to get the library going. "Probably I've become the person most knowledgeable about black genealogy," Haley told the *Wall Street Journal* in 1972. That seemingly harmless boast set him up for later criticism.[34]

*   *   *

REYNOLDS CONGRATULATED Haley on the television deal but warned him, "With no book, your whole house of cards would fall to pieces." Though Haley maintained warm relations with Lisa Drew, by 1974 he felt embittered toward the publishing house. He told Reynolds that he had "a deep canker in my insides" against Doubleday, because it had "consistently pinched, and squinched as if [this book] was some marginal gamble by an unproved writer." Murray Fisher had told him that writers broke contracts all the time to get more money, and Haley wanted to do that. Reynolds dismissed all suggestion that they might get another publisher to buy Doubleday out of the book. "It's known all over New York that you've been writing this book for 7 years. Any publisher is going to wonder whether the next two-thirds of the book can be written and finished within six months or a year." At the same time, Drew was getting constant demands from Doubleday executives to either get a book out of Haley or get the company's money back. She defused the situation by saying the book was almost finished as she tried to get Haley to complete it.[35]

Drew and Ken McCormick, now semiretired, had read the 871 pages of the book delivered in November 1973. They enlisted Reynolds to try to get the book finished. Drew told Reynolds that some of the writing was good but other parts were "simply too long and lose the impact of what Haley is trying to say by excessive repetition." She and McCormick thought the conversations that Haley had created among slaves during the American Revolution were unrealistic and "beyond [the slaves'] scope, given their limited education." Neither of the editors wanted to include a section at the end of the book about Haley's research. The Doubleday staff was relieved when Haley insisted in April 1974 that the book would be submitted in the next few weeks. Reynolds deflated their hopes. "Alex will never deliver in May or June. . . . His problem is money and he's had to go back to lecturing." Sure enough, Doubleday did not receive any more of the manuscript until December 1974, thirteen months after the previous installment had come in.[36]

In the press to finish the book, Haley relied heavily on Murray Fisher. Fisher would later claim to have been Haley's "personal editor" and "deeply involved in the creation" of *Roots*—a fair claim by any standard of measure. In 1969 Fisher had so completely rewritten the African portion of the book—150 pages, almost a fourth of the book—that the prose was probably more his than Haley's. In 1973 Haley had informed Reynolds that he wanted Fisher to get 10 percent of the proceeds of the book in repayment for his great contribution to the work and 5 percent of all movie residuals. The editors at Doubleday had little knowledge of Fisher's role in editing the book until 1974, when, with some desperation, they agreed that Fisher could make the cuts Doubleday wanted in the 871 pages received in November. Fisher was an overbearing and interfering man who exceeded the bounds of editor. He objected to Reynolds that he had not been given an opportunity to edit the copy that *Reader's Digest* was excerpting. A furious Haley told Fisher that he was not to call Reynolds or anyone else handling the production of "Roots." Haley told Reynolds that Fisher was "an aggressive, dominating type of personality, which I regard as fine for his own life, but don't thrust it upon *me*." If Fisher did not back off, Haley would not let him see the second half of the manuscript. If he fired Fisher but had to keep paying him, "I'd regard it as another costly lesson learned." But the fact was that Haley needed Fisher to get the second half of the book out. About three hundred pages of new text reached New York in early 1975. Reynolds thought it was good but needed some cutting. Haley again turned to Fisher to attend to such problems.[37]

Haley kept Drew in the dark about his progress, or lack thereof. She pleaded with Reynolds for information on what Haley was doing. In May 1975, David Wolper expressed concern that "Roots" would not be finished soon enough to appear in bookstores before March 1976, when the television series was scheduled to air. Haley then promised that he would deliver the final manuscript to Doubleday by June 15, 1975. In mid-June Drew went to Jamaica with the intention of giving editorial suggestions to Haley on the spot and then returning to New York with a final manuscript. Drew was surprised to find Murray Fisher also in residence and shocked to discover that the manuscript was far from complete—only about 70 percent of what would eventually comprise the book had been written. Drew worked in one room reading the manuscript while Haley wrote on the porch. He was writing the Chicken George portion of the book in longhand on a legal pad, and when he had written two or three pages, he gave them to a typist. When the typing was complete, Fisher edited the text. "Alex tends to overwrite a great deal," Drew later said. "He had a lot in his head, and he was putting down everything in it." Fisher cut, tightened sentences, moved material around, and then gave the pages back to the typist, who produced a new draft. Drew then read Fisher's edits and made more suggestions, and the manuscript was typed again. Drew thought Fisher's edits were beneficial.[38]

At the end of the first day, Drew asked Haley for a few minutes to go over her edits, and when she left him to read more, Fisher came to Drew and ordered her not to talk directly to Haley. All her comments should go first to him, Fisher said, and he would pass them on to Alex. Furious at his high-handedness, Drew said she would deal with Haley as she saw fit. When she asked Haley if he knew about Fisher's behavior, he replied that he did not and that Drew should come directly to him whenever necessary. Drew and Fisher kept their distance from each other from then on, until Drew was leaving to return to New York, at which point Fisher gave her a set of pages— only the first third of the manuscript. She turned to the title page and saw "Roots, by Alex Haley and Murray Fisher." Drew told Haley that dual authorship was not acceptable. Haley and Fisher had a bitter argument, and Haley told Fisher to leave. Haley told Reynolds that all had gone well among the three of them and that the manuscript would be finished by July 15. He wanted people in New York to believe that he was enjoying smooth sailing toward the completion of the book. In late September he had still not completed the Chicken George chapters, seventeen in all, or about 150 pages of manuscript. But he promised that they would be submitted soon and that in the next six weeks he would push to the end of "Roots." Throughout the entire writing process, this was the only promise of a delivery date that he kept.[39]

In early October 1975 Fisher met with Haley and Stan Margolies, producer of the television series. Fisher interrupted each time Margolies asked Haley a question about the story. Haley angrily left the meeting and informed Fisher that he would finish "Roots" without his help. They were almost opposite personalities, Haley said; Fisher relished conflict and admitted his "private disdain for people who don't meet [you] in confrontations. . . . You all but personify intransigence. . . . Once the manuscript's in your hands, who dares intrude?" Haley despised "any unnecessary confrontations—as I think most are." Haley was angry that Fisher had told Lisa Drew "to keep secret" what she saw in Jamaica, meaning Fisher's heavy involvement in the manuscript's formation. Such a comment, "dropped, seeded, in enough places," could become "the sort of titillating tidbit that can outgrow weeds and outlast dye," and "in time it's heard in cocktail parties in Idaho, 'Look, I happen to know he didn't really write it—.'" On the lecture trail he had been asked regularly if it was not true that a white man had actually written *The Autobiography of Malcolm X.* Haley had been sensitive to gossip about himself since cocktail-party chatter in New York in the 1960s about his failure to get articles published in *Reader's Digest* had gotten back to him. Haley acknowledged that Fisher had greater abilities than he did. Haley said that he himself researched good stories and that "I'm an innate[ly] good story-teller; an adequate author." Maybe he and Fisher could work together in the future, but for the time being they were through.[40]

Nine days later Haley wrote Fisher a letter of reconciliation. Blacks had had many generations to study whites, but whites, he thought, got thin-skinned if they were examined. "Roots" aspired to prove that blacks belonged in the mainstream of society, and if that was accomplished, Haley would come under public examination. "I have got to be able to stand under the spotlight of the scrutiny that will come," he wrote. Fisher, Haley asserted, knew how American society worked on celebrities as they reached the higher rungs of fame: it found ways to "diminish, discredit them back down to size, as if to prove they really hadn't belonged all the way up there." Haley suspected that Fisher had "this discrediting, diminishing potential." There were two ways that black celebrities were brought down: they were found to have been rule- or lawbreakers at some point in their backgrounds or they were somehow found to be controlled by white people. Fisher had to help Haley guard against both kinds of attack. Black critics would demand to know why he relied on Fisher. Didn't he know any black editors? At the end of the long letter, he asked Fisher to return in early November to Jamaica, where, together, they would hammer out the last chapters about Tom Murray during the Civil War and Reconstruction.[41]

The two worked well together from then until the end. Haley now also had the help of Myran Lewis, a graduate student at Ohio State University who was writing a biography of Harriet Tubman. Twenty-six-year-old My was living with Haley and typing the manuscript in exchange for Haley's promise to help her with her book. Haley told Fisher, "This is a very 'heavy' girl, as the saying goes"— meaning that she was accomplished educationally—but she was also "diminutive, black, cute, quiet, sensitive, very, very sharp." Lewis typed 120 words per minute and proofread as she went, but she had an even more active role in composing the book's ending. Each morning she rose early, while Haley was still in bed, and sketched out dialogue and details to be added to the text. Her additions were the foundations of scenes in the book, enabling character development.

Asked later if she deserved to be named as co-author, she replied, "Alex was 30 years older than me. I had such hero worship going. I couldn't imagine being on the same page with somebody like Alex Haley." She would become the third Mrs. Alex Haley.[42]

*   *   *

AT LONG LAST, Haley's financial situation was changing for the better. In October 1975 Wolper had made a payment of $250,000 to Haley for the television series. Haley submitted his final draft of "Roots" to Doubleday in early December, more than eleven years after he had signed a contract for the book. When *Roots* came out, Haley generously acknowledged Murray Fisher. Haley had solicited Fisher's help to structure the book from "a seeming impassable maze of researched materials." Together they established a pattern of chapters and developed the story line. "Finally, in the book's pressurized completion phase, he even drafted some of *Roots*' scenes," Haley wrote, "and his brilliant editing pen steadily tightened the book's great length." It was a generous and accurate tribute.[43]

8

THE BLACK FAMILY BIBLE

L ISA DREW HANDED HALEY THE COPYEDITED MAN-
uscript of *Roots* on January 23, 1976. Promising to return it
with the editor's queries answered a week later, Haley left with
the manuscript and settled into the Commodore Hotel in New
York, where in the next two weeks he rewrote the last 183 pages.
When he returned the manuscript, it was misplaced in the Doubleday building for a few days. The delay was long enough that the
now frantic Lisa Drew did not let Haley see the galley proofs: "I was
frankly frightened of risking having him rewrite any more at that
point." Doubleday was working to get the book out several months
before the airing of the *Roots* television series, which, to great relief
at Doubleday, was soon postponed until early 1977. This meant that
that Haley could travel to promote the book in the fall of 1976.[1]

Though *Roots* was advertised as a book that covered seven generations of Haley's family, it turned out to be far more about slavery
than it was about freedom. Over his long years of writing the book,
Haley's dominant concern was establishing his African past. He
saw that as his greatest contribution to black American history. The

book's focus also reflected the disproportionate time he had spent on researching and writing about the African and Middle Passage experiences. By the time he got to writing about the family members born after Chicken George's time—the last four generations—he had to hammer out the remainder in about two months. The ending feels rushed, because the writing of it *was* rushed. Haley planned to dwell on his family's post–Civil War experience in a separate book.[2]

Haley's attachment to Kunta Kinte overwhelms his interest in other characters and dominates the book. He devoted years of research to creating an idyllic origin for his family in the unspoiled African environment. Kunta's mother, Binta, and father, Omoro, are perfect parents—well born, wise, and loving—symbols for the original natal family of every black American. Kunta is the African hero, fearless at every turn, until he chooses a peaceful life on the plantation over futile and probably fatal rebellion. He contradicts in every way the archetype of Sambo that Stanley Elkins had presented and that had gained so much attention in the 1960s.

Kunta was the second great hero Haley had created on the page. Kunta and Malcolm X both were examples of fierce, independent, and manly characters, and together they formed a new and cherished archetype for black Americans—and, indeed, for many whites. Haley grappled with issues of identity in writing about Malcolm and then Kunta, and the two may have been proxies, on a subconscious level, for the existential struggles of Haley's own life. The autobiographical impulse takes over *Roots* at the end, when Haley narrates his visit to Juffure.[3]

Though the book flows gracefully for at least the first half, Haley frequently tried to tell the reader too much. He relied on slaves' speeches in dialect to narrate the history of race in American history. Their conversations delivered background information on a variety of important historical topics—the death of a president, the invention of the cotton gin—but the means by which slaves acquired knowledge was not always clear, or it was relayed through means that seem contrived, Haley had gathered a vast amount of historical knowledge, and he did not always resist the impulse to show what he knew.

Roots emphasized the patriarchal authority in Haley's family. Each main male character—Kunta, Chicken George, Tom Murray, Will Palmer, Simon Haley, and Alex—directed the action in the narrative more than the women. Haley's men were proud of their heritage and high social standing. They understood how society worked and acquired skills and, some of them, education. Among the women, only Kunta's American-born daughter, Kizzy, emerged as a multidimensional character, but once her master raped her, the book's focus shifted to her son, George. Bell, Kizzy, and Cynthia Palmer had crucial roles in keeping the family stories, but so did the men. The other female characters operated mostly as props for strong, decisive male characters. As Haley portrayed them, slave women in the United States were overly absorbed with whites' lives and passive about slaves' interests, while the men took responsibility for lifting the race.[4]

Haley's portrayal of slave women as passive stands out because it contradicts much of the writing about American slavery since *Roots*. It also opposed the image of slave women that came down from slave narratives. It may have been that the particular pieces of evidence Haley encountered led him in that direction. But because *Roots* was so much a product of his imagination, it had to have resulted to some extent from his own attitude toward women. Notwithstanding his lifelong appreciation for his grandmother and others among his older female kin, he doubted his natal mother's affection for him, and he knew his stepmother did not like him. He had gone through two marriages that ended in protracted and bitter divorces. If time spent with his daughters is an indication, he appears not to have been strongly attached to them. He was charming to women with whom he worked, but he seemed to respect more the views of male colleagues. He spoke proudly of his father, Simon, his brother George, and his colleagues in the publishing business. He admired the integrity of

Malcolm X. Did personal or psychological instincts about women shape his interpretations of the past? The evidence is only suggestive.

But there is no doubt that Haley was determined to develop the theme of the strength of black families. He suggested that over the generations, his family had turned chaos into order, lack of education into accomplishment, and trauma into triumph. Each generation accomplished something vital to the survival of the family. *Roots* captured black slave families' vulnerability under the constant threat of being sold away from one another, but Haley also showed those families' resilience. Kizzy was sold away from her parents, but in her new dwelling, older slaves who had also been robbed of family members created a nurturing community for her to find solace. Kizzy's son, Chicken George, was separated from his family for many years but still managed to lead his children through war and Emancipation and, ultimately, to some security in Tennessee. As a family story, *Roots* has a happy ending, and that accounted for much of its popularity.[5]

Haley's portrayal of patriarchal power in a black family appealed to many blacks because of a decade-long debate about the plight of black families in the United States. In 1965 Daniel Patrick Moynihan, then assistant secretary of labor in the Johnson administration, had prepared a report on black poverty in which he suggested that, despite the great gains of the civil rights movement, African Americans as a group were not progressing economically. In *The Negro Family: The Case for National Action,* Moynihan wrote that the "the Negro family, battered and harassed by discrimination, injustice, and uprooting, is in the deepest trouble." A black child was eight times more likely than a white to be born out of wedlock; the number of black children supported by welfare was rising rapidly, black male unemployment was going up, and there were three times as many female-headed households among blacks as whites. Moynihan listed the historical circumstances—slavery, white supremacy, migration to cities—that accounted for the differences, but still he characterized the black family as a "tangle of pathology capable of perpetuating itself without assistance from the white world." He observed that black men had been emasculated, which Haley contradicted with his creation of strong male characters. A white psychologist spoke for many activists and academics when he denounced Moynihan for "blaming the victim." Moynihan said privately, "Obviously one can no longer address oneself to the subject of the Negro family."[6] But, in fact, that was what Alex Haley had done—addressed himself to the black family—with a compelling account of family strength and survival.

At exactly the same time that *Roots* appeared, Herbert G. Gutman of the City University of New York answered the Moynihan report with *The Black Family in Slavery and Freedom, 1750–1925*, which argued that, while black families did not mirror the structure of white families, they had remained intact through slavery and Emancipation and into the first generation of migration to northern cities. The family was the slaves' salvation through those terrible times. The breakdown that Moynihan described occurred after blacks had been oppressed in urban ghettos for two generations.

Gutman's work was part of a fundamental reinterpretation of American slavery taking place during the last years of Haley's writing of *Roots*. In 1972 John Blassingame of Yale University published *The Slave Community: Plantation Life in the Antebellum South*, which argued that historians of slavery had depended too much on the records of planters to depict slaves' lives. Blassingame used slave narratives to create a portrait of insulated and self-affirming slave communities. He also acknowledged the importance of the family to slaves. "However frequently the family was broken it was primarily responsible for the slave's ability to survive on the plantation without becoming totally dependent on and submissive to his master."[7] In 1974 Eugene Genovese of the University of Rochester also relied heavily on black sources to create *Roll, Jordan, Roll*, a study that placed heavy emphasis on the sustaining power of slave religion. Genovese concluded that slaves were active in pressing for their own well-being.

It is not clear that Haley was familiar with the work of Gutman, Blassingame, or Genovese, though surely, if he knew of them, he had opportunities to review the works of the latter two before he finished *Roots*. If he was not familiar with any of these academic works, Haley should be credited for his intuition in addressing the same question that these professors, and American scholars in general, had been grappling with for two decades by 1976. In the face of an inhumane and immoral system, how had African Americans survived slavery and moved forward in freedom toward a better life? Haley's answer shared many themes with scholars' responses—and was far more influential.

The most significant contribution of *Roots* to society was the one that Haley had identified all along: with this work, he had recovered the black American's African past. Since the nineteenth century, a few blacks had attempted from time to time to recapture their heritage in Africa, but with the emergence of postcolonial nations on the continent in the 1950s and early 1960s, and the rise of black nationalism in the United States after 1965, a more popular and sustained curiosity about blacks' African origins had emerged. Now a black American's history did not begin on a plantation in the South but reached much further back.[8]

*   *   *

BOTH HALEY AND DOUBLEDAY insisted that the book was nonfiction. The book jacket mentioned the stories Haley had heard as a child and then called the writer's research "an astonishing feat of genealogical detection" in which he "discovered not only the name of 'the African' . . . but the precise location of Juffure, the very village in The Gambia . . . from which he was abducted in 1767 at the age of sixteen and taken on the *Lord Ligonier* to Maryland and sold to a Virginia planter." The book jacket claimed not only that Haley had recovered his family's past but that, "as the first black American writer to trace his origins back to their roots, he has told the story of

25,000,000 Americans of African descent. He has rediscovered for an entire people a rich cultural heritage that slavery took away from them, along with their identities."⁹ Though Haley warned against reading the book strictly as objective history, Doubleday's advertising it so emphatically as historical truth opened the book to intense scrutiny.

Asked later if *Roots* was a work of fiction or nonfiction, Lisa Drew said that while there were fictional elements in the book—particularly the made-up dialogues among slaves, the main thrust of which were historically true—"the life of the African . . . the slave ship crossings, the conditions on those ships [were] pretty universally true." Drew had one clear reason for using the nonfiction label: "I was terribly afraid if we called this book fiction, although it had fiction elements in it, the people who are not sympathetic to the viewpoint of the book would use that as an excuse to say . . . this is fiction and it is all made up and it didn't happen that way." In 1978 her colleague Ken McCormick said that he considered the book fiction but that in 1976 he had deferred to Drew. Despite her frustrations in dealing with Haley, Drew was devoted to him personally and may have deferred to his judgment. It is unlikely, however, that she made the determination on her own to call the book nonfiction. At thirty-six she was still a relatively junior editor at Doubleday.¹⁰

Haley and Doubleday might have offered a stronger defense of the historical accuracy of *Roots*. Haley used the neologism "faction," a blend of historical information and imagined thoughts and conversations. They might have drawn an analogy to the New Journalism that had emerged in the mid-1960s and was popularized by such high-profile writers as Gay Talese, Tom Wolfe, Truman Capote, Hunter S. Thompson, and Norman Mailer. Talese, a former *New York Times* reporter, claimed that New Journalism often read like fiction but was more reliable because it sought a "larger truth than is possible through the mere compilation of verifiable facts, the use of direct quotations, and adherence to the rigid organizational style of the older form." Wolfe loved the new genre because it was now possible "in nonfiction, in journalism, to use any literary device." Capote believed that "a factual piece of work could explore whole new dimensions in writing that would have a double effect fiction does not have—the every fact of its being true, every word of its [*sic*] true, would add a double contribution of strength and impact." Capote had already weathered criticism of the method for a decade.[11]

The insistence on categorizing *Roots* simply as nonfiction was a mistake. Some passages of the book were based on Haley's guessing about facts and eliding evidence. By the early 1970s, when he had already drafted and edited the African section of *Roots,* abundant historical evidence contradicted his depiction of Juffure as a kind of Eden. He had been advised that his dating of Kunta Kinte's life was based on doubtful information. Bakary Sidibe, the Gambian national archivist, sent Haley a letter on May 30, 1973, expressing his doubts about Fofana's reliability: "His young days were spent more in sowing wild oats than in studying." He had been a drummer, for which the Mandinka word is *jalli,* which can also mean "griot." Sidibe said that "by birth and his own views he is not a griot but [an] Imam." Fofana had learned his stories from other elders, with whom he often sat in the village. Moreover, Sidibe told Haley that Kebba Fofana was now giving a different account of the history of Kunta Kinte, saying that Kunta was imprisoned at James Island for seven years. Sidibe had also interviewed a griot of the Kinte clan and several of its elders and heard different accounts of Kunte Kinte's genealogy, all of which seemed to locate him several generations later in time than Haley had placed him. Haley chose to disregard Sidibe's information.[12]

When challenged about the veracity of *Roots,* Haley usually responded by talking about his twelve years of research and extensive travel to study archives on three continents. But by admitting that some parts of the book were fictional and using the unfortunate term "faction" to name his genre, he had undermined his claims of historicity. Haley could have defused much later criticism by saying that the village from which Kunta came was the writer's own mythic creation, one that he believed showed the probable character of his ancestor's place of origin. There was ample evidence from the family story to place Kunta in a Mandinka village in the region of the Gambia. The Kinte clan was centered farther up the Gambia River and away from the heavy European presence at Juffure. Indeed, it would have been better to give the village a name other than Juffure. Instead of tying himself precisely to 1767 as the time of Kunta's capture and departure, he could have approximated the dates. The power of *Roots* ultimately lay not in its adherence to historical fact but in its being a new story of blacks' past that included African origins. The book was not competing with empirical studies for the attention of the popular mind but with myths about slavery established by works of pure fiction.

*   *   *

ROOTS CAME AT AN opportune moment in American life. The year 1976 was taken up with continuous, public celebrations of the nation's bicentennial. In 1975 President Gerald Ford had appointed Haley to the Bicentennial Advisory Council, and Haley announced to a reporter his intention "to make certain nobody overlooks what blacks did to make this country." And although he did not say so, he wanted to make sure nobody overlooked his forthcoming book. Haley felt that blacks were not going to be excited about celebrating the anniversary. The typical response might be, "Wow, great, we were slaves in 1776." A fair rendering of the past would note that the South "was built on the back of slaves' labor," but popular history of the country had "obscured, and in some cases eliminated the role of blacks." But Haley diplomatically concluded that "we are marking an historic birthday. In so doing, we're saying who we are. After life and health, the most important thing any living being needs is a sense of security, a sense of pride." Giving that to blacks was Haley's personal mission. In an effort to place *Roots* firmly within the patriotic spirit of the moment, he wrote this dedication for the book: "Just by chance [*Roots*] is being published in the Bicentennial Year of the United States. So I dedicate *Roots* as a birthday offering to my country within which most of *Roots* happened." The historian Willie Lee Rose concluded that *Roots* was "the most astounding cultural event of the American Bicentennial." Almost forty years later, that superlative still seems about right.[13]

Roots also appeared in the midst of the 1976 presidential campaign, in which the Democrat Jimmy Carter challenged President Ford. Carter's open embrace of his southern origins brought an outpouring of media attention to the changes in race relations in the South as a result of the civil rights movement. One observer noted that Carter campaigned "consciously in the context of his family, his town, his region, his religion, his past."[14] If that was true for the peanut farmer from Plains, Georgia, it was doubly so for the author of the other big success from the South in 1976, Alex Haley. The griot from Tennessee spoke in a deliberate, distinctive drawl—different from Carter's but equally identifiable as southern. Each was openly proud of his southern background and appreciative of his southern culture. Each chose to believe that southern human relations were better than they had seemed during the harsh conflicts of the 1960s. The poet James Dickey, recently thrust into national celebrity with the movie production of his southern horror novel *Deliverance,* pronounced that the "southernization" of America would cancel the nation's hypocrisy and impose new simplicity and caring. It was a prophecy that Haley, who had long idealized his Tennessee childhood, could believe.[15]

Roots had in fact caught a big wave of Americans' new absorption with their origins. Irving Howe's *World of Our Fathers* had appeared at the same time as *Roots* and was widely celebrated for recovering the history of America's Eastern European Jews. *Newsweek* reported that genealogical research, once the province of aristocrats, had now "turned ethnic," as new generations looked back on family experience.

Marcus Hansen, a historian of American immigration, wrote, "What the son wishes to forget, the grandson wishes to remember." Another student of immigrants said that a "destruction of memories" had been part of the American assimilation—"assimilate or perish" had been a virtual command. Responding to the black pride movement, other ethnic groups began to explore their own backgrounds. Movements for ethnic awareness had arisen in the 1970s among Poles, Lithuanians, and Italians.[16]

Roots resonated with oppressed peoples outside the United States. Justice V. R. Krishna, judge of the Supreme Court of India, wrote that "the dignity of a race is restored when its roots are known." Mahatma Gandhi was able to resist British imperialism, Krishna said, on the basis of "knowledge of our strength and sustenance from our roots." The Indian nationalist leader Jawaharlal Nehru had been prompted by the same desire to find his origins when he wrote *The Discovery of India*, a book that helped millions of Indians relmagine their past.[17]

*   *   *

IN SEPTEMBER 1976 Haley began a month of promotional events that took him to nineteen major cities. He did scores of interviews, and he was masterful at them. A *Washington Post* reporter described him as leaning back and smoking steadily while he spoke slowly in a soft baritone with a Tennessee accent. "I had always wondered what a million-dollar author was like," Haley told *Publishers Weekly*. "Now I've met two of them, Arthur Hailey and Harold Robbins, and it seems I'll be one myself. . . . The main thing is to be free, and that's something I've always wanted to be." The interviewer inevitably asked how much of the book was verifiable fact and how much was made up, and in his response Haley wandered a bit. "All the major incidents are true, the details are as accurate as very heavy research can make them, the names and dates are real, but obviously when it comes to dialogue, and people's emotions and thoughts, I had to make things up. It's heightened history, or fiction based on real people's lives."[18]

Roots appeared in a season of strong nonfiction works. There were several books about Watergate and John Toland's biography *Hitler,* also a Doubleday book, which at more than a thousand pages was even longer than *Roots.* Book prices were rising, going up by almost 12 percent in 1975. At $12.50, *Roots* was one of the most expensive—as well as one of the longest—books on the *New York Times* best-seller list. *Roots* began at number five on the general nonfiction list in early October. It was second on the list by November 14, 1976, and the following week, it surpassed Gail Sheehy's self-help book *Passages* to become number one.[19]

Many of the reviews of *Roots* were ecstatic. The *Los Angeles Times* echoed the *Roots* jacket copy in calling the book a "fascinating de-tective story." James Baldwin's review in the *New York Times* found no fault and much significance to attach to his old friend's book. Baldwin's constant theme had always been the depravity of American race relations, and he thought *Roots* helped address it. "Alex Haley's taking us back through time to the village of his ancestors is an act of faith and courage, but this book is also an act of love, and it is this which makes it haunting." Baldwin identified in *Roots* the stark contrast between the African dream and the American nightmare. "The density of the African social setting eventually gives way to the shrill incoherence of the American one." The book, for Baldwin, was a study of "how a people perpetuate themselves, how each generation helps to doom, or helps to liberate, the coming one." Christopher Lehman-Haupt's review in the *Times* declared that the book read like "very conventional fiction" but that Haley's extraordinary tracing of his family heritage more than compensated for the ordinariness of the prose. Lehman-Haupt speculated that the main achievement of *Roots* was that its author had created a metaphor "for the vague awareness felt by most American blacks that they are somehow de-scended from people who were abducted from Africa. . . . It is as if he were saying that he knew he was real but didn't really believe it until he discovered corroborating evidence."[20]

Newsweek's reviewer, P. D. Zimmerman, offered the first criticism. He liked "the passion of Haley's narrative, the sweep of its concept and its wealth of largely neglected material," but he was emphatic that Haley and the publisher were not acknowledging the extent of the book's fictional elements: "Even a cursory reading of the book makes clear the invention of countless incidents." Still, despite a "pulpy style," the book gave "a valuable sense of what the black community lost in its acculturation to a slave society."[21]

Willie Lee Rose of Johns Hopkins University, writing in the *New York Review of Books*, thought Haley's opening, with its emphasis on African life, was "beautifully realized," an artistic rendering of an idealized place that reflected the author's mastery of African anthropology. But she insisted that the account was historically incorrect, especially in the pastoral character it gave to Juffure. Rose's colleague Philip Curtin had just published a book on the slave trade in Africa that revealed the ways that European traders had drastically altered the environment and social relations of Juffure. (In 1967 Jan Vansina had consulted Curtin about the African words that Haley had heard growing up, but Haley did not interact directly with Curtin.) In the eighteenth century Juffure was a trading center inhabited by three thousand people, and it was the seat of Ndanco Sono, king of Niumi, who controlled access to the upper Gambia River and in 1767 was at war with British and French traders. Rose surmised that "it is inconceivable at any time, but particularly under these circumstances, that two white men should have dared to come ashore in the vicinity of Juffure to capture Kunta Kinte, even in the company of two Africans, as Haley describes it." Rose conceded that placing Kunta Kinte in a Garden of Eden could suggest a larger truth about African origins that "outdistances any historical fact," for "myth pursues its truth largely outside the realm of reality." A historian of slavery and the American South, Rose found other errors that she said "chip away at the verisimilitude of central matters in which it is important to have full faith." There were anachronisms: cotton was not grown in Spotsylvania County, Virginia, when Kunta Kinte was supposed to have lived there; wire fencing did not exist for another century; and the terms for poor whites, "cracker" and "red-neck," came much later.[22]

Rose's review was the most critical so far, and Haley called her. "Why are you being so hard on me, Willie Lee?" he asked. Then he made a plea, perhaps suggested by the review. "I was just trying to give my people a myth to live by."[23]

* * *

ROOTS FELL INTO a tradition of treatments of American race and slavery that worked together to form what the literary critic Leslie Fiedler called a "popular epic," a tradition that had gone unperceived among intellectuals until Haley's work appeared. The other books were Harriet Beecher Stowe's *Uncle Tom's Cabin,* Thomas Dixon's *The Leopard's Spots* (and its thematic echo, *The Clansman*), and Margaret Mitchell's *Gone with the Wind.* In 1979 Fiedler defined this "popular epic" as being "rooted in demonic dreams of race, sex and violence which have long haunted us Americans," and that determined the people's historical understandings of slavery, the Civil War, Reconstruction, emancipation, and the Ku Klux Klan. Like all leading critics of American letters, Fiedler had earlier dismissed the first three books of the popular epic, but now he said that, with *Roots,* these books advanced a historical myth "unequalled in scope or resonance by any work of High Literature." At exactly the same time, and apparently not influenced by Fiedler, Willie Lee Rose concurred. These four books had given "a vocabulary to American mythologies and demonologies that is generally understood at home and abroad." Each of the four books had clear didactic purposes: Stowe taught the evil of slavery, Dixon illustrated what he saw as the mistakes of emancipation and Reconstruction, Mitchell portrayed the degradation of southerners in the Civil War. All four were success stories.

Haley's family was "victorious over slavery," Stowe's Uncle Tom won a spiritual victory over his oppressors, and Dixon and Mitchell had seen to southern whites' successful recapture of their region from carpetbaggers and evil blacks. Haley wanted blacks to have "a Garden of Eden and Innocence to look back upon," and he imagined one in Juffure.[24]

Harriet Beecher Stowe's *Uncle Tom's Cabin* was the nineteenth century's most famous American novel and Stowe its greatest celebrity among writers. She made a strong statement against slavery, gave a defense of black character, and influenced the sectional crisis of the 1850s. *Uncle Tom's Cabin* sold hundreds of thousands of copies in the United States, in both the North and the South, and perhaps a million in Great Britain. Beaten to the point of death by two black slave drivers, Uncle Tom whispers to a white boy: "I loves every creatur', every whar!—it's nothing *but* love! . . . what a thing 'tis to be a Christian!" It was read by millions of Americans at all ages, including the young, for several generations. "Of course, I read *Uncle Tom's Cabin*," Malcolm X said. "In fact, I believe that's the only novel I have ever read since I started serious reading." Malcolm, like most young black men in the 1960s, rejected the loving, Christian Uncle Tom in favor of the emerging "bad nigger" archetype of which Malcolm was a model. Still, the book had helped shape his understanding of the black past. No one had been more dismissive of the novel than James Baldwin, who detested its self-righteousness and sentimentality. But Fiedler now wrote that Stowe "invented American Blacks for the imagination of the whole world." She created three black archetypes: Uncle Tom, the long-suffering and ever-forgiving Christian slave; Eliza, the heroic mother who escapes slavery; and Topsy, the foolish slave girl. Added to those was Simon Legree, the evil white slave owner and rapist. Over the next century, the three black characters became, Fiedler thought, "for better or worse, models, archetypal grids through which we perceived the Negroes around us, and they perceive themselves."[25]

The next influential and popular interpretation delivered an opposite message. Thomas Dixon Jr.'s novel *The Leopard's Spots,* published in 1902, sold millions of copies. In 1901 Dixon had seen a stage production of *Uncle Tom's Cabin,* the message of which incensed him, and in sixty days he wrote *Leopard's Spots* and sent it to Doubleday, Page and Company. In the novel, an all-knowing preacher warns a racially naïve young white man: "The beginning of Negro equality as a vital fact is the beginning of the end of this nation's life. There is enough negro blood here to make mulatto the whole Republic." In 1905 Dixon reprised the message in *The Clansman*—an anti-Negro melodrama of Reconstruction focused on black soldiers' sexual assault of white southern women. Dixon's black archetype is the soldier-rapist Gus, who violates a virginal white maiden and drives her to suicide. The newly formed Ku Klux Klan then lynches Gus. Dixon's book provoked considerable outrage. He was called "the high priest of lawlessness, the prophet of anarchy," and a provocateur of "enmity between race and race."[26]

Margaret Mitchell's 1936 novel *Gone with the Wind* was a publishing phenomenon, selling a million copies within a year and more than twenty million by the time *Roots* appeared. It was the fastest-selling novel in history. The book offered a view of slaves as happy, simple, and mostly harmless. With the exception of Scarlett's nurse, Mammy, the blacks portrayed in it were not complex characters. Fiedler argued that Mammy was really Uncle Tom redone, "the Great Black Mother of us all." In his autobiography, Malcolm X recalled seeing the film version of *Gone with the Wind* in Mason, Michigan. "I was the only Negro in the theatre," he said, "and when Butterfly McQueen went into her act, I felt like crawling under the rug." (As Prissy, McQueen played a character much like Topsy of *Uncle Tom's Cabin.*) *Gone with the Wind*'s portrayal of Civil War Atlanta was accurate, whereas its depiction of Reconstruction-era Georgia follows the themes of Dixon's work. The lives of black characters in the book were peripheral to the melodrama, but because *Gone with the Wind* was such a huge event in American popular culture, its interpretation of reality influenced American popular thought for several generations after it appeared.[27]

Roots was a complete revision of the myths inherent in the popular epic up until then. The historian Jack Temple Kirby thought it had turned *Gone With the Wind* "inside out," by making whites two-dimensional characters, "widgets in a cruel system," while blacks were "vivid and memorable." The British scholar Helen Taylor thought *Roots* provided a mythology of heroic blacks so compelling that it would be treated as a kind of "Black Family Bible." Fiedler thought Haley's greatest contribution to the popular epic was Kunta Kinte, "an unreconstructed Noble African." Dismissing questions about the authenticity of Kunta, Fiedler said he was "less a portrait of Haley's first American ancestor, legendary or real, than of Malcolm X as Haley perceived him." Both Kunta and Malcolm were "inverted Racist[s], convinced that all Whites not only invariably do evil to all Blacks, but that they have an offensive odor, and are properly classified not as human but as *toubob*, 'devils,' who must be resisted unto death." By the time *Roots* appeared, *The Autobiography of Malcolm X* had sold six million copies, and Malcolm was a heroic figure for many Americans. To make Kunta so heroic, Haley had to depart from historical realism. He barely acknowledged the role of black Africans in the slave trade, leaving whites entirely responsible for its brutality. Fiedler scoffed at Haley's handling of the sexual aspects of the popular epic. Haley made no mention of Mandinka polygamy, and he kept Kunta a virgin until he was thirty-nine—choices that strained the credulity of his narrative but were possibly analogous to the life of Malcolm, who claimed to have been celibate for twelve years.[28]

Roots surely recast the popular epic for American whites. Most blacks had already rejected the contributions to it from Stowe, Dixon, and Mitchell, and they overwhelmingly embraced *Roots*. But most of Haley's audience was made up of whites, and he affected millions of them. Ninety-nine percent of the letters Haley received from the *Reader's Digest* condensed version of *Roots* were from whites, nearly all of them testifying to the book's profound effect on their thinking.[29]

Roots opened readers to a broader empathy with the slave's experience. Charles Todd, a folklorist at Hamilton College and the man mainly responsible for bringing Haley on the school's faculty, had assigned *Uncle Tom's Cabin* to students, and during the 1960s and early 1970s, black students dismissed the book. Some refused to turn in papers on it, and one woman threw the book at Todd's feet and stomped from the class. Often, black students refused to speak about the novel at all, and at other times, discussions of it "reached near riot proportions." But under the influence of *Roots,* students became more understanding of Tom. "One must put the book in the context of its time," many students now said. "Those who talk of 'Tomming' have missed the point." In 1976 one black student compared Uncle Tom to Kunta Kinte, pointing out that his accommodating manner was just a means of survival.[30]

The power of the popular epic created by these novels depended on their transference to other cultural media. Fiedler wrote that what distinguished all popular art from high art was its ability to move from one medium to another. Hundreds of theatrical presentations of *Uncle Tom's Cabin* toured the United States and the world for at least two generations after the novel appeared. Thomas Dixon was only one of millions who first acquired an understanding of the popular epic of race from an *Uncle Tom* play; millions were similarly affected by the treatment of *The Clansman* in *The Birth of a Nation.* Even more acquired a view of slavery and race from *Gone with the Wind.* But the biggest crowd yet would have their views shaped by the televised version of *Roots.*[31]

9

POP TRIUMPH

THE SUCCESS OF *ROOTS* ON TELEVISION SURPASSED anything that Alex Haley, or anyone, had imagined. When he decided to produce *Roots,* David Wolper knew that he was taking a big chance. Blacks had hardly been seen in television drama up to that time. In 1976 the most popular black television personalities were the comedians Redd Foxx (*Sanford and Son*), Flip Wilson (*The Flip Wilson Show*), and Sherman Hemsley (*All in the Family* and *The Jeffersons*). A notable and recent exception was the 1972 production of *The Autobiography of Miss Jane Pittman,* based on Ernest Gaines's novel. Relatively few cinematic dramas had featured black characters. Most of those had appeared since the late 1950s and starred Sidney Poitier—*The Defiant Ones, Lilies of the Field, In the Heat of the Night,* and *Guess Who's Coming to Dinner*—all films with realistic racial messages that were not duplicated on television prior to *Roots.*[1]

In another way, the *Roots* miniseries was part of a new trend in television. It followed *QB VII* (1974), the first miniseries, based on Leon Uris's Nazi-themed courtroom drama, and *Rich Man, Poor*

Man, a family saga adapted from Irwin Shaw's novel that had run in 1976 for seven consecutive Monday nights and won a large audience as well as four Emmys. The trend continued with the 1979 series *Holocaust,* which also won high praise and a big audience. *Roots* would follow the miniseries formula—a cast of established stars, suggestions of sex but nothing explicit, ample violence, and characters of unquestionable heroism. Each of the successful 1970s miniseries explored the experience of a group of "others"—Jews, women, or blacks—who had not been examined positively in popular treatments of American society. This revision of American popular history came in the aftermath of the civil rights movement and in the midst of the women's movement and the rising consciousness among many Americans of European immigrant heritage in the 1970s.

Roots was a departure from past treatments of one of the most disturbing stories of American history, the experience of slavery. Wolper's expectation of a high level of realism set *Roots* well apart from the last screen interpretation of slavery, the 1975 film *Mandingo,* which had dwelt on interracial sex and elicited harsh reviews. Having made that commitment, Wolper worried about how an American audience would tolerate a truly accurate account of the degradation of slaves. He was particularly concerned about scenes in the hold of the slave ship. But he thought the series would be accepted and watched by enough white Americans because it was a family story. The purposeful way that descendants of Kunta Kinte held on to their African heritage and survived slavery intact as a family gave the story the good feeling that offset the inhumanity—the beatings and family break-ups—that was necessary to portray. A master of the genre of documentary film, Wolper thought of himself as a "visual historian." He insisted that his documentaries were especially effective educational instruments because they were also entertaining, and thus he made no apology for his didactic purposes in *Roots.* Wolper and Stan Margulies, his manager of daily production, had most recently enjoyed success with the cinema comedies *Those Magnificent Men in*

Their Flying Machines, If It's Tuesday This Must Be Belgium, and *Willy Wonka and the Chocolate Factory.* They had the confidence to try something new and, for the time, daring, by producing *Roots.*[2]

Wolper approached the American Broadcasting Company (ABC), whose executives were intrigued but also concerned that there had never been a successful black dramatic series on television and doubted that advertisers would support one. ABC agreed to go ahead but set a relatively low production budget—given the length of the series and the size of the cast—of $5 million, later raised to $6 million. The producers' first concern in casting *Roots* for television was how whites would receive the show. Wolper said he was "trying to appeal to whites" since "they make up 90% of the audience," and thus "to reach and manipulate" whites' minds so they would watch the miniseries and not think of it as a "black" show. He lined up white television stars to win over white audiences. The ABC executive Brandon Stoddard said the network used actors whom white viewers had seen a hundred times before, "so they would feel comfortable." The most familiar white actors included some who had starred in long-running television series: Lorne Green (*Bonanza*), Sandy Duncan (*Funny Face*), Lloyd Bridges (*Seahunt*), Chuck Connors (*The Rifleman*), Edward Asner (*The Mary Tyler Moore Show*), Ralph Waite (*The Waltons*), Macdonald Carey (*Days of Our Lives*), Doug McLure (*The Virginian*), and Yvonne De Carlo (*The Munsters*). The promotional trailers before the broadcast included many shots of those stars.[3]

To create the teleplay, the screenwriter William Blinn used drafts of the unfinished book. Haley had little to do with the writing of the script, although Wolper insisted that Haley controlled the story. He said that Haley never objected to or complained about the changes in character and plot: "He understood that a movie and a book differed and he trusted us." Haley visited the set and advised on cultural matters: "How does a Gambian child address his mother? What animals are found in the village?"[4]

Shooting began in June 1976 in Savannah, Georgia, where rep-licas of an African village and a slave ship had been built. The ship's hold was so authentic that the extras crammed into it cried during the shooting. One early effort for verisimilitude was to have African women shown naked from the waist up; the women were shown from a distance. Most viewers accepted the scenes without objec-tion or even notice, but the mother of a twelve-year-old extra, who volunteered to appear nude in a scene, sued Wolper. The producers identified her in every frame of film and made sure that she was not exposed.[5]

Wolper cast many well-known black actors in the series. John Amos (*Good Times*) played the mature Kinte; Leslie Uggams (*The Leslie Uggams Show*) was Kizzy; Cicely Tyson (*The Autobiography of Miss Jane Pittman*) portrayed Kinte's mother, Binta; and Richard Roundtree (*Shaft*) was a carriage driver and Kizzy's lover. Though he had not worked in television, Ben Vereen had just won two Tony Awards for starring roles in *Jesus Christ Superstar* and *Pippin*. If the producers wanted mostly identifiable black actors, they sought an un-known for the role of the young Kunta Kinte. Stoddard said that "from a purely casting standpoint it was essential that Kunta Kinte be seen not as an actor being Kunta Kinta" but as embodying Kunta entirely. They cast LeVar Burton, who had no acting credits, in the role, and he proved to be a great success. Haley's only input on the casting was to encourage the selection of a dark-skinned actor to play Kunta. He had gotten a strong impression in Africa of the blackness of the native people, as compared with the shades of brown found among most African Americans. Haley imagined Kunta to resemble the Gambian student Ebou Manga. For their work in *Roots*, nine black actors were nominated for Emmy Awards, and Olivia Cole (Mathilda) and Louis Gossett Jr. (Fiddler) received awards for, re-spectively, best supporting actress and actor. Leslie Uggams (Kizzy) won a Golden Globe Award. The large black cast of *Roots* hoped that the series would bring more opportunities for them in Hollywood.

But neither *Roots* nor its sequel, *Roots: The Next Generations,* opened many new doors. In 2007 Uggams said the miniseries had very little long-lasting effect: "We all had high expectations and thought the world was going to be everyone's oyster. It didn't happen that way."[6]

Each of the eight episodes of *Roots* followed a separate theme, and most ended on an upbeat note. For example, at the end of the first, when the captives are at the end of the Middle Passage, an African leads a chant by the captives: "We will live!" At the end of the second, when the overseer has beaten Kunta, the Fiddler character tells him, "There's gonna be another day!" At the end of the third, after slave catchers have cut off part of Kunta's foot and the cook Bell is trying to raise his spirits, Kunta says, "I'm gonna do better than walk. *Damnit!* I'm gonna learn to *run!*" In the fourth, Kunta tells Kizzy, "Your name means 'stay put'—but it don't mean 'stay a slave.'" Each episode thus reinforced the series' overarching theme of blacks' individual endurance and strength, as well as the persistence of black families. When he chose not to attempt an escape to the North, Kunta affirmed his commitment to his family over the possibility of freedom. But the inhumanity of slavery provided a constant tension throughout the series. The fifth episode ended with Kizzy vowing vengeance against Tom Lea, the man who raped her. The sixth stopped with Chicken George's owner, who has sold George's family away while George fights cocks in Europe, saying that the returning slave will not be able to do anything about such cruelty. "He'll come back a nigger. . . . And what's a nigger to do?" The seventh ended with Tom Murray facing an ominous future for having killed the white man who raped his wife. After he has faced down the brother of the man he killed, Tom's gaze looks fierce and unconquered. The eighth and final episode showed Chicken George and his progeny escaping from peonage and making their long journey to Tennessee, where the last generations of the family enjoy peace and prosperity, and ended with Alex Haley telling of his triumphant twelve-year quest to find his family's history.

The script adaptation made the emphases in the miniseries drastically different from those in the book. Almost the first fourth of the book dwells on the African environment, but the television series devoted only part of the first episodes to it. The rich anthropological material that Haley used in the book was almost entirely lost. Stoddard of ABC explained that "what seems to interest Americans most are Americans. . . . In *Roots,* we got out of Africa as fast as we could." The characters arrive in America early in the second episode. *Roots* on television hardly challenged the Eurocentric cultural perspective of Africa as the "dark continent." In the book, Haley made a point of emphasizing the survival of African cultural elements among American slaves. That was lost on television. The script made some white characters "good," whereas in the book there are almost no admirable white figures. The book said almost nothing about Captain Davies of the slave ship, but he was portrayed on television by Edward Asner as a religious man with a tortured moral character. Davies was paired in the plot with the seasoned slave trader called Slater, a violent, abusive character whose inhumanity makes Davies seem like a good white man in comparison. When Slater thrusts a young African girl on Davies for his sexual pleasure, and Davies accepts her, Davies seems human in his sinfulness and vulnerability. Asner won an Emmy for his performance.

The television interpretation of *Roots* diminished Haley's black characters. Three characters who mentored Kunta were collapsed into one, eliminating the nuances that came from multiple black perspectives in the book. The producers and writers decided that they needed the continuity of a single, strong influence on Kunta, and Fiddler, played by Lou Gossett Jr., performed that function. On the other hand, the television script created a character, the slave woman Fanta, who is forced to have sex with Davies on the slave ship and later, in Virginia, becomes Kunta's first love interest. She seems to have been inserted to titillate viewers. When she argues loudly with Kunta the morning after their night together, her explosion leads to his entrapment. This characterization seems false because a consistent point of *Roots* was that slaves were always careful in keeping their thoughts and emotions from whites.[7]

Nonetheless, *Roots,* as both book and the miniseries, was such a departure from previous popular interpretations of slavery that it shifted mass culture to a new understanding of slavery and the black family. More than a decade after *Roots* aired, the cultural historian Donald Bogle, perhaps the most astute critic of African Americans in film and television, thought that the series was rare among television dramas in that neither the black characters nor the actors in the series were "standard, comfy, middle-class, reassuring types" but were instead figures "larger than life with aches, pains, or struggles that filled the viewers with a sense of terror or awe. . . . None pulled back from a moment that might disturb or upset a viewer." Bogle thought the weakest part of the series was the African portion: Kunta's manhood rites looked like a "frat initiation." Binta, Kunta's mother, was a richly developed character in the book, but on television she was less fully realized and influential on Kunta, even as portrayed by the talented Cicely Tyson. On the other hand, John Amos as the mature Kunta and Madge Sinclair as Bell played off each other deftly, evoking real humanity. Louis Gossett Jr. took the Fiddler character to a high level, "displaying in turn Uncle-Tomish deference, fatherly care for Kunta, and strutting showmanship as the musician." Bogle concluded that the black experience was "far wider, far denser, far more complicated, far more unmanageable than *Roots* implied" but that the series still "captured the raw, archetypal, mythic essence of human experience." Seeing on commercial television the atrocities of American slavery but then "witnessing the victorious spirit of those who survived it all, audiences have been affected in unanticipated ways." Bogle considered *Roots* a "pop triumph."[8]

*   *   *

THE QUESTION REMAINED whether *Roots* would have a significant impact on Americans. Would the mass of Americans really entertain a whole new interpretation of their history? To be sure, the civil rights movement had brought *Gone with the Wind* and its racial interpretations into question for many people. But a new cultural exemplar was needed to override that work's influence on the American cultural understanding.[9]

Fred Silverman, head of entertainment programming at ABC, decided to run the show on consecutive nights rather than once a week for eight weeks. He said that to run the series over eight or ten weeks would have dissipated its emotional impact. That way, if the series was a failure, its effects on ABC's ratings would be minimized. Wolper Productions and ABC had done something no one in television had ever done before, he said, so, "Let's show it in a way that no one has ever shown television before!" ABC hoped that over those eight nights, *Roots* would garner fifty million viewers in total, not a big overall audience, and the network was not confident that it would do even that. It sold advertising on the promise of a 30 "share," or percentage of television viewers watching the show. The network decided not to broadcast the series during the "sweeps" period, when network ratings were recorded and then used to set subsequent advertising charges. Advertisers paid $120,000 per minute for a spot during *Roots,* whereas the rates for a broadcast like the Super Bowl, which had the biggest audience of any program, pulled in $150,000 per minute of commercial time. This miscalculation would cost the network millions of dollars.[10]

Roots was broadcast from January 23 to January 30, 1977, in the midst of one of the hardest and most prolonged cold spells in American history, which, some commentators speculated, may have accounted for the huge viewership it earned from the first night. At least fifty million viewers, the audience that ABC hoped the entire series would generate, tuned in the first night. Nielsen Ratings service reported that the show received between a 62 and 68 share of those Americans watching television each night. Eighty million Americans, "the largest television audience in the history of the medium," Nielsen reported, watched the final episode of *Roots*. That figure represented 51.1 percent of all television sets in homes across the country, or 36,380,000 homes, and exceeded by 2.4 million the audience reached by the first half of the television release of *Gone with the Wind* the previous fall. ABC estimated that 130 million viewers, about 85 percent of all homes with televisions in the United States, saw some part of the series.[11]

"For eight days and nights, the most talked-about men in the country were a middle-aged writer named Alex Haley and his great-great-great-great-grandfather, Kunta Kinte," *Newsweek* reported. Regular patrons of a Harlem bar watched every episode together and became angry after one show when someone tried to play the jukebox. "They just wanted to talk it out," the barkeeper reported. "It wasn't until they had talked for a very long time that they finally remembered they were in a bar." An ABC executive said the phenomenon was "like millions of people reading the same book simultaneously, instead of privately, making it a shared experience." Vernon Jordan, executive director of the National Urban League, called *Roots* "the single most spectacular educational experience in race relations in America." All over the United States, *Roots* dominated chats among friends and colleagues, preachers' sermons, radio call-in shows, bull sessions in bars, and classroom discussions. During the time that *Roots* was running on television, the *New York Times* reported that a black man in business attire stepped on to an elevator and was greeted by a white colleague, "Good morning, Kunta Kinte." The black fellow lowered his head and said, "Toby."[12]

Almost nine of ten blacks watched some portion of the series, and more than seven in ten whites did. Blacks watched an average of six episodes, whites more than five. Eighty-three percent of the watchers thought *Roots* was one of the best television programs they had ever seen. Black and white viewers both thought the show was accurate in its portrayal of both blacks and whites, although blacks rated it a little higher for accuracy. The overwhelming feeling prompted by the show was the same for blacks and whites—sadness.

White viewership tended to be a more liberal segment of the white population. Polls found that whites who did not watch the show were hostile to laws against housing discrimination and believed blacks were inferior to whites in intelligence and trustworthiness. A third of white viewers thought blacks' historical experience was no worse than the struggles of European immigrants.[13]

Roots, both the book and the miniseries, was used as the syllabus for new college courses. By February 1977, 250 colleges were offering credit courses based on Roots. Random House sold 150 institutions a Roots curriculum. Black Studies departments were seeing a sudden upsurge of interest in their curricula.[14] Travel agencies around the country reported a surge of interest in "heritage" tours to Africa, and some offered the special destination of Juffure.[15] "[Roots] has produced a virtual explosion of American interest in travel to Africa," said the marketing manager for Air Afrique. In New York City in the days after Roots aired, twenty black newborn babies were named Kunta Kinte or Kizzy; so were fifteen in Los Angeles, ten in Detroit, and eight in Atlanta. In Cleveland a pair of twins, male and female, were so named.[16]

A phenomenon so pervasive naturally drew some dissenters. Time magazine's critic, Richard Schickel, was the most noted naysayer, calling the production a "Mandingo for middlebrows." A well-to-do white woman in Atlanta thought Roots was awful: "The blacks were just getting settled down, and this will make them angry again." David Duke, national director of the Knights of the Ku Klux Klan, charged ABC with airing a "vicious malignment of the white majority in America and a serious distortion of the truth." A white woman in Queens complained, erroneously, that Roots did not have any good white characters. Her husband answered, "The good whites had their day with Gone with the Wind." He added, "How good could any whites look to a slave? And that's whose eyes we're seeing it through." The black journalist Chuck Stone called Roots "an electronic orgy in white guilt successfully hustled by white TV literary minstrels."

Haley knew Stone and had told him in 1974 that "the book aspires to be the symbol saga [*sic*] of all of us of African ancestry." Perhaps so, but Stone thought the television drama "was aimed at a white market" and produced "to sell advertising for the enrichment of white TV executives."[17]

A poll of one thousand Americans, half of them black and half white, taken a month after *Roots* aired, found that 42 percent of those who had watched at least two episodes thought the series would be "inflammatory." But also important, 60 percent of blacks and whites thought they had an increased understanding of the psychology of black people. Respondents thought the most memorable scenes were those of violence—the capture of Kunta, the cutting off of his foot, the rape of Kizzy. Ninety-five percent of viewers believed *Roots* was realistic, and 77 percent thought it was relevant for contemporary race relations.[18]

The rape of Kizzy was cited for prompting a fight between black and white teenagers in Hot Springs, Arkansas, and disturbances occurred at schools in Michigan, Pennsylvania, and Mississippi. Chanting "Roots, roots, roots," a gang of black boys attacked whites at Detroit's Ford High School. William "Fella" Haley, who was now an army sergeant specializing in race relations counseling in the military, had gauged the responses to *Roots* and found that it "gave some black people feelings that they just couldn't handle all at once. They had to vent their feelings in words to 'debrief' themselves and their kids."[19]

*   *   *

ALL ALONG, Doubleday executives expected the television series to boost sales of the book, but they did not imagine the scale of television's impact. On the third day of the broadcast, *Roots* sold sixty-seven thousand copies. Doubleday had originally planned to print fifty thousand books. Stoddard responded, "Fifty thousand? That's what I plan to buy. How many are you going to print for everybody else?" Afterward, Doubleday raised the print run to two hundred thousand. The television executives were sure that Doubleday was still underestimating the results of what was, in effect, twelve hours of prime-time advertising for the book. In fact, *Roots* sold one million hardback copies in 1977.[20]

During the airing of *Roots,* Haley was traveling every day from appearance to appearance, coast-to-coast, signing books. Wolper called him every morning to report on what the previous night's audience count had been, and they shouted their joy to each other. Haley saw the last episode, after which he spoke on camera to eighty million viewers. At 3:30 the next morning, Haley was asleep in his hotel room when his door buzzer sounded. When he opened the door, a young white bellboy stood before him and said, "Sir, I want to thank you for what you've done for America." At airports and on streets, Haley was mobbed by well-wishers and celebrity hounds.[21]

Amid the brouhaha, Haley was a likeable and adept celebrity. On February 2, 1977, just as the broadcast of the miniseries ended, Haley appeared on *The Tonight Show with Johnny Carson,* whom he had interviewed for *Playboy* in 1968. He presented Carson with a bound book of Carson's family's genealogy. Carson was visibly moved by the gesture. At five bookstores in Los Angeles during the week after *Roots* aired, thousands of people stood in line to get Haley to autograph their copies of the book. He sat for hour after hour in each place, greeting people: "How you doing, (sister, babe, honey)?" he asked each one. "Thank you for the book," the typically awed person said quietly. "Thank you very much," Haley said. He started out by writing personal inscriptions, but the Doubleday sales staff stopped him because it was taking too long. A pregnant woman bought a book for her unborn child. "Bless your heart," Haley said to many who expressed their admiration. "Haley seemed as overwhelmed by his near deification as were his admirers," a reporter observed.[22]

The celebration of *Roots* continued for the remainder of 1977. In May a New York department store held "Roots Week" during which it offered consumers tips on researching their genealogy and learning about their heritage. "Heritage tours" to the Gambia and other points in Africa became popular. The number of letters of genealogical inquiry shot up at the National Archives. Haley received a stream of honorary degrees during commencement seasons in 1977 and 1978. He was named the third most admired black man among black American youth, behind only Muhammad Ali and Stevie Wonder. Fifty cities declared a "Roots Week." Governor Ray Blanton of Tennessee declared "Alex Haley Days" in May 1977, and Haley led his family and friends on a triumphal return to Henning.

Roots was viewed as a driving force for a broad cultural movement toward Americans' greater appreciation of their past. *Newsweek* reported on July 4, 1977 that "the quest for personal origins has turned phenomenal in the past six months," prompted in part by Haley's work. "Roots" travel had become big business, with Continental Trailways now offering a $75 fare to any United States destination and Pan American World Airways promoting international travel with the ad campaign slogan: "All of us came from some place." The elitist British agency DeBrett's Peerage had even opened a United States office to serve "the masses" in their quest for information regarding genealogy. Haley said that "very, very few people in their own lifetimes have the blessing to play a major role in something that is [as] patently affirmative for society," as the new quest to find origins. "I work now with a sense of meant-to-be-ness, a sense of mission to tell people how much we have in common."[23]

For the next year after the publication of the book and the airing of the miniseries, Haley took part in a continuous stream of talk shows, press conferences, autograph sessions, and events held in his honor. He received keys to cities, honorary degrees, and citations from Congress. He had lunch with former secretary of state Henry Kissinger, President Jimmy Carter, and the queen of Iran. The famous actors Elizabeth Taylor and Marlon Brando sought to meet him. But he also got pleas for money, requests for help in getting others' work published, and still more invitations for public appearances. For one six-month period, Haley had 802 lecture invitations. He still liked to lecture, but he declined far more invitations than he accepted. His fee was now at least $4,000.[24]

In February 1977 Haley, now fifty-six, was the biggest celebrity in the United States. "There ain't no hashish powerful enough to make you dream up something like this," he told Hans J. Massaquo, a reporter for *Ebony* magazine, long the primary publication for the celebration of black celebrity. "It's bewildering when—literally over night—you become a person whom people recognize wherever you go." Massaquo asked him about his new wealth. The money was rolling in. A publisher in Germany had paid $260,000 for the rights to publish *Roots* in that country, reportedly the highest figure ever paid for European rights to an American book. Haley told Massaquo, "It's like that question, 'How many slaves were brought from Africa?' Who knows? My accountants tell me that I'm now a bona fide millionaire, maybe twice a millionaire." He discounted the money's importance to him. "I was broke so long that I got used to being without money. . . . All I'm concerned with is just being comfortable, being able to pay my debts, and having a little margin to buy something or make a gift to somebody." He told of giving a Los Angeles waitress a fifty-dollar tip on a six-dollar tab. "She didn't know me from Adam," he said, but he admired her friendly way and her eagerness to please her customers. He was in the process of signing over all royalties to *The Autobiography of Malcolm X* to Betty Shabazz. He was funding the American education of students from Juffure and the building of a mosque in the village.[25]

Massaquo reported "the steep escalation of attention which women of all races and ages" were paying Haley. "Deluged with kisses, hugs, love letters, marriage proposals and plain invitations to 'get it on,'" Haley demurred, saying he was too busy to take up any of the offers. He asked if Haley planned to marry again. "Marriage is the best state for a person," Haley answered, glancing toward My

Lewis, his editorial assistant and "close companion for three years."
He had already found his prospective third wife in Lewis, whom
he called "the most comprehensively compatible woman I have ever
known." Haley and Lewis were married later in 1977.[26]

Haley had reached the height of the celebrity for which he had
longed. He had expected that the benefits of big success would be
freedom from money worries and the liberty to travel as he desired.
From his many interviews with famous people, he knew something
of the perils of celebrity, but writing about fame and coping with
it were two separate matters. Two years later Haley would tell the
readers of *Playboy*, "There are days when I wish it hadn't happened."
Perhaps explaining what had happened, he said, would "serve as a
reminder that our great god 'success,' with its omnipotent trinity
of fame, wealth, and power, is something we should learn to *respect*
rather than to worship—lest it enslave us." Haley was still rushing
around the country when the most troubling of all celebrity problems
suddenly appeared, almost all at once, in April 1977.[27]

10

ROOTS UNCOVERED

HALEY ENJOYED THE HEIGHTS OF CELEBRITY FOR only a short while. In the spring of 1977, he faced conflicts with his publisher, journalists determined to expose his mistakes in *Roots,* and two authors who alleged that he had copied parts of *Roots* from their work. For the next two years, he would spend much of his time defending himself in both the court of public opinion and the federal courts of the Southern District of New York. At the end of 1978, Haley felt that he had been maligned and persecuted for being a successful black writer. To a large extent, that was true, but he had also caused his own undoing in some important ways.

In March 1977 Haley sued Doubleday for $5 million in California state court, alleging that the publisher had failed to sell the book properly and asking that the paperback contract be renegotiated. The complaint argued that Doubleday had not provided book distributors with sufficient copies of *Roots* to satisfy the clearly foreseeable public demand. As a result, copies were not available for sale in Los Angeles and other metropolitan areas during and after the television program ran. Another part of the complaint contended that Doubleday's premature announcement that Dell, which it now owned, would soon produce a paperback had undermined hardback sales and reduced Haley's royalties. There was a lot of money at stake. Haley got $1.87 for each hardback sold but only about fifteen cents for a Dell mass-market paperback, priced at $2.95. It was not clear whether Dell would publish a paperback sooner than a year after the hardback release, the traditional timing for paperback publication.[1]

Haley had held a grudge against Doubleday since at least 1967, when, during his worst financial struggles, he had become resentful of the publisher's unwillingness to raise his advance. "My quarrel is not with my friends on the editorial side of Doubleday," he said at the time of the lawsuit. "My quarrel is with the corporate Doubleday." In the lawsuit, he was "speaking symbolically for two groups—black people and others struggling to make it in the country, and writers, who are like sharecroppers." Then after casting his complaint in this racial context, he said, "I hasten to add that there is nothing racial involved in the case." But he wrote privately that he had heard "within the trade" that Nelson Doubleday was "anti–black folk." Suspicions about the owner were understandable, given the publisher's sudden cancellation of *The Autobiography of Malcolm X* in 1965. Haley considered it indicative of a "hardrock corporate perspective" to hold him to the "time-of-hunger" contract he had originally made for "Before This Anger." He thought Nelson Doubleday was "dealing with me now as when I was desperate during the years I was working on the book." Now he had produced "the most talked-about book in the country," and the biggest-selling book in Doubleday's history, one that added "luster to the Doubleday corporate name." He thought he should be treated differently.[2]

A Doubleday corporate spokesman expressed dismay about the accusation of mismanagement. The book had been number one on the best-seller list for several months, and it had sold more than 1.5 million copies in 175 days, facts that drove the man to observe drily, "We must have done something right." The publisher pointed out that, over the course of the twelve years of Haley's writing, it had increased his advance from $5,000 to $96,000. The book had been a success "in large measure as a result of the editorial assistance rendered by Doubleday" and the publisher's promotion efforts.[3]

The lawsuit, filed by Lou Blau, was a strategic measure to elicit a better paperback deal. In the world of Hollywood, lawsuits were often filed as negotiating tactics. Blau and Haley had good reason to want a different arrangement for the paperback editions. Paperback rights had been sold to Dell in 1967 for $18,000, of which Haley got half. It was now worth far more than that. The 50-50 split was normal at that time, but by 1977 the split on big-selling paperbacks was often 60-40 or even 75-25 in the author's favor. "Mr. Doubleday is electing to hold me glued fast to what, by a comparison, in virtually *everyone* else's opinion, is an obviously ridiculous, ludicrous paperback deal," Haley said. The Doubleday takeover of Dell meant that its interests were no longer identical to the author's, as would have been the case had the hardcover publisher dealt with an outside paperback publisher. To complicate matters, Haley was contracted with Doubleday for his next book, "My Search for Roots." Haley told his agent that, as the author of two books now being called "classics," he would have to consider "enticement" offers if Doubleday refused to rewrite the original contract.[4]

It is not clear exactly what the lawsuit yielded. Dell kept the paperback rights and sold millions, and they may well have given Haley a larger royalty. Doubleday kept the contract for "My Search for Roots," but the book never appeared. In August 1977 Haley quietly withdrew the suit. He told the *New York Times* that he regretted the legal action. He had sued, he said, on the advice of attorneys in the film industry, where people "sue each other and then have lunch," but he found that business was not done that way in the publishing world. "It was my naiveté. I felt terrible." He was, after all, a person who did not like interpersonal conflict, and by then, he was mired in plenty of conflict coming from other directions.[5]

*   *   *

ON APRIL 10, 1977, Mark Ottaway, a travel writer for the *Sunday Times* of London, wrote in an article entitled "Roots Uncovered" that the United States was "in the grip of 'Rootsmania.'" *Roots* had been presented as fact, and that "above all else accounts for the book's phenomenal success." But Ottaway, who had gone to the Gambia to write about tourism, claimed to have happened on information that exposed Haley's research as fraudulent. He wrote that Kebbe Fofana was a man of "notorious unreliability." Residents of Juffure were involved with the slave trade not as victims but as collaborators. Ottaway claimed that Haley's Gambian advisers had not found an informant in Baddibu, further to the east in Gambia, but when they looked in the ancient Kingdom of Barra at Juffure, they found someone who would tell Haley's family story. Ottaway had discovered what Bakary Sidibe, the Gambian archivist, had told Haley in 1973, that by birth Fofana was not a griot but an imam, and in reality something of a playboy: "His young days were spent more in sowing wild oats than in studying." Ottaway wrote that in Juffure, "No villagers can remember the name of any ancestor captured by slavers. Except, miraculously, that of Kunta Kinte." Several Juffure people told Ottaway that on the day in 1967 when Haley visited, everyone there knew he was coming and why. Ottaway questioned whether the "year the King's soldiers came" was in 1767, because many soldiers sent by British, French, and Portuguese kings had been coming for a hundred years before then, and some came years afterward. The British were allowed to trade in Juffure "only under one condition: that no subjects of the King of Barra should ever be captured as slaves." Ottaway doubted that the person Haley said was taken to America in 1767 was in fact Kunta Kinte. But Haley chose 1767 on the basis of his American research, not on evidence from the Gambia.[6]

When Ottaway put the factual problems before Haley on the day before the article ran, Haley conceded that there were probably mistakes in the book, but he said he had been "misled during his researches in Gambia." Haley told the reporter that everyone in the Gambia "casts doubts on everyone else and in the end he had to believe someone. So he [chose] to believe Fofana." But Haley admitted that the mischaracterization of Juffure was a conscious decision. "You must understand, this book is also symbolic. I know Juffure was a British trading post and my portrait of the village bears no resemblance to the way it was. But the portrait I gave was true of nearly all the other villages in Gambia." Blacks, he said, "need a place called Eden. . . . I wanted to portray our original color in its pristine state, and I know it is a fair portrayal."[7]

Based on a week of research in the Gambia, Ottaway was certain that Haley's story was wrong. "The probabilities that [Kunta Kinte] disappeared much later than 1767, that he was never shipped as a slave to America, and that he was not an ancestor of Haley far outweigh any possibilities that he did or was." If it happened at all, Kunta Kinte's disappearance was more likely to have taken place in 1829, when the village more nearly fit Haley's description.[8]

Ottaway's alleged exposure of *Roots* hardly amounted to evidence that undermined the whole story of Haley's ancestral origins in the Gambia. Haley probably had imposed his idea about chronology on those aiding him in Bathurst, but the family story provided plausible leads that at some point in the past an African of the Kinte clan had been taken into slavery and ended up in Virginia. But by insisting on such a specific account, Haley had opened himself to condemnation if even some of that account was not literally true. Newspaper reporters typically strived for a standard of pure objective truth, as did most academics. To such critics, a few mistakes of fact damned the whole work. But Haley was trying to counter the West's image of Africa as being uncivilized and without culture or morality. Still, even academic critics sympathetic to Haley thought it was a mistake to depict the village inaccurately.[9]

Haley insisted that he had made no errors knowingly, but he did not acknowledge that he had received Sidibe's warning about Fofana more than two years before *Roots* was published. He told Ottaway he had been tempted to call the African part of the book an historical novel, "but in the end I felt I could only write what I was told." No one knew exactly what happened, but he stood by *Roots* "as a symbol of the fate of my people."

Ottaway's story was big international news. On April 10 Haley was on his way to London when the *New York Times* asked him to comment. He fought back immediately. "People are seeking now to explode 'Roots.' . . . It would be a scoop to beat all hell if 'Roots' could be proved to be a hoax, and that's one of the reasons why it was so important to me to document as best I could."[10] By the time he got to London, Haley's indignation had turned to feelings of persecution. He told the *Times* of London that he had spent twelve years on his research, and he resented any opportunist "spending seven days in Africa and then writing a story which seeks to blemish the deepest, strictest, most honest research I could do, given the materials I had to work with." Haley said what mattered was that Ottaway had put on *Roots* "a mark of doubt" and that "people won't remember what the specifics are, but they'll remember that it has been questioned." He had just been interviewed on radio by someone not familiar with the substance of Ottaway's criticism but who "just knew it raised questions."[11]

By the end of that week, Haley had returned to Juffure with fifty American visitors, including his brothers, Lou Blau, and a large contingent of photographers, some of them there to gather film footage for the next miniseries, *Roots: The Next Generations*. In Juffure the villagers had never seen television, which was not yet available in the Gambia. The Ottaway story had followed the visitors. "Mr. Haley's visit comes at a time of mounting controversy over his phenomenally popular best seller," reported the *New York Times*'s Africa correspondent. The *Times* of London story had "angered and dampened the spirit" of the Haley party and encouraged journalistic skepticism. "At times, the commercial aspects of the trip seemed to overshadow all others, as some 38 members of the Kinte clan were assembled around the author, who was handed a baby to bounce on his knee for the benefit of the movie camera." A television director asked Haley several times to explain what Juffure meant to him in order to film Haley's response from different angles. "Juffure is not the paradise that the village portrayed on television is," the *Times* reporter concluded. "Back on the yacht, [Haley] discussed the visit with his brothers. 'A helluva welcoming. You couldn't stage that if you wanted to.'"[12]

The more doubtful his critics were, the more adamant Haley became that *Roots* was factual. At the end of his Gambian visit, Haley expressed anger that Ottaway was "headline grabbing" and that he had "deliberately distorted and slanted" what Haley had said. "But what really upset me most was that, also, by implication, it clearly sought to impugn the dignity of black Americans' heritage." Could not blacks have "one case where we are able to go back to our past without someone taking a cheap shot to torpedo it?" He told a reporter for *People* magazine: "When you consider how many blacks were taken out of here, it seems like the Good Lord would let one of us trace his family tree back to his ancestors. It just incenses me that if one *was* able to do it—after nine *years* of research—some s.o.b. would come here and question it."[13]

Haley still had plenty of admirers. During the week after the Ottaway article appeared, ABC television brought a group of Gambians to appear on its *Good Morning America* show to defend Haley. On April 11 the National Book Award Committee gave him a special award: "Because Alex Haley's 'Roots' does not accommodate itself to the category of history, but transcends that and other categories, members of the history panel were unable to name it as one of the nominees in history. They are at one, however, that its distinguished literary quality justifies according it a special citation of merit."[14]

Leading historians, including Bernard Bailyn and Robert Fogel from Harvard, came to Haley's defense. Bailyn thought that "this account is the author's perception of the meaning of slavery, and the account is one of sensibility. I don't think it turns on details. It turns on a state of mind, and there's no documentation of that." Fogel said he would not hold it to the same standard that he applied to history by professional historians. David Brion Davis and Edmund S. Morgan of Yale also stepped up. Davis thought *Roots* was a work of history and still excused the errors: "We all need myths about the past." Morgan suggested that the debate about factual accuracy did not matter. "You can point out errors to your heart's content and it won't affect people's attitudes. It [will] just make them mad." Oscar Handlin at Harvard was the main academic dissenter: "A fraud's a fraud." Handlin said that historians were reluctant to mention errors "when the general theme is in the right direction; that goes for foreign policy, for race and for this book."[15]

The syndicated columnist Ellen Goodman gave perhaps the most spirited defense of *Roots*. She said Haley was not a historian but a "witness bearer." She thought the doubts about the historicity of *Roots* carried the implication that if some of Haley's facts were wrong, then the book was a fraud. "Perhaps we can comfortably close our eyes to the most vivid picture of slavery written in our lifetimes," Goodman wrote, but she was sure that that would be a bad outcome. "By looking at the heart of slavery," she wrote, "Haley looked evil in the eye," when the natural human impulse would have been to "look away, to deny evil when possible and to reject it as part of our heritage as human beings." This was as true for Americans dealing with the slave past "as it is for those who carry the memory of the Nazi holocaust." The victims of evil and their descendants were among those most prone to ignore it. Haley did not attempt to explain slavery but instead wrote about "the experience of evil," a subject that did not "pivot on the 'reliability' of a *griot* in a small Gambian village."[16]

The Ottaway article spurred most of the hard scrutiny of Haley's research that was to come in the years ahead. Virtually every commentator after April 1977 noted Ottaway's criticism, and few gave Haley's response or questioned Ottaway's reasoning. In May, Eliot

Fremont-Smith, who had reviewed *The Autobiography of Malcolm X* with glowing praise in the *New York Times,* now used Ottaway to build an exposé of Haley in the *Village Voice* under the headline "Alex Haley and The Rot in 'Roots.'" Fremont-Smith characterized Haley as "defensive of late" and claimed that he "ranked his book with the Bible," which Fremont-Smith thought "smacks of absurdity and possible dementedness." This was an absurd criticism, because Haley had said no more than that *Roots* was based on oral history as much of the Old Testament was. Fremont-Smith recounted Ottaway's accusations of inaccuracy without a moment's skepticism, making Haley seem like a self-righteous egomaniac.[17]

*   *   *

THE FINANCIAL SUCCESS of *Roots* opened the possibility of copyright infringement claims, a common occurrence in publishing. Haley spent much of 1977 and nearly all of 1978 working on his defense in five such suits. One was quickly dismissed, and another, about which little is known, was defended successfully by Doubleday. Margaret Walker Alexander, a poet and novelist, brought two of them, the primary one having to do with her novel *Jubilee* and a second suit based on her essay "How I Wrote *Jubilee.*" She sued Haley in mid-April 1977 in federal court in the Southern District of New York, charging that Haley had taken his depictions of the Waller and Lea plantations from portraits drawn in *Jubilee.* A few days later in the same jurisdiction, Harold Courlander, a folklorist, filed a claim that there were numerous similarities of theme, structure, and language between *Roots* and his book *The African,* published in 1967 and described in the *New York Times* as "a novel dealing with freedom in Africa and slavery in Georgia." Haley responded that he had spent twelve years writing the book, "and if I were copying I'd type faster than that."[18]

At the announcement of his suit, Courlander issued a list of "thematic parallels" between the two books, to which Haley replied: "Anybody who writes about something as thematic as slaving knows that the whole slave trade was thematic, the middle-passage . . . was thematic. You take 100 men, put them in the hold of a ship, all in chains and all going through more or less the same thing I would venture to say that their experience would tend to be thematic." Haley's agent and editor came immediately to his defense. Paul Reynolds said that "the book is original and is Haley's. . . . This is perfect nonsense." Margaret Walker Alexander's suit in particular, Lisa Drew said, was the "most ridiculous thing."[19]

The accusations involving *Jubilee* and *The African* are usually referred to as charges of plagiarism, which in the academic world refers to using published material without giving attribution, whether or not the copied material was in the public domain. In the law of copyright, material in the public domain can be copied freely. In Haley's case this included many of the eighteenth- and nineteenth-century sources on which *Roots* was based—such as slave narratives, the debates on slavery in the House of Commons, and the notes of physicians who treated slaves during the Middle Passage. Although all of these books drew from sources in the public domain, the plaintiffs argued that Haley had also copied their original work. The two governing legal issues in the case turn on the question of "access"— whether the alleged copier had access to the source from which the borrowed material came, and whether there was "substantial similarity," which meant that a large portion of the alleged copier's text was so similar to the original that it was presumably copied.

Margaret Walker Alexander—known professionally as Margaret Walker—was born in Birmingham in 1915 and educated in Chicago, where she worked on the Federal Writers Project. She was a good friend of Richard Wright, though she believed that Wright had appropriated some of an unpublished novel for *Native Son*.[20] She became recognized as a poet with the publication of her 1937 poem "For My People."

Walker's research and writing of *Jubilee* bear striking similarities to those Haley did in *Roots*. *Jubilee* was the story of Walker's family, which she had learned from her grandmother, the child called Minna in the novel. Because the grandmother lived until Walker was an adult, the writer had had years to interview her for factual details about her life and that of her mother, the Vyry character in the novel, from whose perspective the story is mostly told. Walker started composing the story in 1934 while still an undergraduate at Northwestern University. As a graduate student in 1939 and 1940 at the University of Iowa's Writers' Workshop, she did more research, reading widely in the history of the South and consciously viewing material from three perspectives—those of southern whites, northern whites, and blacks. Then her peripatetic teaching career began, and her research mostly stopped, but with a Rosenwald Fellowship, in 1944, she examined the backgrounds of free blacks in antebellum Georgia, looking specifically for her great-grandfather Randall Ware, so named in the novel. In 1948 Walker began teaching at Jackson State University in Mississippi. With a Ford Fellowship, in 1953 she did six months of research in Alabama and Georgia, backtracking her family's locations from the time she was born in Birmingham to the moment her relatives had left Georgia just after the Civil War. In 1954, with the birth of her fourth child, Walker's progress on the novel stopped for seven years, but then in 1961 she returned to Iowa to work on a PhD. She completed all of the coursework and language study for her doctorate. From 1964 to 1966 she wrote the remainder of *Jubilee*, submitting it as her dissertation.[21]

Jubilee is an excellent novel with realistic characters, a plethora of interesting details about black folk life and culture of the nineteenth-century South, sharp observations of white racism, and a plot that keeps the reader focused until its end. It was an immediate success as literary fiction, a book that held its own with the works of Wright, Zora Neale Hurston, and Ralph Ellison, to which it was rightfully compared. Like Haley, Alexander had written a didactic work, meant to recount "the history that my grandmother had told me, and to set the record straight where Black people were concerned in terms of the Civil War, of slavery, segregation and Reconstruction." For her, the role of the novelist was the same as that of the historian. "More people will read fiction than . . . history, and history is slanted just as fiction may seem to be." As a work of art, *Jubilee* is superior to *Roots*. But that did not mean Haley had infringed on Walker's work.[22]

There are important differences between *Jubilee* and *Roots*. Walker's novel covers a much shorter time frame, about 1850 to about 1870, with a main focus on one generation. Still, it is a long book, about four-fifths the size of *Roots*. Walker's female characters are much more fully developed, and her men are treated more critically, although not without sympathy. She was shrewder about the fact-or-fiction question, perhaps because she was always a novelist and knew from the start that hers was a work of fiction, whereas Haley had spent most of his career as a journalist. Her basic story was true, but "imagination has worked with this factual material . . . for a very long time."[23]

Walker and Haley were acquainted, because he had lectured at Jackson State in 1971. Haley freely acknowledged that Walker was an admired writer and that he himself held her in esteem, although he said he had never read *Jubilee*. Walker had tried to get *Jubilee* adapted for film or television, and she had seen what she considered lesser works than her own produced. Certainly she put *Roots* in that category. She had been laboring for decades at a poorly funded black college in Mississippi, and she felt, with justification, that her work was underappreciated. That *Roots* got *so* much more attention than *Jubilee* clearly galled her.

Walker asserted 112 instances of Haley's allegedly borrowing of language from *Jubilee*. While there are many examples of the same words and phrases used, her evidence was not persuasive that the two writers' use of the same common southern and black folk terms amounted to an instance of copying. She concluded that her novel was "the first from the slave's point of view . . . first as an example of the oral history-genealogical genre. There has not been prior to *Jubilee* another civil war novel written by a black person from that point of view. . . . Customs, expressions, daily life and manners in the slave community had never before appeared in any novel." And then she made a large leap of logic: "Therefore, *Jubilee* must be the model for *Roots*. There is no other book like it prior to 1966." If Haley had admitted using her book or copying from *Jubilee,* Walker asserted, "that would have been another matter. To claim that *Roots* is first is an impostor's claim. *Roots* is usurping what belongs to *Jubilee*."[24]

The Walker case was heard by Judge Marvin E. Frankel, who had been an accomplished lawyer in defense of First Amendment rights, including the landmark libel case *Times v. Sullivan* in 1964. President Lyndon Johnson had appointed Frankel to the federal court in 1965. From Los Angeles Lou Blau found a New York expert on copyright law, a forty-two-year-old NYU graduate named George Berger, to represent Haley. Berger later characterized Frankel as "acerbic, arrogant, and intellectual," and especially astute in his understanding of copyright law. Berger argued that the nonfiction writer should have "free access to the facts of history without fear of losing his profits." Berger's reasoning was close to that inherent in the freedom-of-expression argument that had triumphed in *Times v. Sullivan*.[25]

Berger said Walker's examples were merely "a catalogue of alleged similarities that is strained, insignificant, and devoid of factual or legal substance" and did not prove a violation of copyright law. One category of alleged copying that Judge Frankel noted in his opinion was that of passages based on folk custom—for example, the phrase "jumping over the broomstick," which signified slave marriage. Walker also alleged that Haley's use of the term "making mud pies" was an unlawful appropriation. Haley had said that he made mud pies as a child, and Berger successfully argued that such usage was clearly part of Americana and thus in the public domain. Another category of non-protectable material was *scènes à faire,* scenes in a book that are necessary or obligatory for the plot. Judge Frankel wrote that "attempted escapes, flights through the woods pursued by baying dogs, the sorrowful or happy singing of slaves, the atrocity of buying and selling human beings . . . are all found in stories at least as old as Mrs. Stowe's. This is not, and could not be, an offense to any author. Nobody writes books of purely original content." Walker also claimed that Haley had borrowed clichés like "poor white trash" and "everything went black" (for a slave who has just been whipped). Frankel declared that "words and metaphors are not subject to copyright protection," nor were "phrases and expressions conveying an idea that can only be, or is typically expressed in, a limited number of stereotyped fashions." Berger asked for summary judgment in the suit, and in September 1978 Frankel granted it, thus ending the case.[26]

The next case against Haley would be far less straightforward. Harold Courlander's *The African* told the story of a young man captured in Dahomey in 1802 and taken first to St. Lucia in the Caribbean and then to Georgia. Compared with his works of folklore, which comprise a long and impressive bibliography, *The African* was not very good. But Courlander was an interesting man. Born in 1908, the son of a not very successful Jewish tailor who gained some fame as a painter, Courlander grew up in a Detroit neighborhood of ethnic and racial diversity. He was a successful undergraduate at the University of Michigan, winning prizes for playwriting and criticism. He worked for the Office of War Information during World War II and then after the war for the Voice of America, retiring in 1974. Along the way he took research leaves financed by three Guggenheim fellowships. He wrote eight novels, fourteen scholarly works on various aspects of American and Caribbean folklore, fourteen collections of folktales, and twenty-two scholarly articles, and he assembled fifty-two albums of folk music recordings. His early books were interpretive retellings of folktales from Haiti and West

Africa that were well reviewed as children's literature. His 1939 book, *Haiti Singing*, won plaudits from its *New York Times* reviewer for its "truly scientific spirit" and its "quiet sympathetic tact."[27] *The Cow-Tail Switch and Other West African Stories*, published in 1947, won a Newbery Honor Award. His 1963 *Negro Folk Music U.S.A.* became a standard textbook in college folklore classes.

Courlander and Haley had corresponded and may have met prior to the case. Courlander had written to Haley after reading the 1972 *New York Times* piece, "My Furthest-Back Person, The African," which he found "enormously interesting." He asked about Haley possibly appearing on a Voice of America program and contributing the *Times* piece to an anthology of Afro-American literature Courlander was putting together. He was sure that Haley's book would be out before this anthology appeared, in 1974 or 1975, and so "there is no question of my getting ahead of you in any way."[28] There is no record of a reply from Haley.

But Haley knew of Courlander even earlier. In 1970 Haley had lectured at Skidmore College, in Saratoga Springs, New York, on "Before This Anger." In the audience was an English professor, Joseph Bruchac, a specialist in Native American literature who also had a strong interest in African history. Bruchac had taught in Ghana from 1966 to 1969 and knew many African writers, including Chinua Achebe, author of the internationally renowned anticolonialist novel *Things Fall Apart*. He also knew Courlander personally and admired both his collections of Native American folklore and *The African*. Forty-five years later, Bruchac had a remarkably clear recollection of meeting Haley at Skidmore. He had found Haley's lecture interesting and talked with him for some time at the reception that followed. Haley asked Bruchac what books he used in teaching about Africa, and Bruchac mentioned *The African*, which he thought "dealt so well with so many aspects of the slave experience in Africa, on ship, and in America." Haley seemed not to have heard of it. "I then drove the three miles home, grabbed my personal copy (that I'd annotated) and came back to the reception where he was waiting for me—with his overcoat on. I pointed out a few things in the book to him, then gave it to him. He placed it in his right coat pocket, shook my hand, thanked me, and said he was sure it would be useful, that he would read it on the plane ride home and let me know what he thought of it."[29]

Courlander was astonished at and perplexed by the success of *Roots*. "How can I say it calmly," he wrote to his editor at Crown Publishers in February 1977, "without feeling too much?" *Roots* was selling "so fast they can't keep track of how many. But where is *The African*, which scooped *Roots* by ten years?" Courlander's book was now out of print. He had been pleading for a reissue since at least 1975 to no avail. In February 1977 he noted the similarities between the two books and sent his publisher examples of what he thought were Haley's "borrowings," but after talking with the publisher, he was "satisfied that there is no legal redress." Any author who has seen a book he believes to be lesser than his own gain greater fame, or who has felt that his work has been neglected by his publisher, can identify with Courlander's resentment. Soon after he wrote to his publisher, that feeling turned into a lawsuit alleging copyright infringement. Crown soon did reissue *The African*, no doubt with the intention of capitalizing on the interest in the slave experience caused by *Roots* and the emerging conflict over copyright infringement.[30]

Haley had to turn over many boxes of research notes to Courlander, which violated Haley's sense of privacy and authorial privilege, but he and George Sims assembled the files.[31] There were no notes on novels anywhere in the material. Still, Courlander came away with ninety-eight instances of what he alleged was copying, although nearly all of them were examples of common words and phrases and not passages of a sentence or longer. But Courlander identified four passages that he believed showed that Haley had copied from *The African*. In the first, Courlander's captive character says, "The sun rises in Africa, and whenever we see it we shall remember the place of its daily birth," while Kunta recalls an old man saying, "Each day's new sun will remind us that it rose in our Africa, which is the navel of the earth." A second example from *The African* reads, "'We are different tribes,' Doume said. 'We bear different marks upon our skins. But as of today we are one village.'" And from *Roots:* "The voice of an elder rang out, 'Hear me! Though we are of different tribes and tongues, remember that we are the same people! We must be as one village." A third example from *The African:* "'First thing to learn,' Old Ned said, 'is to forget all that African talk. Old Master, he don't like it. Overseer, he don't like it neither.'" And from *Roots:* "'I'm tellin' you, boy, you got to forgit all that African talk. Make white folks mad an' scare niggers.'" A fourth example from *The African:* "In my young days, I run away three times. . . . That time I got no place to get away, I fight with 'em right here. . . . How do I do this thing? Do it by bein' a no-good, lazy, shiftless, head-scratchin' nigger, that's how." And from *Roots:* "My young days, I run off so much dey near 'bout tore my hide off 'fore I got it in my head aint nowhere to run to. . . . Sooner later you gets cotched an' nearly kilt. . . . Reckon since you been born I been actin' like de no-good, lazy, shiftless, head-scratchin' nigger white folks says us is."[32]

George Berger understood that Judge Robert Ward, a recent Nixon appointee to the court, knew little about copyright law, but he seemed like an affable fellow, so when Berger suggested during an early trial conference that Ward hand off the case to Frankel, Berger was taken aback when Ward said, "You pulled the wool over Judge Frankel's eyes, but you won't pull the wool over mine." Ward told the lawyers that he would let them explain the evidence. At one point Berger referred to a federal appeals court decision, and Ward asked, "What idiot wrote that?" Berger replied, "Judge Learned Hand"— widely considered the most influential American jurist not to have served on the U.S. Supreme Court. At one point, Ward volunteered,

"I don't read a lot," and admitted that his most serious reading was *Reader's Digest*. Berger suspected then that he was in trouble, but his hunch became a certainty when Ward pressured Courlander's lawyer, Robert N. Kaplan, to drop the ABC television network as a defendant. The basis for this action appeared to be that Ward identified with the Edward Asner character in the *Roots* miniseries, the morally tortured Captain Davies of the slave ship. Kaplan let ABC out of the case. There was no limit on such judicial impetuousness, regardless of how irresponsible, short of appeal.

The trial started in early November 1978. In his opening statement, Kaplan told the court that it was "incredible" for Haley to maintain that he had never read *The African*. "Mr. Haley has taken over the language and dramatic mood of this novel." Kaplan pointed to verbatim replication, including text from page 128 in *The African*, which tells how the slave captive "awoke one morning more lighthearted than he had felt since leaving his village. He carried his knowledge secretly as a treasure." In *Roots:* "Kunta awakened more lighthearted than he had felt since leaving his village. He carried his knowledge secretly as a treasure." Another example from *The African*, on the same page: "There were some in the south camp who saw Wes smile for the first time." *Roots:* "There were those in the slave quarters who declared to others that they had just seen him smile for the first time." The two books used an identical field call: "Yooo-hooo-ah-hooo." Courlander and Crown asked for more than half the profits from *Roots*.[33]

Berger responded that, notwithstanding a few examples, "the evidence here will show that there is no substantial similarity between the two books within the meaning of the copyright law," which required that "the alleged copying must be readily apparent to the average lay reader." *Roots* was the "result of a colossal research effort and dedication by Mr. Haley, much of it completed before *The African* was published."

Most of the persuasive examples of copying came from the sec
tions on the Middle Passage. This was ironic, because Haley's rendering of the Middle Passage was long, electrifying, and horrific,
whereas Courlander's was relatively brief, flat, and almost boring.
Courlander also claimed that he had done no research for *The African*, a statement that strained credulity, given the clear reflection
of some well-known primary documents in his text. In both books,
there were scenes of slaves being made to dance in chains on ships,
probably inspired by British antislavery broadsides, although the language in the two books differs.

Haley spent several days in the witness box answering questions
from Berger about how he researched the book. He explained that
he often received notes with research leads from people who had attended his lectures. "In the midst of a reception, with people sort of
crowding about, someone would say, 'here's something of interest to
you, I think.' . . . It might be anything from a 3 × 5 index card which
might contain the name of a book and author. It might be something
they had Xeroxed. It might be something in longhand." After he
finished a lecture tour, he would put the notes collected in a box, and
eventually he would look through the material and decide whether to
make use of it. By the time he did this, however, he usually had lost
all sense of a note's provenance. George Sims reputedly read virtually
everything that Haley read, and he was said to have a photographic
memory. Like Haley, Sims said in deposition that he had never read
The African.[34]

From the bench, Judge Ward was skeptical that Haley had never
read Courlander's book. "If he saw it and read it and made a couple of
notes from it, and wrote a 600-plus-page book, you have one thing,"
the judge said, but Haley's contention that he never saw the book
"leaves me a little cold." Haley had sworn that he had never read it—
he had made the same claim about *Jubilee*—and Berger said he believed him. "I trust at the end of the case you will believe him, too,"

he told the judge. Berger may have been whistling past the graveyard, because he already knew that Ward was hostile to his client.[35]

Haley's testimony was widely reported, and Joseph Bruchac at Skidmore College assumed that Haley was lying when he claimed not to have read *The African*. "The idea that someone would lie about something so important upset me deeply, especially because Haley had set such store on telling the real truth about slavery and then undercut his own work by stealing from others and then lying. It led me to write a letter to Harold about my having discussed and then given the book to Haley some 5 or so years before." It was, of course, possible that Haley had not read the book, but it was unwise of him not to acknowledge he had been given it. Courlander and Kaplan each contacted Bruchac and asked him to testify at the trial, but Bruchac did not want publicity and instead gave an affidavit attesting to what he knew.[36] The document was not submitted at the trial, at least not as a matter of record; affidavits are not admissible evidence once a trial has begun because the affiant is not available for cross-examination.

The trial took on a bizarre character. Judge Ward's wife, Florence, sat in a wheelchair in the courtroom through much of the proceeding, perhaps because she was very ill. From the bench, Ward alternately smiled at her and berated her. His nastiness to the sick woman shocked others in the courtroom. The trial was frequently interrupted for short periods for Ward to handle criminal arraignments, mostly for men brought up on drug charges. Shackled prisoners and their attorneys shambled in to hear Ward tell the accused that they could plead not guilty, but if they did so, the court would deal more harshly with them if they were found guilty. Most pleaded guilty on the spot. The lawyers waiting on the sides for the Courlander case to resume noted that Ward's sentences for the blacks pleading guilty were twice as long as those for the whites.[37]

As the trial continued, Ward's hostility to Haley became more apparent. He heard expert testimony from two Columbia University

English professors who thought they had found evidence of copyright infringement, but Ward made it clear that he would decide if there was substantial similarity in the books based on "my reading of them," because he represented the "average reader" referred to in the laws governing cases of copyright infringement. "I know where I sit."[38] He set a standard that Haley had to prove that he had gotten a passage from somewhere other than Courlander—in effect, that he was guilty of copyright infringement until he could demonstrate his innocence. Several times Ward insinuated that Haley had "cleaned up" his notes—i.e., rewritten them to take out copied passages. In private meetings with lawyers, Ward made clear that he thought "Haley could not have written this." Lawyers hearing this understood it to mean that he did not think that a black man could have done something so powerful or so successful and that he must have stolen the book. A lawyer observing the trial said: "Judge Ward is the master and Alex is Toby."[39]

When the plaintiff's case was finished, Ward tried to force a settlement. He suggested two different dollar figures for a settlement, both of which Haley rejected. The trial recessed for the Thanksgiving holiday, but Ward ordered the parties to appear on Friday in his chambers for a settlement conference, which continued on Saturday and Sunday. At times Ward met with all parties, at other times alone with Haley and then with Courlander, and then with the two of them together, without counsel. He then told the lawyers that because he had had such extensive discussions beyond the evidence in the case, he would recuse himself and grant a mistrial if it was requested. On the Monday after Thanksgiving, Robert Callagy, the Doubleday lawyer, told Ward that because he had pressed so hard for a settlement, "and since you have been presented with documents by the other side, documents not in evidence"—this referred in all likelihood to the Bruchac affidavit—"defendants do not feel now that they can receive a fair trial from here on in."[40] Not surprisingly, the plaintiff's lawyers did not want Ward to step aside; he clearly seemed headed toward a finding for them. Ward denied the motion for his recusal.[41]

Then Ward turned more pressure on Haley. In a meeting outside the courtroom, he threatened Haley, although Haley was not present. "If Haley doesn't settle the case, I am going to ruin *Roots*." He meant that his ruling would be so harsh that the book would lose all legitimacy in the public's eyes. He admitted that his decision might get overturned, but news of a reversal on appeal would merely appear on the back pages of the *New York Times,* and that only years later, after the damage to *Roots* would long since have been done. The message was relayed to Haley. Ward's tactic was similar to the one he used with persons charged with drug trafficking: make the compromise the judge demanded, or face a much more costly outcome.[42]

The journalist Phillip Nobile later wrote that Ward threatened Haley with a charge of perjury, and that precipitated the settlement. Haley's lawyer never heard such a threat. Berger was sure later that such a threat, if in fact it was made, was not why Haley settled. On reflection, he did not think Ward would have pursued that course, because it would have brought unwanted scrutiny to his conduct in the case. But Ward probably knew of Bruchac's affidavit, even though it was not entered in the trial record, and he may have threatened Haley with it in their private meeting.[43]

Haley was exhausted by the trial and fearful for his reputation. *Roots: The Next Generations* was set for broadcast the following February. A bad judgment would distract from its promotion. According to Nobile, Robert Callagy heard Haley say, "I can't take the press on this. . . . I can't have a case that I copied." Haley reportedly was frequently on the telephone to "his advisers," most likely Lou Blau in Hollywood, a man who knew that wealthy celebrities were subject to lawsuits and that money usually solved the problem.[44]

A settlement was reached on December 14, six weeks into the trial. "The suit has been amicably settled out of court," the sides announced. "Alex Haley acknowledges and regrets that various materials from *The*

African by Harold Courlander found their way into his book *Roots*." Haley said that "somewhere, somebody gave me something that came from 'The African.' That's the best, honest explanation I can give."

The settlement agreement contained a confidentiality provision, which Judge Ward ordered all to observe—before trying to get Berger to tell him the figure. Berger refused. A figure of $650,000 was widely reported and never denied, but also never confirmed. If that number was correct, it represented $2.34 million in 2015 dollars. Haley paid the settlement and his legal fees himself, with no help from the publisher. His legal fees were probably between $300,000 and $500,000 to defend both the Alexander and Courlander suits. Whatever the amount of the settlement and the legal fees, they surely consumed much of what he had earned from *Roots*. On the other hand, Haley was paying federal income tax at a rate of 70 percent on income over $182,200 in 1978. If the settlement and legal fees cost him $1 million, they were most likely deducted as business expenses. He may have received a tax benefit of $700,000. Thus the net loss from the suits may not have been as bad as it seemed. This is the kind of calculation that Lou Blau could certainly have made for Haley.

Neither Berger nor Robert Collagy, the Doubleday lawyer, thought that the settlement was the right decision. The six or seven nearly identical passages did not constitute "substantial similarities" for a book of 688 pages. Even if all eighty-one of Courlander's instances of copying were conceded—and they were not—it would have amounted to less than one percent of the *Roots* text. Almost forty years later, Berger wrote, "I greatly admired Alex Haley for what he had accomplished and then believed and still believe that he would have ultimately won the Courlander case."[45] Unfortunately for Haley's reputation, most observers later interpreted the settlement as an admission that he had plagiarized part of *Roots*.

Haley had already imagined such an outcome. He had told Murray Fisher in 1975 that black celebrities were under special scrutiny, and much of the public anticipated their fall. In the Courlander trial, he acted to forestall his demise by handing over a lot of money. He hoped it would end the scrutiny and preserve his success.[46]

* * *

MOST OF THE ACADEMIC WORLD refrained from comment on Haley's research until 1981, when two historians and a professional genealogist stepped forward. Donald R. Wright, a historian at the State University of New York at Cortland, had done research on the Niumi region in the Gambia, where Juffure is situated. He interviewed ninety-six griots, among them Kebba Fofana. Like Ottaway, Wright had found that Fofana was not a true griot, but a "local entertainer and teller of stories." Wright quickly added that that did not mean that his information about Kunta Kinte was incorrect. Wright doubted Fofana's bona fides as a historian, because he recited no family histories and gave no answers like he reportedly had provided Haley. Moreover, none of the informants on the history of the lower Gambia River considered him a good source on the local history. "The oral traditions of the lower Gambia simply do not contain specific information about real people living before the nineteenth century—except now, of course, for the story of Kunta Kinte." To Wright, it was "quite incredible that anyone would remember a story about sixteen-year-old boy . . . when no one remembers stories about anyone else, including older men and leaders of society, from that time on or much later." The story Fofana told Wright about Kunta Kinte was more elaborate than what he offered Haley in 1967—and it was different. He said that Kunta was held on James Island for six years after his capture before he was taken to America. Asked how he knew the boy went to America, Fofana did not have a good answer.[47]

Wright believed Haley's research was "a virtual scenario of how *not* to conduct fieldwork in oral societies," because he had told his family story to all he met in the Gambia, and "in doing so he made it all too clear just what he hoped to hear in return." Wright believed that Haley had misunderstood the real purpose of the griot, which was not to record in his memory an accounting of a family's history. Griots were "dependents of important families and their role in life was to entertain, to praise members of their patron families, and perhaps most importantly, to remember and recite the kinds of things their patrons wanted to hear, all for recompense." Wright thought Haley's Gambian advisers could have found any number of storytellers with connections to the Kinte clan, some of them real griots. They found Fofana in Juffure because that was the first place they looked. Thus, Haley established Juffure as his ancestral home on the basis of his Gambian advisers' happenstance in locating Fofana. Wright faulted Haley for not recording his interview with Fofana, although it was recorded by Gambian national radio, and for basing his research on a single interview. He noted Haley's failure to include the information from the Gambian national archivist Bakary Sidibe, received in 1973, that cast doubt on Fofana's account. Wright thought that was an instance of Haley disregarding information that "did not serve the purposes he wanted it to." Wright concluded that the defects in Haley's research were "sufficient to demolish" his account of Kunta's capture in Juffure in the 1760s. He thought Kunta was either "a wholly fictitious figure" or, more likely, someone who lived somewhere in the lower Gambia region in the 1800s. "For centuries oral historians everywhere have been manufacturing and manipulating genealogies and personal stories to meet the needs of their patrons," Wright wrote, and "Fofana probably did for Haley just what any good griot might have done for an African ruler several centuries before his time."[48]

At the same time in 1981, the American portion of Haley's research came under close scrutiny by Gary B. Mills, a history professor at the University of Alabama, and his wife, Elizabeth Shown Mills, a professional genealogist. Gary Mills was an active neo-Confederate at the same time that he was a respected scholar of the free black experience in the antebellum South. The Millses were skilled researchers in family history with a strong commitment to following established procedures. They believed all serious genealogists needed to be skeptical about using oral history for genealogy. "Family traditions are surrealistic images of the past, blurred by time, colored by emotion and imagination. They are valuable as cryptic maps that can lead to rewarding personal revelations; but the careful researcher must decode them through dogged exploration of the actual documents our ancestors left us." They cited Haley's statement that "in plantation records, wills, census records, I documented a bit here, shreds there," and that by 1967, he believed he had "seven generations of the U.S. side documented." The Millses said that, in fact, the documents Haley referred to "not only *fail to document* his story, but they *contradict* each and every pre–Civil War statement of Afro-American lineage in *Roots!*"[49]

Haley had first discovered the slave called Toby (Kunta Kinte in *Roots*) in a 1768 deed conveying him from John Waller of Spotsylvania County, Virginia, to his brother William Waller. This was the document on which Haley based Kunta's departure date from Africa as 1767. The Millses discovered documents that placed Toby in Virginia as early as 1762, and, noting his absence from William Waller's 1782 tax declaration, they presumed that Toby died at some point before 1782. Thus, according to the Millses, this Toby could not have been Kunta, because he was in Virginia five years before Kunta allegedly arrived and died eight years before his daughter Kizzy was born. They found no conclusive evidence of the existence of Toby's wife, Bell, but clear evidence that "Missy Anne" Waller was far too old to have been Kizzy's white playmate, a relationship central to the *Roots* narrative. Indeed, they could find no evidence of a Waller slave named Kizzy. They found no evidence of William Waller's marriage to Priscilla or his alleged 1789 will, but they did discover his 1763 relinquishment of all his property to his brother John, an action commonly taken, the Millses explained, when an incapacitated person was in need of someone to care for him.

The Millses conjectured about various scenarios other than Haley's explanation that could have accounted for the events in *Roots*, but, they said, "Speculations aside, there remains the inarguable conclusion that the 182 pages and thirty-nine chapters in which the Virginia lives of Haley's 'ancestors' are chronicled have no basis in fact." Neither the marriage of Toby to Bell nor the identity of Kizzy—"the two relationships that are crucial to [Haley's] pedigree"—could be established by genealogical research. With regard to the subsequent generations of the family, the Millses provided evidence that Haley had misrepresented the makeup of the white Lea family of North Carolina, whence came Chicken George. Either Haley had gotten the names wrong or his ancestors did not belong to Tom Lea, who, as Chicken George's biological father, was Haley's great-great-great grandfather. Chicken George's biography was problematic, they pointed out, because during his sojourn in England in the 1850s slavery was illegal, and he would have been free on arrival there. Yet he came home a slave and stayed one for many years, according to *Roots*. The Millses questioned whether Haley had "misadvised the thousands of trusting black Americans who have turned to him for guidance and for standards of their own work."

*   *   *

BEING A BEST-SELLING AUTHOR did not bring Alex Haley the peace and freedom that he had imagined. He had worked hard, struggled against formidable odds, treated most people well, and thought he deserved success. He did not disdain the expertise of academics, but neither did he believe he should be held accountable to their standards of objectivity when he was aiming for a higher, symbolic truth. He believed that many critics simply wanted to deflate someone whose celebrity had grown large, and he was right about that. In some instances, the provocation for disparaging him was simply racial prejudice. But it was also true that he had made a fundamental mistake in proclaiming the historicity of *Roots* when he knew that the book was not, at least in some of its parts, strictly true. His account of his use of *The African* was not plausible, in the view of many observers. Did the alleged misrepresentations warrant the onslaught of attacks he was enduring? Were they so grievous as to rightly undo the salutary effects of *Roots* on the American popular mind? No, they were not, but in the world of American celebrity, fair and correct judgments often do not prevail.

11

FIND THE GOOD
AND PRAISE IT

THE OTTAWAY EXPOSÉ AND THE COPYRIGHT SUITS
left scars on Haley. His old friend Leonard Jeffries, with whom
he had worked on a black genealogy project in the early 1970s,
described him as "shell-shocked." Haley had won all the suits
except one that he had settled, but he took no consolation from that.
"The one who really lost was me," he said, because what the public
remembered was not the substance of the findings in the cases but
that he was sued. "What I learned was if you're fortunate enough to
do anything that becomes highly acclaimed, especially if it makes
money, you can almost bet that somebody is going to come along
and say, 'You took something from me,'" he told the *New York Times*.[1]

Haley had settled the Courlander case because he wanted to sal-
vage his reputation, but he did not really succeed, in part because
of the inconsistent way that America's celebrity culture dealt with
accusations of plagiarism. In 1989 Thomas Mallon, a noted writer
of historical fiction, published *Stolen Words*, an analysis of several

leading cases of alleged plagiarism—although not Haley's. "It seems plagiarism is something people get off with scot-free or it's a career killer, the single thing they're known for," Mallon said years later. "What we need . . . is a certain proportionality." Whether "somebody takes a kind of delight in an icon's being reduced to a bum in the space of a week, ought to be factored into people's reputations. It should diminish our overall estimation of him, but we should not run him out of the human race." Haley saw a reputation for plagiarism as a possible "career killer."[2]

Accusations of plagiarism were a phenomenon common in Hollywood, where Haley lived from the mid-1970s to the early 1980s. The financial stakes were higher and much was to be gained from claiming theft of intellectual property. There, such accusations did not carry the same opprobrium that they did in intellectual and literary circles in New York. A number of successful films—*Nosferatu, A Fistful of Dollars, Rocky, Coming to America,* and *The Terminator*— were allegedly based on misappropriated ideas. In Hollywood, the victim whose intellectual property was poached was often well compensated for it after the fact. Such settlements were seen as merely the cost of doing business in the entertainment industry. Most people in Hollywood understood the Courlander case as Haley's cost of fame.

It was ironic that, while Alex Haley was dealing with the accusations of factual inaccuracy and copyright infringement in 1977 and 1978, he was also working on another, and some thought better, recounting of his family's past. In long interviews with producers and scriptwriters that were far easier for him to render than a book, he supplied information for *Roots: The Next Generations,* broadcast in early 1979. The miniseries was fourteen hours long (two hours longer than the original *Roots*) and was shown over seven consecutive nights. The production cost $18 million, three times as much as the first *Roots.* It followed Haley's family from the 1880s through World War II, which was the time covered in the last thirty pages of *Roots,* and then touched on the decades that followed, culminating in

Haley's trip to Africa. As in the first *Roots* broadcast, white characters were created who had not appeared in the book, but here they were necessary to develop important themes about race relations and to tell the true story of the black experience after Reconstruction. Much of it adhered to the facts Alex had made well known since the 1960s, including his troubled marriage to Nan. But it also contained many new characters, mostly whites, and scenes created just for television that filled out the narrative of black history from Emancipation in the 1860s to the civil rights movement of the 1960s.

"*Roots* II" emphasized several new themes. It explored the ways that race complicated romantic love among blacks and between blacks and whites, suggested mostly with characters not present in Haley's writing. It created an unlikely interracial marriage between a white planter's son and a well-educated black teacher in Henning. The series rendered in realistic scenes the ugliness of post-Reconstruction race relations, including segregation, the convict-leasing system, lynching, disenfranchisement, the persistent racism of working-class whites, and the amorality and arrogance of white paternalism, portrayed chillingly by Henry Fonda. It captured the demeaning compromises that blacks had to make to survive in the white supremacist South. It took the narrative of black history through the important events of the twentieth century, covering the nuances of white supremacist customs; the exploitation of the sharecropping system; the conflict between Booker T. Washington and W. E. B. Du Bois; the discrimination against blacks in the U.S. Army; the racial terrorism in American cities after the war; the rise of the all-black Pullman porters union; and the reemergence of the Ku Klux Klan in the 1920s. White hatred provided the main tension of the plot, but there were enough conflicts in the Haley family saga to keep the momentum of the series rolling. A few benevolent whites were inserted in the story to relieve the otherwise unrelenting malevolence of the dominant majority. There were some false steps in the plot. The writers devoted almost a whole episode to white bigots in Alabama in the 1930s who were violently enforcing exploitation of black sharecroppers over Simon Haley's fierce opposition. Such violence existed, although not where the script located it, and there was no evidence in Alex Haley's research that Simon was involved in anything like it. This part of the story contradicted what was known about Simon's personality. The last episodes, focusing on Alex's rise as a writer, felt slow and a lot like typical television melodrama. The history lessons seemed more forced than in the earlier episodes. So, too, did the recalling in each episode, almost by rote it seemed, of the Kunta Kinte heritage.

"*Roots* II" had a large cast of black actors. The main male characters—Tom Murray, Will Palmer, and Simon Haley—were played as overburdened men, without much texture, although all were on screen for long stretches. Most important, the miniseries dispensed entirely with Simon's extroverted, crowd-loving nature. On the other hand, several of the smaller parts were played brilliantly: Ossie Davis as a Pullman porter, Bernie Casey as a World War I soldier, and Paul Winfield as a black college president stole their respective scenes. James Earl Jones, Haley's old friend, played Haley as a grown man. Donald Bogle found Jones unconvincing because he "overacted"; he made Haley more demonstrative than he was in fact, especially in the expression of anger. But when Beah Richards as Cynthia Palmer spoke to Alex about his ancestors, Bogle thought "her power and convictions lifted the drama completely out of TV land." He concluded that, in contrast to the way actors in the first series "pushed for big emotions and big emotional responses from the audience . . . the sequel was frequently a quieter drama focusing partly on class struggle and espousing the American work ethic and a belief in the American Dream." More white star actors filled the cast of "*Roots* II" than were in its predecessor. Henry Fonda as a former Confederate colonel, Olivia de Havilland as his wife, Andy Griffith as Alex's helpful Coast Guard commander, and Marlon Brando as the American Nazi George Lincoln Rockwell raised the illustriousness of the cast higher than that of the white actors in the first series. Brando, having recently starred in *The Godfather,* had begged for a part, and his few minutes on screen were riveting.[3]

Airing from February 19 to February 25, 1979, *Roots: The Next Generations* was viewed by one hundred and ten million Americans, just twenty million fewer viewers than the first miniseries. It got better reviews. *Newsweek* said it was "richer in physical sweep and psychological shadings, graced with acting seldom seen on the tube." The reviewer in the *New York Post* said it was "a fuller, sweeter, more agonizing story, and its conflicts cut deeper into our twentieth century sensibility." Whereas the first series was largely the story of a rebellious black man challenging white authority, "*Roots* II" focused on blacks' accepting American values about progress and success. The overarching message, as in the first *Roots,* was the continuity of survival and hope in black families.[4]

The judgments of historians made decades later matter less in evaluating the historical significance of the series than the impact when it aired. "*Roots* II" completed Haley's "saga of a people" on television, and with the help of David Wolper, he had given more than a hundred million Americans a new understanding of the black experience in the United States. Together the two *Roots* miniseries had filled in huge gaps in the public's knowledge of black history, and it had given Americans vivid images that would enable them to hold on to that new awareness.

*   *   *

BOTH *ROOTS* SERIES were autobiographical, and so was Haley's next television production, *Palmerstown, USA,* a weekly series that ran in 1980 and 1981 and comprised seventeen episodes. Haley collaborated with the producer Norman Lear, who had enjoyed great success in the 1970s with several television series, most notably *All in the Family.* Haley suggested the plots of the episodes and collaborated on some scripts. *Palmerstown* finally realized the plot and themes of the novel "The Lord and Little David," which Haley had begun writing in the early 1950s and tried to get published well into the 1960s. It incorporated the original presumption of "Before This Anger," that there was a time in the South, the 1930s, when blacks and whites got along more amicably than they would in the 1960s. *Palmerstown* drew on Haley's life, but it was not as explicitly auto-biographical as the two *Roots* miniseries. He named the town after a branch of his family and modeled it on Henning. The main premise of the series, a relationship between two boys in a southern town during the Great Depression, was also personal. Haley had had a white friend in Henning, Kermit, with whom he spent much time until age twelve. That relationship had ended badly, when Kermit tried to assert his supposed racial superiority over Haley. In *Palmerstown*, the boys remain friends throughout the course of the story.

Haley's notes for the scripting of *Palmerstown*, provided to guide writers, revealed his understanding of the sociology of the South: "This series reaches for something deep within the American culture which has not been accurately portrayed." It focused on two of "America's most bedrock" groups, each of them exploited—blacks and poor whites. Haley put these groups side by side in a small town, much like Henning, that comprised five hundred folks evenly divided by race. "One of the secrets of small towns is they contain no anonymous individuals, as cities do," Haley wrote. "Anyone who is raised in a small town can tell you something singular, something salient, about everyone else." One telling instruction to the writers was not to "belabor racial inequities." A recent docudrama about Martin Luther King Jr.'s career had done that, which was why, Haley said, it had failed with white audiences. "Deal obliquely with race matters; as *Roots* did, permit viewers to derive their own subjective editorials."[5]

In *Palmerstown*, black Booker T. Freeman and white David Hall are sons of a blacksmith and a grocer, respectively. The two boys observe the racial tensions among adults. The boys' fathers argue over a grocery bill, and the tension trickles down to them. Racial epithets are thrown about. The series explored the theme of class through the way that poor whites were the source of conflict in Palmerstown; it continued the persistent theme in Haley's work of the strength of black families. Each episode developed a crisis in the town and then resolved it. The series was nostalgic about the South of the 1930s and romantic in its treatment of racial issues. Donald Bogle insisted that the show ignored the ugly realities of the segregated South and the abiding cultural distinctions that sustained blacks. But even if it was a much less satisfying program than "*Roots* II," Bogle thought that black audiences would be happy to watch another black drama, especially if it came from Alex Haley.[6]

By the end of *Palmerstown*'s run, Americans had been given forty-three hours of Alex Haley's family history on television in four years. Such attention won him great admiration among many Americans, especially blacks, who as a group knew that television had slighted them before Haley came along. His stories treated the black experience seriously, whereas such popular programs as *Good Times*, in which the actor Jimmie Walker often shouted "Dy-no-MITE!" were seen by many as demeaning blacks.

Haley had moved on from *Roots* to celebrate equality in American life and good human relations in the South, but his largest impact on American culture probably was his encouragement of black nationalism. The black media critic Herman Gray believed that *Roots* had enabled discourse on blackness in a way that caused the "rearticulation of the discourse of Afrocentric nationalism." Gray thought the work had also brought about a renewed interest in black studies and the development of "African-centered rap and black urban style." *Roots* encouraged a racial nationalist temper in the archetype of Kunta Kinte. The rappers Lil Wayne and Missy Elliott made reference to Kunta Kinte in song. Filmmakers John Singleton and Spike Lee referred to Kunta in *Boyz n the Hood* and *Do the Right Thing*, respectively.[7]

In 1994 four cultural anthropologists wrote in an academic journal that "Afrocentricity could not have existed without *Roots*." Afrocentrists believed and taught that European civilization was derived from African origins—an understanding of history that Elijah Muhammad and the Nation of Islam had advanced. Afrocentrist history was often condemned as ahistorical, and it caused a furor on some American college campuses in the 1980s. Afrocentric history was not what Alex Haley had presented in *Roots,* but he paved the way for men like his friend Leonard Jeffries, who did teach it. Afrocentrists were "preaching to the already converted," the anthropologists said, because *Roots* had already taught black Americans they had "their own stories of origin and identity." Haley and Malcolm X "wanted to use Africa in this crucial manner in order to shield the American Black against the ego deficiency produced by White racism."[8] Many Americans thought Haley and Malcolm had succeeded.

* * *

HALEY DID LITTLE WRITING in the early 1980s. "Even as the *Roots* madness died down, I continued to do too much speaking and not enough writing," he recalled. "Because I don't like to turn people down—it bothers me to hurt anyone's feelings." Lecturing was easy and lucrative—he was now paid $10,000 per lecture—and it gave him good reason to indulge his wanderlust, although he said he did not keep up the frenetic speaking pace of the late 1960s and early 1970s. By the late 1980s his income from royalties had declined to the point that he needed to lecture to maintain a high standard of living. Haley continued to make freighter trips in the 1980s, ostensibly to write. He usually sailed for four to six weeks at a time, often over the Christmas holidays. He sailed along the Pacific side of Latin America in 1984 and from Savannah to Rotterdam the following year. In 1988 he went to Australia, taking along a friend, Tennessee former governor Lamar Alexander. At some point Haley leased an apartment in Seattle. It is not clear what the attraction was there, but he visited the city regularly.[9]

What writing he produced usually followed a familiar pattern—it was autobiographical and meant to end up on television. The one story that was not autobiographical was about a mountain man and his son, called "Appalachian." In 1985 *Reader's Digest* published "Easter in Henning," an excerpt from Haley's forthcoming book, "Henning, U.S.A.," which in fact never appeared. He also discussed a project called "Queen," about his paternal grandmother, which would, as he said, "square another debt" to his father; Simon Haley had hinted for years that the story of his side of the family, particularly his mother, Queen, would make a good book. Queen had cared for Alex and his brothers for a time after the boys' mother had died. He had heard many stories about her and her white father, Colonel Jackson.[10]

In 1986 Haley decided to return to his roots in Tennessee. He had lived in California, mostly in Los Angeles, since the early 1970s, and with Haley now at age sixty-five, the move represented a large shift in lifestyle. He and his brothers had reacquired the family home in Henning, which they had sold after Aunt Liz died. The property had fallen into disrepair and been damaged by a fire, but now they renovated it and, thanks to Alex's fame, had it named a state historic landmark. The Haley brothers planned to turn the house into a tourist site. Alex Haley was drawn home for Tennessee Homecoming '86, a yearlong celebration that promoted tourism by urging those who had left Tennessee to discover the progress that the state had made in their absence—and spend money they had earned elsewhere. The celebration hearkened back to the tradition at southern evangelical churches of setting aside one Sunday in the month when former members returned to visit old friends. It also reflected the lasting impact of *Roots* on American culture: many people had been prompted to reconnect with their past through "roots travel," and the growing phenomenon, especially among blacks, of both family and community reunions. People who had migrated to the North traveled in big groups to the towns or rural communities where they had been born. They often wore t-shirts announcing such events as "The Haley Family Reunion" or "The Henning, Tennessee Reunion." The phenomenon continues to this day.

Tennessee Homecoming '86 also formed committees to do research on local history in preparation for the state's bicentennial, in 1996. The national bicentennial of 1976 had put Americans in the mind of celebrating two-hundredth anniversaries. Tennessee Homecoming was the idea of Governor Lamar Alexander, a young, progressive-minded Republican. In Tennessee politics of the mid-1980s, Alexander projected a modern approach to government, a break with the old one-party Democratic control of the segregationist South. He supported education and opposed racial divisiveness. Alexander accomplished the shift in political perception so successfully that he became popular enough for Tennesseeans typically to refer to him simply as "Lamar," a familiarity he encouraged by habitually donning a checkered flannel shirt, almost regardless of occasion. What better way was there to demonstrate a "new Tennessee" than to engage its newest celebrity, a genial black writer, in celebration of the old Tennessee? Alexander and Haley were already acquainted, and the young governor liked the writer's positive attitude, especially his oft-repeated slogan, "Find the good and praise it." Alexander drew him into the project, making him the honorary co-chair of the celebration, along with the country-music comedian Minnie Pearl. Haley and Alexander traveled across the state on a train during Tennessee Homecoming.

In the fall of 1986, Haley bought two condominiums in Knoxville, home of the University of Tennessee and the Tennessee Valley Authority, in the Appalachian Mountains area of eastern Tennessee. In his 1946 book *Inside U.S.A.,* the writer John Gunther had called Knoxville the ugliest city in the United States, but it was undergoing a renaissance of late, having a hosted a well-attended World's Fair in 1982. In Knoxville Haley created a circle of friends composed mainly of prominent white men, most of them local celebrities. They included John Rice Irwin, a school superintendent and folklorist who had founded the Museum of Appalachia and thus could help Haley with his miniseries, "Appalachian"; Alexander, who in 1988 became president of the University of Tennessee; the Harvard professor Richard Marius, formerly of the University of Tennessee faculty, who ran a writing program for high school students in Knoxville each summer; Jim Clayton, an industrialist; and David White, a media entrepreneur. Edye Ellis, a black television newscaster, was the notable exception to the white, male character of Haley's crowd. "I don't go to parties," Haley told the *New York Times* in 1988. "I live very well with myself." Perhaps so, but he was known to *give* big parties in Knoxville, especially after he bought a mansion on Cherokee Boulevard, Knoxville's most prestigious address.

He also hosted parties at a 130-acre farm he bought from Irwin, next door to the Museum of Appalachia. There, he renovated an old farmhouse and built several buildings to accommodate visitors. He created a two-acre lake with a dock leading to a gazebo at its center. He hired a decorator specializing in African American–themed art, but when she hung an image of a black fist, he fired her and put up his Hollywood memorabilia and scenes from Appalachia.[11] In the next few years, he entertained his publishing friends from New York, among them Lisa Drew, and his television friends from Hollywood, including Lou Blau.

Haley was a good citizen of Knoxville, a constant promoter of the joys of Tennessee life. He accepted many invitations to speak for free. Once he spoke to a student honor society that as a service project sponsored the local home for unwed mothers, and afterward he posed for pictures with a dozen pregnant teenagers. He agreed to teach a course at the University of Tennessee, and the university administrators asked the English department to name him an adjunct professor. But the English professors, often struggling with plagiarism by students, thought he might have already set a bad example. The journalism department did take him on, but his service did not last long because he often failed to make it to class, and his unreliability was reported in the student newspaper.[12]

* * *

HALEY HAD ATTRACTED a biographer who learned perhaps more than anyone else about the inner life of the writer. Anne Romaine was a pretty and extroverted forty-three-year-old North Carolina native who had studied history in graduate school at the University of Virginia in the mid-1960s. While there, she turned to civil rights activism in the Southern Student Organizing Committee, which led to her create the Southern Folk Cultural Revival Project, a racially mixed troupe of traditional singers and musicians who toured the South performing protest songs. She also wrote, produced, and recorded folk music. She and her activist husband, Howard Romaine, lived in Nashville in the mid-1970s, and there she worked as a curator for the Tennessee State Museum, becoming involved in the naming of the Haley home in Henning as a state landmark. She met Haley in 1986, and they agreed that she would write his biography. By the time she was seriously at work on it, in the mid-1980s, she and Howard Romaine were divorced.

Anne Romaine did a massive amount of work collecting documents and conducting interviews, but her research was not a comprehensive quest for sources, and her interviews were not systematic inquiries and usually were poorly transcribed. Eventually she got access to Haley's personal papers, which might have yielded a good biography. But she died suddenly of a burst appendix in 1995, before she could write much of her book. Her papers, containing her research on Haley, were deposited at the University of Tennessee archives. Romaine's curiosity about Haley was intensely personal, and her findings revealed his personal side in a way that his almost continuous autobiographical writing and talking never had.

Romaine spent a lot of time with Haley, although not as much as she wanted. She said he found "one obstacle after another" to delay the biography. But they were, she later said, "close friends for six years." He told her of his first sexual encounter and recounted the two times in life he had had angry confrontations. She knew his tastes in music and appears not to have approved of his affinity for Mel Torme, Billie Holiday, Billy Eckstine, and Arthur Prysock. She witnessed his friendships in Knoxville with rich, Republican men, of which, again, she did not approve. She witnessed his "status as a folk hero." She noted that once, in Nashville, a black woman stopped him on the street and castigated him for wearing polyester pants: "A man of your stature who represents success for those of us who are black should dress like he is *somebody*—not like some ordinary, old-timey man." Haley asked Romaine what was wrong with polyester pants, and she explained that natural fibers were more stylish. He now understood, but the problem was, "I just ordered seven more pairs from the Sears catalog. I got them in every color. . . . They come already hemmed to my length."[13]

Romaine freely speculated about Haley's psyche. She agreed with Nan Haley that "Alex is a master at not showing his feelings." He did not appreciate Simon Haley's "outgoing, free wheeling" manner, much preferring his grandfather, Will Palmer, "the strong silent type." Romaine asked about Haley's marital woes just as he was getting divorced from My Lewis. He was "too intensely private in his marriages," he admitted to Romaine. She interviewed Haley's daughter Lydia Anne, his first child and Romaine's exact contemporary. Lydia Anne Haley was "a reformer and spiritualist," but Romaine thought she was an embarrassment to her father, going against his view of "what a woman ought to be," quiet and demure like the three he had married. Lydia Anne Haley was a "flashy and brassy" woman who helped people "understand why they are here."

Romaine recounted spending late nights interviewing Haley at his Knoxville homes, just the two of them, with the writer lying on a sofa. Then in a private note, she wrote, "He told me he had been in love with me for a long time[,] since we first met in 1986." She does not say they became lovers, nor does she deny it. She sensed his insecurities: "I am a Greek chorus to Alex. 'Here are the things I admire about you. You are wonderful.'"

Romaine's curiosity about Haley's inner self led her to pose personal questions to the dozens of people she interviewed. She discovered that "he surrounds his outer professional life with white women and men and his close circle with black men and women." She got intimate details of Haley's first marriage from Nan. She elicited from William "Fella" Haley his bitterness about Alex's neglect of him, which was less surprising than William and Nan's belief that Alex and Nan were never legally divorced. While Romaine was interviewing Alex's half-sister, Doris, his stepmother, Zeona, suddenly appeared, and Romaine captured Zeona denouncing Alex as a lout—and confirming the shrewish character that some saw in her but that Alex would not comment on. She learned of Leonard Jeffries's pain over Haley's failure to acknowledge his contributions toward advancing black genealogy. She listened as David Wolper, who adored Haley, expressed his bafflement at Haley's contradictions. Wolper told Romaine he wanted her to find out why Alex, "the ultimate symbol of the family," could not "keep a family together. . . . Why is he such a wanderer, and why he didn't write any more than he's done, why he can't meet deadlines. . . . Why you go in his houses and he has not one picture of his children, no picture of his wife, there's no picture of his mother and father." Those were good questions, but even the ever-personal, ever-penetrating Anne Romaine never got the answers.

After all her interviews and her intimate conversations with Haley, Romaine had put together a portrait of a likable narcissist, although she did not call him that. "Everybody likes Alex," Betty Shabazz had said many years earlier.

*　　*　　*

HALEY FINALLY ENDED his long dry spell of writing in 1988. That year he published a novella, *A Different Kind of Christmas,* about a slave's escape on the Underground Railroad. He also worked on *Roots: The Gift,* a 1988 Christmas television special. Neither was a creation of much import, and each depended a lot on Haley's celebrity for its limited success. Haley told David Wolper that the miniseries *Queen* was what got him writing again. He wrote a seven-hundred-page outline of *Queen* for Mark Wolper, David's son, who was producing the series, and the Australian screenwriter David Stevens, who was writing the eight hours of television script. *Queen* told the story of the relationship between Simon Haley's maternal grandparents, the Confederate Colonel James Jackson and a slave woman, and then the life of their child, Queen. Haley had met white Jackson family members in Florence, Alabama, and got information about the family from them. Some critics thought Haley soft-soaped the relationship between Queen's parents, perhaps making it a story of more romantic love than had actually existed. Still, the commitment to marry exclusively within one's race, an imperative of both black nationalists and white supremacists, was certainly waning in the broader culture, a truth the program perhaps sought to reflect. Or Haley might have been returning to the truth that blacks and whites had always had intimate relations in America, even if many such relationships were not undertaken by choice.[14]

Haley watched with detachment in 1991 and early 1992 as Spike Lee's production of a biopic, *Malcolm X,* revitalized black nationalism. Lee and Amiri Baraka, the preeminent poet of black nationalism, engaged in a public argument over Lee's treatment of the slain icon's life. Haley said that Lee had every right to project his "vision of Malcolm." The movie sparked a revitalization of interest in its subject. The renewed appreciation of Malcolm focused to a large extent on the autobiography, a text for which Haley was mostly responsible. That fact was not usually acknowledged amid the controversy over whether Lee had "gotten Malcolm right."[15]

In its February 1992 issue, the black celebrity magazine *Essence* celebrated Haley's return to writing, discussing *Queen,* which Haley had been talking about for a decade by then. The article noted that the writer's speaking engagements enabled his philanthropy—the full scholarships he provided for needy Tennesseans and Gambians to attend college. *Essence* concluded the piece with this paean: "Alex Haley is a national treasure, and his importance to the world, and to African-Americans in particular, was perhaps best expressed by Haley himself when . . . he wrote that in Africa 'when a griot dies, it is as if a library has burned to the ground.' Fortunately, Alex Haley, our griot, lives!"

But not for long, because the *Essence* piece had just reached the newsstands when readers were shocked to learn that Alex Haley had died on February 10, 1992, at a hospital in Seattle. He had been admitted to the emergency room late on a Sunday night in the midst of having a heart attack. He had gone to Seattle for a speaking engagement, having met earlier that day with Mark Wolper in Los Angeles to discuss the *Queen* script. His family reported that he suffered from diabetes and a thyroid condition, but they thought he was otherwise in good health. Haley had long been a smoker, a high risk factor for heart disease, although it was not clear whether he was still smoking at the time of his death.[16]

His funeral was held in Memphis, because there was no church large enough in Henning to accommodate the throng that assembled to honor him. Among the attendees were LeVar Burton and Cicely Tyson from the *Roots* cast; Dick Gregory; Betty Shabazz; Lamar Alexander, now U.S. secretary of education; and representatives from Senegal and the Gambia. All three of his wives were there, and the last, Myran Lewis Haley, eulogized him: "Thank you, Alex, you have helped us know who we truly are." Also speaking were Malcolm's daughter Attallah Shabazz, who was Haley's goddaughter, and Jesse Jackson. "He made history talk," Jackson said. "He lit up the long night of slavery. He gave our grandparents personhood. He gave *Roots* to the rootless." Haley was buried on the front lawn of Will Palmer's home in Henning, just a few feet from the porch where he had heard the family stories. The funeral received coverage around the world and was the subject of a five-page spread in *Jet* magazine.[17]

As is typical for a major celebrity in the United States, Haley's death inspired a fascination with his estate. According to his will, his brothers and his children were to inherit the bulk of his assets in trust. The will provided for cash gifts of $30,000 each to George Sims; Haley's half-sister, Doris; Nan; and Haley's longtime Los Angeles assistant, Jackie Naipo. Newspaper and magazines soon reported, however, that Haley was $1.5 million in debt when he died and that no money would go out anytime soon. According to the *New York Times,* the debts resulted from losses in real estate, and the article also cited Haley's cash gifts to friends and students. In fact, Haley's finances were a mess. The figure of his indebtedness almost matched what he had spent on his farm. He told people in the mid-1980s that his income was about $3 million a year, but that figure had fallen by 1991 to about $750,000, so that his lectures were his main source of income. Before he died, the debts were burdensome enough that he had put the farm up for sale. The indebtedness resulted in part from a decline in his income from royalties and from rising expenses connected to support staff in a Knoxville office, caretakers on the farm, and assistants in Los Angeles. Haley's lawyer blamed Haley's overpayment of staff and general mismanagement of money for the insolvency of his estate when he died: "People took advantage of him. Something that he could buy for a dollar, he paid six."[18]

When his will was probated in Knoxville in March 1992, a long line of creditors formed, led by banks, but also including furniture suppliers, a tractor company, and the Memphis morticians who conducted his funeral and now presented a bill for more than $39,000. George Haley, his brother's executor, announced that the estate would eventually return to solvency with the reduction of expenses. He believed that income from writing projects that were in the works when Alex died, particularly *Henning* and *Queen,* would bring in hundreds of thousands of dollars.[19]

There then emerged a series of challenges to the will. Myran Haley had a prenuptial agreement with Alex and alleged that George

Haley was withholding money that was due her. She said that she had been Haley's literary collaborator for many years and that a 1991 contract, signed after she had sued for divorce but before the divorce was granted, entitled her to a third of the estate and the right to finish *Queen*. The executors of the estate argued that the contract was unenforceable because Haley had signed it under duress. George Sims sued the estate for nonpayment of his salary as Haley's research assistant, for money Alex owed him for debts he had covered, and for half the royalties of both *Roots* and *The Autobiography of Malcolm X*. "I was with him for 32 years and [George Haley] knew nothing about his writing life," Sims told a journalist. "They treated me like shit." William and Nan Haley claimed that she should be the sole wife to inherit money, because she had never been legally divorced from Alex. His death certificate listed Nan as the surviving spouse. Betty Shabazz sued to get half-ownership of an early draft of the manuscript of *The Autobiography of Malcolm X*. There was much confusion over which items in Haley's personal papers were of value. In September 1992 in Knoxville chancery court, the estate was settled with Myran's and George Sims's interests recognized, along with those of Haley's family members.

George Haley then moved to liquidate as much of the estate as possible to reduce the debt. This decision angered Haley's Hollywood friends Blau and Wolper, who thought there should be a major museum devoted to his life and work, filled with the articles that George was selling. The farm was sold to the Children's Defense Fund, and the sale of home decorations and memorabilia got much press attention. Except for the $50,000 paid for the Pulitzer Prize, the bidding for manuscript material, especially the Malcolm X drafts and tapes of *Playboy* interviews, brought the most money. Gregory Reed, a Detroit dealer in literary property, bought the three chapters of Malcolm's autobiography that were removed before publication. The University of Tennessee bought much of the manuscript material to go with the large deposit of his files Alex Haley had made not long before his death. Haley's housekeeper watched the auction with deep sadness, saying, "If he could see what was happening now, he'd be shaking his hand and saying, 'Aw, babe, I can't believe what a fuss they're making. 'Cause Mr. Haley didn't want people to bother and fuss."[20]

*   *   *

ROOTS HAD BEEN mostly supported by public opinion in the face of doubters about its authenticity. In the 1980s and 1990s, that support dissipated, as memories faded and both *Roots* miniseries went on the shelf. A few detractors kept hounding Haley even after his death. The opening of his papers at the University of Tennessee library was probably the prompt for an exposé written by the journalist Philip Nobile and published under the headline "Uncovering Roots" in the *Village Voice* in February 1993, exactly a year after Haley's death. The *Voice* had published Eliot Fremont-Smith's critical article in May 1977, and Nobile himself had already written a skeptical editorial piece for the *New York Times* about Haley's genealogical claims. The 1993 article was a full-scale assault on Haley's career and character, drawing together a compendium of allegations of professional malfeasance—essentially all that had been made over the years and then some. Nobile called *Roots* "a hoax, a literary painted mouse, a Piltdown of genealogy, a pyramid of bogus research," and a fraud successful only because a "massive perjury" had covered it up. Nobile called *Roots* "an elegant and complex make-it-up-as-you-go-along scam." He repeated the Ottaway charges about inaccuracy in Haley's Gambian research, and he found a transcript of a recording made during Haley's first visit to Juffure that contradicted Haley's account of it in *Roots*. Nobile alleged that all of the events of that day had been staged. Nobile interviewed Ebou Manga, who provided information that confirmed that Haley had given an inaccurate chronology of his research. Nobile then asserted that Haley had not even written the sections of the book detailing the African background. He found in the Haley papers a file called "Fisher-edited copy" that showed how thoroughly Murray Fisher had rewritten the African section of *Roots*.

Nobile rounded up many of Haley's detractors. Margaret Walker called the deceased writer a "hack." Even the words of Haley's best friends were used for character assassination. John Hawkins, Haley's literary agent after Paul Reynolds retired, told Nobile that "Alex was a man with many compartments and nobody knew them all," sort of "a literary Kim Philby." Extending that analogy, Nobile wrote: "Like a master spy, Haley could persuasively lie about anything." He quoted Haley's oldest friends as saying things that implied dishonesty on the part of the writer. George Sims, embittered over the disposition of Haley's estate when Nobile talked to him, said, "Alex didn't know 10 blacks or 10 whites in Henning. I was there for 18 years and he was there for 18 months. Those were *my* stories, but Alex could tell them better."

Some of Nobile's accusations were misleading or simply incorrect. He wrote that Haley had copied eighty-one pages of Courlander's book when in fact Courander alleged that eighty-one *passages* had been copied. Most of the allegations were simply not convincing. Nobile reported from a secondhand source, for example, that Haley had said Margaret Walker Alexander might have won her suit if she had had a better lawyer than her son. It is doubtful that Haley said it, but if he did, he was clearly wrong. Haley's lawyer, George Berger, later said that Walker would not have prevailed before Judge Frankel if "Oliver Wendell Holmes had been her lawyer." Nobile dismissed as a lie the claim that Haley had slept in the hold of the *African Star* on his way from Dakar to Florida in 1973, basing the accusation on a sailor's insistence that Haley could not have done so because of the noxious cocoa beans in the hold. But in fact Haley had made that trip on the *African Star* two years earlier, and Nobile had no information about what was in the hold of the ship then.

Nobile ended his article with a long quote from an interview that Haley gave near the end of his life to Charles Thomas Galbraith, a

New York genealogist and originally a Haley admirer. Haley admitted to Galbraith that he had made errors in *Roots* and, by way of explanation for not admitting or correcting them earlier, said: "The quest for the symbolic history of a people, just swept me like a twig atop a rushing water." Then he made an unfortunate change of metaphor. "I guess it was sort of like riding a tiger . . . you always remember, you ride this tiger and the crowds [are] cheering, [you] always remember if you fall off the tiger, you's eaten."[21]

But Nobile did not elicit the outrage he seemed to expect. His article got only a brief mention in the *New York Times,* and while it was the basis for a British Broadcasting Corporation documentary exposé, the BBC never got the film shown on American television. Today that film is a lost artifact, not found in American research repositories. Millions of Americans had been educated and moved emotionally by *Roots,* and they simply may not have wanted the work's meaning destroyed by a character assassination.

By 2002 Nobile had moved into unconstrained ad hominem attack mode. On the website History News Network, read widely by professional and lay historians, Nobile wrote a snarky public letter in the guise of Haley to Doris Kearns Goodwin and Stephen Ambrose, two historians who had been accused of plagiarism. "Don't worry, be happy," Nobile wrote. "There is life after literary disgrace. Look at me. They nailed me for copying the main plot and character for Roots from Harold Courlander's slave novel . . . and for fabricating a family tree stretching back to 18th century Gambia. (Luckily, nobody found out that I relied on a well-paid white-ghostwriter, too, the same one who secretly revised *The Autobiography of Malcolm X*.)"[22]

By 2000 the neglect of Nobile's exposé had become fodder in the culture wars, allegedly an example of political correctness among the liberal elite to protect a miscreant black writer. The failure to "get" Haley was offered as evidence that liberal intelligentsia had little regard for historical truth or honesty. In 2002, when NBC broadcast a twenty-fifth anniversary retrospective on *Roots,* Stanley Crouch, a black cultural critic, wrote that the truth about *Roots* was still ignored because blacks were "obsessed with being a 'lost' people in America. . . . Younger black people were told they were not Americans, but victims of Americanism." *Roots,* he wrote, was an "insult to black people, and no amount of excuses will change that harsh fact." Crouch's view did not represent those of many blacks, but a strong and growing contingent of American conservatives liked hearing such criticism from an important black intellectual. A 2005 book, *Hoodwinked: How Intellectual Hucksters Have Hijacked American Culture,* relied mostly on Nobile to assign Haley much responsibility for Afrocentrism and to link him to "the myriad lies and half-truths that America's progressive elite has used to hijack an entire culture."[23]

* * *

NOBILE'S ATTACK mattered in weighing the historical significance of Haley, because it narrowed the range of assessment. Loud accusations of lying and theft have to be addressed before a more sober, fair, and balanced assessment can emerge. Nobile's article registered with academics. He had caught Haley in misrepresentations of facts, and few professors countenanced that. The British literary scholar Helen Taylor used Nobiles' critique in her fair-minded 1995 review of the work of "the griot from Tennessee." Jan Vansina, the African historian who had helped Haley in 1967 and whom Haley referred to time and again as his authority on Mandinka language, quoted Nobile in his 1994 biography to the effect that *Roots* was "a willful fabrication" for personal advantage. In 1999 Haley's Knoxville friend Richard Marius wrote the entry on Haley for the *Tennessee Encyclopedia.* He called Nobile's article "measured" and "a devastating final shot" at Haley.[24]

It was easier to ignore Haley than to sort out the details of his alleged wrongs. Haley was all but left out of the creation of a canon of black American literature. When the *Norton Anthology of*

African-American Literature, a work of almost three thousand pages covering hundreds of literary excerpts, appeared in 1997, no passage from *Roots* was included. "We didn't exclude Alex Haley from the canon, he just didn't make the cut," said Henry Louis Gates Jr., editor of the anthology. "[There were] a lot of people who were good who just didn't make the cut."[25]

Gates and his advisers thus excluded a work that sold more than any other, that arguably touched the racial sensibilities of more Americans than any other, and that recast Americans' popular understanding of slavery more than any other. This decision seems short-sighted at the very least, and probably reflected the influence of Nobile, although Gates denied such an influence. To another reporter, Gates admitted that "most of us feel it's highly unlikely that Alex actually found the village from which his ancestors sprang. *Roots* is a work of the imagination rather than strict historical scholarship. It was an important event because it captured everyone's imagination." That accurate assessment of Haley's work was perhaps justification for including it in the canon of African American letters, since all the works in the anthology were, after all, works of imagination. The anthology did include an excerpt from *The Autobiography of Malcolm X* (with the wrong publication date given), which carried only a brief mention that Haley had helped with the book. By then, virtually all students of black literature were crediting Haley with creating and preserving Malcolm's story, even if they thought he had depicted Malcolm inaccurately in regard to some particulars.[26]

Ultimately Gates paid a silent tribute to Haley with a successful series of television programs on the genealogy of celebrities. In 2005 and 2006 he produced and hosted a miniseries, *African American Lives.* On that program, through historical evidence and DNA testing, the lineage of black celebrities—including Gates himself—was traced and revealed to those celebrities on camera, among them Whoopi Goldberg, Oprah Winfrey, Quincy Jones, Tina Turner, Morgan Freeman, and Maya Angelou. The show was so popular that

Gates returned in 2010 with another miniseries, *Faces of America,* which traced the genealogy of white celebrities of various ethnic backgrounds. Then, in 2012 and 2014, the series morphed into *Finding Your Roots—with Henry Louis Gates Jr.* It might have been Haley's fate to do the show, had he lived. It might never have emerged under the astute direction of Gates had Haley not done *Roots.* Haley was at least partly responsible for the ongoing exploration of Americans' roots.

To be sure, Haley's friends remembered him and his accomplishments. In 2007, on the thirtieth anniversary of the *Roots* miniseries, *Reader's Digest* produced a slick, full-color book with a dozen selections of his pieces from the magazine. Haley had meant a lot to the *Digest,* and it to him, and the book was a tribute to his work and that relationship.[27] In 2005 Al Martinez, a *Los Angeles Times* reporter, wrote an article entitled "He's the Man That February Forgot." Another Black History Month had passed without offering any accolades for Haley. "His fall from grace was abrupt and humiliating," Martinez said. But the memory of Haley "shines brightly in my mind," Martinez wrote, because they had "told stories together, but mostly, we shared each other's company without demands or impositions." Even after Haley became "a racial icon, he was the same self-effacing man I had always known. This distinguished him and, perhaps, also in a way diminished him. He wasn't your average hero."[28]

One tribute came from Haley's old friend and traveling companion Lamar Alexander, who in 2013 was the United States senator responsible for organizing the second inauguration of Barack Obama as president. Speaking briefly in front of the U.S. Capitol, Alexander complimented the peaceful reaffirmation of Obama's leadership, even as the senator knew that a large segment of whites in his home state freely expressed their hatred of the first black president. "The late Alex Haley, the author of 'Roots,' lived his life by these six words: 'Find the good and praise it.'"

*   *   *

ALEX HALEY happened to rise to celebrity in America at a time when American popular culture was fascinated when heroes were knocked off their pedestals. In the 1980s Martin Luther King Jr. had been shown as a plagiarist in his sermons and his dissertation. John F. Kennedy's womanizing was the subject of endless stories. Presidents Eisenhower and Franklin Roosevelt were posthumously taken to task for extramarital affairs, and longtime FBI director J. Edgar Hoover for bizarre private behavior. As Haley's detractors knew, the rules of American celebrity dictated that, once a person came under scrutiny, he or his defenders fought an uphill battle to regain his standing. In Haley's case, there was too little reflection about whether the allegations were as bad as some alleged, whether the punishment for wrongdoing fit the crime, or what, exactly, were the motives of the accuser.

The positive impact of Alex Haley's writing on the thinking and attitudes of Americans was lost—lost, at least, on the popular media. If, however, one measures that impact by the tens of millions who have read *The Autobiography of Malcolm X* and *Roots,* and the hundreds of millions who have seen the television and film renderings of those works, then Haley wrote the two most important works in black culture in the twentieth century. More than any other writer, he changed the way the masses of Americans understood the black experience. He gave whites a compelling reminder of the ugliness of racial exploitation and blacks a sense of ownership of their past, with all its travails but also its triumphs. His work was a great contribution to American culture and race relations, and it deserves to be remembered.

NOTE ABBREVIATIONS

FREQUENTLY CITED SOURCES

AHP   Alex Haley Papers, University of Tennessee Libraries, Special Collections

ARC   Anne Romaine Collection, University of Tennessee Libraries, Special Collections

MXC-S   Malcolm X Collection, Schomburg Center for Research in Black Culture, New York Public Library

KMP   Ken McCormick Papers, Container 11, Papers of Doubleday and Company, Library of Congress

FREQUENTLY CITED WORKS

MM, *MX*   Manning Marable, *Malcolm X: A Life of Reinvention* (New York: Viking, 2011).

AMX   *The Autobiography of Malcolm X* (New York: Ballantine, 2003). Currently, this is the most widely available edition.

McCauley   Mary Siebert McCauley, "Alex Haley, a Southern Griot: A Literary Biography" (unpublished Ph.D. dissertation, George Peabody College of Vanderbilt University, 1983).

FREQUENTLY CITED NAMES IN THE NOTES

AH   Alex Haley
AR   Anne Romaine
MX   Malcolm X
PR   Paul Revere Reynolds Jr.

NOTES

CHAPTER 1: GRANDMA'S BOY

1. Unless otherwise cited, the information on the Palmer and Haley family in this chapter is drawn from the many interviews that Alex Haley gave in the 1960s and 1970s and from his various autobiographical works, only some of which were published but all of which can be found in his papers at the University of Tennessee's Special Collections. Alex and George Haley gave lengthy interviews to researchers. See especially Anne Romaine interviews of Alex and George Haley, Anne Romaine Papers, University of Tennessee Library Special Collections, MS 2020, box 1, folders 1, 2, 7, and 8. See also Mary Seibert McCauley, "Alex Haley, a Southern Griot: A Literary Biography" (unpublished PhD dissertation, George Peabody College of Vanderbilt University, 1983). This work contains long quotes from McCauley's interviews of Alex Haley. The author interviewed George Haley on May 11, 2014.
2. Transcript, Haley "Roots" lecture, n.p., AHP, MS 1888, box 30, folder 18.
3. *Search for Roots* manuscript, AHP, MS 1888, box 34, folder 55.
4. Alabama A&M Reports, 1932–34, Alabama A&M University Archives, Normal, Alabama.
5. Charles S. Johnson, *Shadow of the Plantation* (Chicago: University of Chicago Press, 1934).
6. George Haley, interview by AR, ARC, MS 2032, box 2, folder 34.
7. Donald Bogle, *Blacks in American Films and Television: An Encyclopedia* (New York: Garland, 1988), 295.

CHAPTER 2: THE COOK WHO WRITES

1. Roy Byrd, interview by AR, March 10, 1993, handwritten notes, ARC, MS 2032, box 2, folder 26.
2. Logan Lannon, interview by AR, February 3, 1993, handwritten notes, ARC, MS 2032, box 2, folder 26.
3. AR, "Alex Haley Notes," 1991, ARC, MS 2032, box 4.
4. George Webb, interview by AR, January 21, 1993, handwritten notes, ARC, MS 2032, box 2, folder 26.
5. AR, "Alex Haley Notes," 1991, ARC, MS 2032, box 4; "*Roots* II" file, AHP, MS 1888, 38, 12.

6. AH, "Why I Remember," *Parade*, December 1, 1991.

7. Nan Haley, interview by AR, February 22, 1992, ARC, MS 2828, box 1, folder 6.

8. AH, "The Most Unforgettable Character I've Met," *Reader's Digest*, March 1961, 73–77.

9. *The Seafarer*, vol. 1, no. 17, February 1944, ARC, MS 2828, box 2, folder 19.

10. *The Seafarer*, vol. 1, no. 9, n.d. (but probably late 1943), ARC, MS 2828, box 2, folder 19.

11. Byrd, interview by AR.

12. Ibid.

13. *New York Times*, May 21, 1950; Kenneth Black, interview by AR, February 20, 1993, handwritten notes, ARC, MS 2032, box 2, folder 26.

14. *New York Post*, August 2, 1943; Dominic J. Capeci Jr., *The Harlem Riot of 1943* (Philadelphia: Temple University Press, 1977).

15. MM, *MX*, 108.

16. Horace R. Cayton, "Fighting for White Folks?" *Nation*, September 26, 1942.

17. "*Roots* II" file, AHP, MS 1888, box 38, folder 12.

18. Ibid.

19. James Playsted Wood, *Magazines in the United States* (New York: Ronald Press Company, 1956), 154, 222, 201.

20. *Alex Haley: The Playboy Interviews*, ed. Murray Fisher (New York: Ballantine, 1993), viii.

21. Notes, "The Lord and Little David," AHP, MS 1888, box 9, folder 2.

22. Peggy Dowst Redman to AH, July 17, 1954; Maryse Rutledge to AH, January 22, 1954, both in AHP, MS 1888, box 9, folder 4.

23. John H. Johnson with Lerone Bennett, Jr., *Succeeding Against the Odds* (New York, 1989), 207,155–59.

24. John B. Mahan, interview by AR, March 14, 1993, handwritten notes, ARC, MS 2032, box 2, folder 26.

25. William Earle, interview by AR, March 1, 1993, handwritten notes, ARC, MS 2032, box 2, folder 26.

26. Barnaby Conrad, *Name Dropping: Tales from my Barbary Coast Saloon* (New York: HarperCollinsWest, 1994), 60–66.

27. Barnaby Conrad, interview by AR, n.d., ARC, MS 2032, box 2, folder 28; C. Eric Lincoln, interview by AR, April 21, 1993, ARC, 3041, 2, 1; Nan Haley, interview by AR, February 22, 1992, ARC, MS 2828, box 1, folder 6.

CHAPTER 3: PEOPLE ON THE WAY UP

1. Nan Haley, interview by AR, February 22, 1992, ARC, MS 2828, box 1, folder 6.

2. Haley diary entry, July 12, 1963, AHP MS 1888, box 19, folder 8. Fella apparently had sex with an underage girl. At the time he was sixteen years old. It is not clear whether it was the girl or her parents who accused him. Haley refers to the charge as one of statutory rape, but in 1962 the closest designation the New York Penal Code had to statutory rape was rape in the second degree, or sex with a girl under eighteen without force, coercion, or mental incapacity. The code makes no explicit provision for sex between minors. There is no evidence that what took place was forcible rape; nor is there evidence that it was not.

3. "Origins of Roots" manuscript, AHP, MS 1888, box 34, folder 8; Logan Lannon, interview by AR, February 3, 1993, handwritten notes, ARC, MS 2032, box 2,

folder 26; McCauley, 46–8; Ronald Wells, interview by AR, March 8, 1993, handwritten notes, ARC, MS 2032, box 2, folder 26; Jeffrey Elliot, "The Roots of Alex Haley's Writing career," *Writer's Digest,* August 1980.

4. McCauley, 49.
5. Biographical information, AHP, MS 1888, box 19, folder 8.
6. "Search for Roots" manuscript, AHP, MS 1888, box 19, folder 8.
7. "Roots: The Second Hundred Years," story meeting, January 9, 1978, AHP, MS 1888, box 38, folder 6.
8. AH, "Negro Entertainer's Contribution to the American Way of Life," *Cosmopolitan,* 1962.
9. Haley autobiography typescript, AHP, MS 1888, box 19, folder 8.
10. AH, "She Makes a Joyful Noise," *Reader's Digest,* November 1961.
11. Miller Williams, letter to the editor, *Readers Digest,* and Alex Haley, January 22, 1963; Miller to Haley, January 28, 1963, ARC, MS 2083, box 3, folder 23; AH to Barney McHenry, February 11, 1963, ARC, MS 2032, box 3, folder 28.
12. AH to PR, July 14, 1964, AHP, MS 1888, box 44, folder 14; McCauley, 45.
13. MM, *MX,* 139.
14. MM, *MX,* 117.
15. MM, *MX,* 113–123.
16. "*Roots* II" file, AHP, MS 1888, box 38, folder 12; *AMX,* 390.
17. MM, *MX,* 160–61; *New York Times,* March 12, 1961; James Baldwin, *The Fire Next Time* (repr. New York: Dell, 1963), 72.
18. C. Eric Lincoln, *The Black Muslims in America* (Boston: Beacon Press, 1961).
19. AH, "Mr. Muhammad Speaks," *Reader's Digest,* March 1960.
20. Nat Hentoff, "Through the Looking Glass, *Playboy,* July 1962.
21. Thomas Weyr, *Reaching for Paradise: The Playboy Vision of America* (New York: Times Books, 1978), 171–172; *Los Angeles Times,* June 5, 2002; *Playboy,* September 1962.
22. M. A. Jones to DeLoach, memo, October 9, 1962, ARC, MS 2032, box 2, folder 16.
23. AH and Alfred Balk, "Black Merchants of Hate," *Saturday Evening Post,* January 27, 1963.
24. MM, *MX,* 232.
25. McCauley, 68.

CHAPTER 4: THE FEARSOME BLACK DEMAGOGUE

1. See books by Paul R. Reynolds: *The Writer and His Markets* (New York: Doubleday, 1959), *The Writing and Selling of Non-Fiction* (New York: Doubleday, 1963), and *The Middle Man: The Adventures of a Literary Agent* (New York: William Morrow, 1972); *New York Times,* June 11, 1988; PR to AH, April 8, 1963, AHP, MS 1888, box 44, folder 13; AH to PR, April 9, 1963, AHP, MS 1888, box 44, folder 14.
2. *New York Times,* February 11, 1978; Handler, Introduction to *AMX,* xxvi.
3. Reynolds, *Middle Man,* 199–200; *AMX,* 463; MM, *MX,* 248.
4. MM, *MX,* 247; PR TO AH, June 26, 1963, AHP, MS 1888, box 44, folder 14.
5. PR to AH, May 14, 1963, AHP, MS 1888, box 44, folder 14.
6. MX to PR, June 3, 1963; AH to PR, June 3, 1963; PR to AH, June 4, 1963; AH TO PR, June 27, 1963, all in AHP, MS 1888, box 44, folder 14.
7. PR to AH, July 3, 1963, AHP, MS 1888, box 44, folder 14.

8. AH to PR, September 5, 1963, October 3, AHP, MS 1888, box 44, folder 14.
9. Russell J. Rickford, *Betty Shabazz: A Remarkable Story of Survival and Faith Before and After Malcolm X* (Napierville, IL: Sourcebooks, 2003), 80, 152; Betty Shabazz, interview by AR, January 27, 1989, ARC, MS 2032, box 3, folder 6.
10. *AMX*, 394-95; AH to MX, September 25, 1963, MXC-S, folder 3, box 6.
11. *AMX*, 396.
12. Ibid., 396–398.
13. Ibid., Handler introduction, xxvii.
14. Ibid., Epilogue, 406.
15. MM, *MX*, 238; *New York Times,* May 12 and 19, June 4 and 25, July 28, 1963.
16. AH to PR, June 27, 1963; AH to Wolcott Gibbs Jr., October 10, 1963, both in AHP, MS 1888, box 44, folder 14.
17. PR to AH, September 18, 1963, AHP, MS 1888, box 44, folder 14; James F. Dwyer to Wolcott Gibbs, Jr., September 16, 1963, KMP.
18. PR to AH, October 1, 1963, AHP, MS 1888, box 44, folder 14.
19. AH to PR, October 10, 1963, AHP, 1888, box 44, folder 14.
20. W. E. B. Du Bois, *The Souls of Black Folk,* pp. 116, 126, 127, 132, 133, 169, 170, 204, and 227 in the 1903 edition, which can be found at several web locations, including: https://archive.org/details/cu31924024920492 and http://web.archive.org/web/20081004090243/http://etext.lib.virginia.edu/toc/modeng/public/DubSoul.html; W. E. B. Du Bois, *The World of W.E.B. Du Bois: A Quotation Sourcebook,* ed. Meyer Weinberg (Westport, CT: Greenwood, 1992), 208; George Bornstein, "W. E. B. Du Bois and the Jews: Ethics, Editing, and The Souls of Black," *Textual Cultures* 1(Spring 2006): 64–74.
21. AH to Wolcott Gibbs, Jr., October 27, 1963, AHP, MS 1888, box 44, folder 14.
22. AH to PR, September 22, 1963; AH to Wolcott Gibbs, Jr. September 25, 1963; AH memos to McCormick, Gibbs, and Reynolds, November 11, 14, 1963, and January 6, 1964; AH to Wolcott Gibbs, Jr., October 27, 1963, all in AHP, MS 1888, box 44, folder 14.
23. AH to Wolcott Gibbs, Jr. October 11, 1963; AH Memo to McCormick, Gibbs, Reynolds November 14, 1963, both in AHP, MS 1888, box 44, folder 14.
24. PR to AH, December 12, 1963 AHP, MS 1888, box 44, folder 14.
25. MM, *MX,* 26–32, 260.
26. PR to AH, December 4, 1963; PR to AH, December 12, 1963; AH memo to McCormick, Gibbs, and Reynolds, December 12, 1963, all in AHP, MS 1888, box 44, folder 14.
27. *AMX,* 411–13.
28. MM, *MX,* 283–84.
29. *AMX,* 416–18.
30. AH to PR, December 11, 1963; AH memos to McCormick, Gibbs, and Reynolds, January 19 and March 21, 1964; AH to PR, March 26, 1964, all in AHP, MS 1888, box 44, folder 14; AH to PR, February 6, 1964, KMP.
31. AH memo to McCormick, Gibbs, and Reynolds, February 18,1964, ARC, MS 2032, box 3, folder 24; AH memos to McCormick, Gibbs, and Reynolds, February 10,1964; March 21,1964; and March 25, 1964, all in KMP.
32. *New York Times,* March 9, 1964.
33. MM, *MX,* 301–303.
34. Davis quoted in MM, *MX,* 324.
35. *AMX,* 418.
36. PR to AH, May 14, 1964, AHP, MS 1888, box 44, folder 14; *AMX,* 419.

CHAPTER 5: MARKED MAN

1. *AMX*, 338-339, *New York Times*, May 8, 1964.
2. *AMX*, 420.
3. MM, *MX*, 352.
4. MM, *MX*, 178–179, 200.
5. McCormick to John Appleton, May 13, 1964, KMP; PR to AH, May 14, 1964, AHP, MS 1888, box 44, folder 14; AH to Ken, Tony and Paul, June 14, 1964, AHP, MS 1888, box 44, folder 14.
6. AH to MX, June 21, 1964, MXC-S, box 3, folder 6.
7. AH to PR, June 21 and July 8, 1964, AHP, MS 1888, box 44, folder 14.
8. "Search for Roots" manuscript, 2nd draft, January 18, 1979, n.p., AHP, MS 1888, box 34, folder 3; PR to AH, July 9, February 5, 1964; AH to PR, January 28, 1964, AHP, MS 1888, box 44, folder 14.
9. PR to AH, June 23 and July 9, 1964; AH to PR, July 14, 1964, both in AHP, MS 1888, box 44, folder 14.
10. *New York Times*, March 1, 1964.
11. *New York Times*, September 21, 1964.
12. AH to Phoebe [PR secretary], November 7, 1964, AHP, MS 1888, box 44, folder 14.
13. Ken McCormick testimony, *Alexander v. Haley*, 915–16, ARC, MS 2032, box 6; *Los Angeles Times*, February 15, 1977.
14. Robert Penn Warren, "Malcolm X: Mission and Meaning," *Yale Review* 56 (December 1966): 167.
15. *Saturday Evening Post*, September 12, 1964; *AMX*, 426.
16. *New York Times*, September 8 and October 11,1964; *Saturday Evening Post*, September 12, 1964.
17. *New York Times*, October 4 and November 8, 1964.
18. *AMX*, 426–27.
19. Ibid., 428–29.
20. Ibid., 430; Russell J. Rickford, *Betty Shabazz: A Remarkable Story of Survival and Faith Before and After Malcolm X* (Napierville, IL: Sourcebooks, 2003), 298.
21. *New York Times*, February 22, 1965; *AMX*, 433.
22. *AMX*, 431.
23. AH to PR, November 15, 1964; PR to AH, January 28, 1965; AH to PR, February 8, 1965; PR to AH, February 9, 1965, all in AHP, MS 1888, box 44, folder 14.
24. AH to PR, February 21, 1965, AHP, MS 1888, box 44, folder 14.
25. John Doar to the Director, FBI, February 24, 1965, http://www.columbia.edu/cu/ccbh/mxp/pdf/aag.pdf.
26. Lisa Drew to author, May 9, 2014.
27. *AMX*, 459–62.
28. *New York Times*, February 22–27, 1965.
29. AH to PR, February 21, 27, 1965, AHP, MS 1888, box 44, folder 13.
30. PR to AH, March 11, 1965; Timothy Seldes to PR, March 15, 1965; Ed Kuhn to PR, March 22, 1965; James N. Perkins to Malcolm Reiss, March 26, 1965, all in AHP, MS 1888, box 44, folder 15.
31. Malcolm Reiss to Percy Sutton, April 14, 1965, AHP, MS 1888, box 44, folder 15.
32. "Search for Roots" manuscript, 2nd draft; PR to AH, May 11, 1965, AHP, MS 1888, box 44, folder 15.

33. PR to AH, May 11, 1965; PR to AH, July 7, 1965; AH to PR, July 9, 1965, all in AHP, MS 1888, box 44, folder 15.

34. *AMX,* 463.

35. *New York Times,* November 5, 1965; *Washington Post,* November 14, 1965; Warren, "Malcolm X: Mission and Meaning," 164; *New York Review of Books,* November 11, 1965.

36. "What They're Reading," *Change in Higher Education* 1 (May–June 1969): 9.

37. *Christian Science Monitor,* January 22, 1969; *Atlanta Daily World,* January 22, 1970.

38. MM, *MX,* 466; *A Lie of Reinvention: Correcting Manning Marable's Malcolm X,* ed. Jared A. Ball and Todd Steven Burroughs (Baltimore: Black Classic Press, 2012); V. P. Franklin, "Introduction: Reflections on the Legacy of Malcolm X," *Journal of African American History* 98 (Fall 2013): 562–64; *The Cambridge Companion to Malcolm X,* ed. Robert Terrill (New York: Cambridge University Press, 2010).

39. Burroughs, "Doda: Objectivity vs. Memory," in *A Lie of Reinvention;* David Remnick, "The Making and Remaking of Malcolm X," *New Yorker,* April 25, 2011.

40. *The Norton Anthology of African American Literature,* ed. Henry Louis Gates Jr. and Nellie Y. McKay (New York: Norton, 1997), 1860–1876; Robert E. Terrill, "Introduction," *The Cambridge Companion to Malcolm X,* ed. Robert E. Terrill (Cambridge: Cambridge University Press, 2010), 3.

41. Carol Ohmann, "*The Autobiography of Malcolm X:* A Revolutionary Use of the Franklin Tradition," *American Quarterly* 22 (Summer 1970): 133; Robert B. Stepto, *From Behind the Veil: A Study of Afro-American Narrative* (Urbana: University of Illinois Press, 1991).

42. *The Autobiography of W. E. B. Du Bois: A Soliloquy on Viewing My Life from the Last Decade of Its First Century* (International Publishers, 1968), 12.

CHAPTER 6: BEFORE THIS ANGER

1. "Origins of Roots" manuscript, AHP, MS 1888, box 34, folder 28; AH to PR, January 30, 1965, AHP, MS 1888, box 3, folder 10.

2. "Origins of Roots" manuscript.

3. AH to PR, January 30, 1965, AHP, MS 1888, box 3, folder 10.

4. "Origins of Roots" manuscript.

5. Stanley M. Elkins, *Slavery: The Problem in Americqn Institution and Intellectual Life* (Chicago: University of Chicago Press, 1959), 82, 88.

6. "My Search for Roots—A Writer Goes Back to Africa," *Tuesday Magazine,* a supplement to the *Philadelphia Sunday Bulletin,* October 12, 1965.

7. McCauley, 113–114; "Origins of Roots" manuscript.

8. *New York Times,* September 26, 1976; "Origins of Roots" manuscript.

9. Karel Arnaut and Hein Vanhee, "History Facing the Present: An Interview with Jan Vansina," H-AFRICA, November 1, 2001, http://www.h-net.org/~africa/africaforum/VansinaInterview.htm; Jan Vansina, *Oral Tradition: A Study in Historical Methodology* (Chicago: Aldine Publishing, 1965), 186.

10. AH to "Jim," February 17, 1966, ARC, MS 2032, box 3, folder 25; AH to Lucy Kroll, Jill D'Argent, Ollie Swann, and James Earl Jones, December 18, 1967; AH to PR, December 19, 1967; PR to AH, December 22, 1967, all in AHP, MS 1888, box 45, folder 1.

11. Malcolm Reiss to Betty Shabazz, June 17, 1966, AHP, MS 1888, box 45, folder 1.

12. *Playboy,* April 1966.

13. *Playboy,* December 1966.

14. AH to PR, August 8, 1966, AHP, MS 1888, box 3, folder 10; Ebou Manga, interview by AR, May 13, 1989, in ARC, MS 2032, box 3, folder 15.

15. AH to PR, October 24, 1966, AHP, MS 1888, box 45, folder 1; AH to PR, October 18, 1966, AHP, MS 1888, box 3, folder 10.

16. *New York Times,* January 27 and July 9, 1967; May 13 and October 5, 1969; January 27 and August 16, 1970; AH to PR, October 29, 1966, AHP, MS 1888, box 45, folder 1.

17. McCauley, 112.

18. "Origins of Roots" manuscript; Haley notes on "Encounter with Africa," AHP, MS 1888, box 34, folder 38.

19. "Gambia," AHP, MS 1888, box 29, folder 1.

20. AH to Maurice Ragsdale, December 14, 1966, AHP MS 1888, box 3, folder 10.

21. KM to PR, January 12, 1967; PR to KM, January 16, 1967; KM to PR, January 18, 1967; AH to PR, March 5, 1967, all in AHP, MS 1888, box 45, folder 1.

22. PR to AH, March 8, 1967, in AHP, MS 1888, box 45, folder 1.

23. AH to PR, March 9, 1967, in AHP, MS 1888, box 45, folder 1.

24. PR to AH, March 10 and April 10, May 16 and April 25, 1967, AHP, MS 1888, box 45, folder 1; Lawrence Hughes to John Hawkins, May 15, 1974, ARC, MS 2032, box 3, folder 27.

25. AH notes, AHP, MS 1888, box 34, folder 26; John Gunther, *Inside Africa* (New York: Harper's, 1955), 744–45.

26. AH to Edward Sowe, March 16, 1967, AHP, MS 1888, box 3, folder 10.

27. Haley notes on "Encounter with Africa.".

28. Ibid.

29. AH to PR, April 23, 1967, in AHP, MS 1888, box 45, folder 1; Jan Vansina to AH, April 29, 1967, AHP, MS 1888, box 3, folder 10.

30. Manuscript of AH in Africa, May 1967, p. 515, in AHP, MS 1888, box 34, folder 33.

31. Ibid.

CHAPTER 7: THE AMERICAN GRIOT

1. AH to PR, May 27, 28, June 16, August 5, 1967; PR to AH, May 29, July 11, September 29, 1967; PR to AH, 1967, AHP MS 1888, box 45, folder 1.

2. AH, *Roots* (Garden City, NY: Doubleday, 1976), 682–83.

3. Ibid., 684–85.

4. Ibid., 672–73.

5. Haley direct examination, *Courlander v. Haley,* ARC, MS 2828, box 6, folders 16–17; *Publisher's Weekly,* September 6, 1976.

6. McCauley, 141.

7. AH to PR, December 27, 1967, AHP, MS 1888, box 45, folder 1; Lucy Kroll to Oliver Swan, December 14, 1967, AHP, Ms 1888, box 45, folder 1; *New York Times,* March 8, 1968.

8. Haley direct testimony, *Alexander v. Haley,* AHP, MS 1888, box 45, folder 2; *Playboy,* January 1977.

9. Anne Romaine interview with Louis Blau, August 9, 1989, ARC, MS 2032, box 2, folder 25.

10. Richard Marius, "Alexander Murray Palmer Haley," *Tennessee Encyclopedia,* https://tennesseeencyclopedia.net/entry.php?rec=586; *New York Times,* June 27,

1976; Helen Taylor, "The Griot from Tennessee: The saga of Alex Haley's *Roots*," *Critical Quarterly* 37 (1996): 57.

11. *New York Times,* June 27, 1976; *"Roots* II," autobiographical narrative, AHP, MS 1888, box 38, folder 12.

12. *"Roots* II," autobiographical narrative, AHP, MS 1888, box 38, folder 12; William Van Deburg, *New Day in Babylon: The Black Power Movement and American Culture, 1965–1975* (Chicago: University of Chicago Press, 1992), 78; *Newsweek,* February 10, 1969; Peniel Joseph, "Dashikis and Democracy: Black Studies, Student Activism, and the Black Power Movement," *Journal of African-American History* 88 (Spring 2003): 182–2003; *New York Times,* June 9, 1968.

13. *Newsweek,* May 6, 1968; *U.S. News and World Report,* February 24, 1969.

14. *Washington Post,* June 6, 1968, December 8, 1971; *Wall Street Journal,* March 9, 1972; *Hartford Courant,* April 4, 1969, February 21, 1973.

15. *Lost Angeles Times,* May 25, 1969; *Cleveland Plain Dealer,* February 13, 1969; *Washington Post,* January 6, December 8, 1971; *Wall Street Journal,* March 9, 1972.

16. AH to PR, February 15, 1971, AHP, MS 1888, box 45, folder 2; Ken McCormick affidavit, December 30, 1991, KMP.

17. "Lecture on Roots," AHP, MS 1888, box 30, folder 18.

18. Ibid.

19. Ibid.

20. *Wall Street Journal,* March 9, 1972.

21. *"Roots* II" file, AHP, MS 1888, box 38, folder 12; Charles Thomas Galbraith quoted Haley, reported in Philip Nobile, *Village Voice,* 1993.

22. AH to Helen B. Wilkins, September 13, 1969, AHP, MS 1888, box 21, folder 11; AH to PR, August 8, 1969; AH to "Mrs. Williams" [Reynolds agency], March 27, 1970, AHP, MS 1888, box 45, folder 2; J. Martin Carovano to Paul Reynolds, October 9, 1974, ARC, MS 2032, box 3, folder 27; *"Roots* II," autobiographical narrative, AHP, MS 1888, box 38, folder 12.

23. AH to Hillel Black, March 5, 1969; AH to Lawrence Hughes, July 29, 1969, Hillel Black to AH, July 31, 1972, AHP, MS 1888, box 45, folder 2; AH to PR, August 24, 1969, AHP, MS 1888, box 45, folder 2; "Fisher-edited copy," AHP, MS 1888, box 25, folder 4.

24. AH to PR, September 16, 1970; KM to PR, September 21, 1970; AH to PR, November 28, 1970, AHP, MS 1888, box 45, folder 2; AH to PR, May 20, 1971; PR to George Sims, July 2, 1971, AHP, MS 1888, box 45, folder 3.

25. AH to PR, June 19, May 20, 1971, AHP, MS 1888, box 45, folder 3; PR to AH, April 30, 1971, AHP, MS 1888, box 45, folder 2.

26. AH to PR, May 18, 1971, ARC, MS 2032, box 3, folder 25; McCauley, 148.

27. *Chicago Tribune,* February 18, 1973.

28. Personal Video Interviews Given by and Given to Alex Haley, Alex Haley website, http://www.alex-haley.com/alex_haley_video_interviews.htm; *Christian Science Monitor,* April 24, 1972; "My Furthest-Back Person—'The African,'" *New York Times* July 16, 1972.

29. PR to AH, August 7, 1972, AHP, MS 1888, box 45, folder 2; AH to PR, October 5, 1972; PR to AH, August 7, 1972; PR to Rubin Clickman, May 29, 1973 AHP, MS 1888, box 45, folder 3.

30. Donald Bogle, *Blacks in American Films and Television: An Encyclopedia* (New York: Garland, 1988), 208–209.

31. AH to PR, May 5, 1973, ARC, MS 2032, box 3, folder 25; AH to PR, July 11, 1973, AHP, MS 1888, box 45, folder 3.

32. "*Roots* II," autobiographical narrative, AHP, MS 1888, box 38, folder 12; PR to Rubin Glickman, May 29, 1973; AH to PR, August 10 and 16, October 24, November 3, 1973; PR to AH, August 16, 1973, AHP, MS 1888, box 45, folder 3.

33. David L. Wolper with Quincy Troupe, *The Inside Story of T.V.'s "Roots"* (New York: Warner Books, 1978), 34–35; David L. Wolper with David Fisher, *Producer: A Memoir* (New York: Scribner, 2003), 227.

34. AH to PR, September 7, 1974, AHP, MS 1888, box 45, folder 4; *Wall Street Journal,* March 9, 1972.

35. PR to AH, September 25, 1974, ARC, 2032, 3, 27; PR to AH, December 30, 1974, AHP, MS 1888, box 45, folder 4; PR to AH, August 20, 1973, AHP, MS 1888, box 45, folder 3; AH to PR, March 10, 1974, AHP, MS 1888, box 45, folder 5; Lisa Drew to author, December 9, 2014.

36. PR to Lisa Drew, April 19, 1974; Lisa Drew to Paul Reynolds, April 17, December 11, 1974, AHP, MS 1888, box 45, folder 5.

37. Murray Fisher to Anne Romaine, [n.d.], ARC, MS 2032, box 3, folder 28; AH to PR, March 11, 1973, AHP, MS 1888, box 45, folder 3; PR to AH, February 10, 1975, ARC, MS 2032, box 3, folder 28.

38. Drew to PR, February 3, 1975; AH to PR, May 16, 1975; PR to AH, May 28, 1975, AHP, MS 1888, box 45, folder 5; Lisa Drew letter to the author, December 8, 2014.

39. Lisa Drew letter to the author, December 8, 2014; AH to PR [dated July 18, 1975, but he probably meant June], AHP, MS 1888, box 45, folder 4; AH to PR, September 20, 1975, AHP, MS 1888, box 45, folder 5.

40. AH to Murray Fisher, October 9, 1975, ARC, MS 2032, box 3, folder 28

41. AH to Murray Fisher, October 18, 1975, ARC, MS 2032, box 3, folder 28.

42. Ibid.; *Norfolk Virginian Pilot,* February 5, 2013.

43. AH to Ardis Leigh, October 28, 1975, ARC, MS 2032, box 3, folder 28.

CHAPTER 8: THE BLACK FAMILY BIBLE

1. Lisa Drew deposition, 985, in *Alexander v. Haley* ARC, box 5.

2. David A. Gerber, "Haley's Roots and Our Own," *Journal of Ethnic Studies* 5 (1977–78): 90.

3. Ibid., 100; see also Selwyn R. Cudjoe, "Maya Angelou and the Autobiographical Statement," in *Black Women Writers,* ed. Mari Evans (London: Pluto, 1985), 6; and Merrill Maguire Skaggs, "Roots: A New Black Myth," *Southern Quarterly* 17 (Fall 1978): 43–48.

4. Skaggs, "Roots: A New Black Myth," 42–50.

5. Gerber, "Haley's Roots and Our Own," 91–94.

6. Office of Policy Planning and Research, United States Department of Labor, *The Negro Family: The Case for National Action* (March 1965), 3–47; Lee Rainwater and William L. Yancey, ed., *The Moynihan Report and the Politics of Controversy* (Cambridge: The MIT Press, 1967), 410; Nicholas Lemann, *Promised Land: The Great Black Migration and How It Changed America* (New York: Knopf, 1991), 175–176, 181; *New York Times,* November 15, 1965.

7. John Blassingame, *The Slave Community: Plantation Life in the Antebellum South* (New York: Oxford University Press, 1972; rev. ed., 1979), 151.

8. Gerber, "Haley's Roots and Our Own," 95.

9. AH, *Roots* (Garden City: Doubleday, 1976).

10. Drew deposition, 1004–1005, *Alexander* trial documents, AHP, MS 1888, box 48, folder 6.

11. Gay Talese, *Fame and Obscurity* (New York: Bantam, 1970), vii; Wolfe quoted in *A Brief History of Literature and Journalism Inspirations, Intersections, and Inventions from Ben Franklin to Stephen Colbert,* ed. Mark Canada (New York: Palgrave Macmillan, 2013), 15; M. Thomas Inge, ed., *Truman Capote Conversations,* (Jackson: University Press of Mississippi, 1987), 40.

12. Donald R. Wright, "Uprooting Kunta Kinte: On the Perils of Relying on Encyclopedic Informants," *History in Africa* 8 (1981): 212–13.

13. *Washington Post,* March 27, 1975; Willie Lee Rose, *Race and Region in American Historical Fiction: Four Episodes* (Oxford: Clarendon, 1979), 5.

14. *Washington Post,* January 31, 1977.

15. Jack Temple Kirby, *Media-Made Dixie: The South in the American Imagination* (Baton Rouge: Louisiana State University Press, 1978), 172–73.

16. *Newsweek,* July 4, 1977.

17. Judith Mudd, "Returning a Theft of Identity: This Is Also Me: Two Indian Views of *Roots,*" *Indian Journal of American Studies* 10 (July 1980): 50.

18. *Washington Post,* March 27, 1975; *Publishers Weekly,* September 6, 1976.

19. *New York Times,* August 29, October 17, and November 14 and 21, 1976.

20. *Los Angeles Times,* January 2, 1977; *New York Times,* September 26 and October 14, 1976.

21. *Newsweek,* September 27, 1976.

22. Willie Lee Rose, "An American Family," *New York Review of Books,* November 11, 1976.

23. Philip Nobile, "Roots Uncovered," *Village Voice,* February 23, 1993.

24. Leslie Fiedler, *The Inadvertent Epic: From Uncle Tom's Cabin to Roots* (New York: Simon and Schuster, 1979), 17, 84; Rose, *Race and Region in American Historical Fiction,* 2–3, 8–9.

25. Fiedler, *The Inadvertent Epic,* 27; Jane Smiley, *Thirteen Ways of Looking at the Novel* (New York: Anchor, 2006), 369–371.

26. Joel Williamson, *The Crucible of Race: Black-White Relations in the American South Since Emancipation* (New York: Oxford University Press, 1984), 151–58; Thomas Dixon Jr., *The Leopard's Spots: A Romance of the White Man's Burden—1865–1900* (New York: Doubleday, Page & Co., 1902), 244, 263; Dixon was quoted in Fiedler, *The Inadvertent Epic,* 44.

27. Robert May, "*Gone with the Wind* as Southern History: A Reappraisal," *Southern Quarterly* 17 (Fall 1978): 51; Fiedler, *The Inadvertent Epic,* 61.

28. Fiedler, *The Inadvertent Epic,* 80; Kirby, *Media-Made Dixie,* 166, 169; Helen Taylor, "The Griot from Tennessee: The Saga of Alex Haley's *Roots,*" *Critical Quarterly* 37 (1996): 48.

29. Fiedler, *The Inadvertent Epic,* 52.

30. Todd explained this change in a letter to the editor in the *New York Times,* December 5, 1976.

31. Fiedler, *The Inadvertent Epic,* 40.

CHAPTER 9: POP TRIUMPH

1. John De Vito and Frank Tropea, *Epic Television Miniseries: A Critical History* (Jefferson, NC: McFarland, 2010), 30.

2. David L. Wolper and Quincy Troupe, *The Inside Story of T.V.'s "Roots,"* (New York: Warner Communications, 1978), 179.

3. C. Richard King, "What's Your Name? *Roots,* Race, and Popular Memory in Post–Civil Rights America," in *African Americans on Television: Race-ing for*

Ratings, ed. David J. Leonard and Lisa A Guerrero (Santa Barbara: Praeger, 2013), 73.

4. Marty Bell, "Tale of a Talker," *New York*, February 28, 1977; David Wolper, *Producer: A Memoir* (New York: Scribner, 2003), 230; Wolper and Troupe, *The Inside Story of T.V.'s "Roots,"* 174.

5. *New York Times*, June 27, 1976; Leslie Fishbein, "*Roots:* Docudrama and the Interpretation of History," in *American History American Television: Interpreting the Video Past*, ed. John E. O'Connor (New York: Frederick Ungar Publishing, 1983), 287.

6. Hemant Shah and Lauren R. Tucker, "Race and the Transformation of Culture: The Making of the Television Miniseries *Roots*," *Critical Studies in Mass Communication* 9 (1992): 325–36; *Seattle Times*, July 15, 2007; *New York Times*, March 18, 1979.

7. AH, *Roots* (Garden City, NY: Doubleday, 1976), 276; Shah and Tucker, "Race and the Transformation of Culture," 331.

8. Donald Bogle, *Blacks in American Films and Television: An Encyclopedia* (New York: Garland, 1988), 340–344.

9. Pauline Bartel, *The Complete Gone with the Wind Trivia Book: The Movie and More* (Taylor Trade Publishing), 64–69, 161–172.

10. Fishbein, "*Roots:* Docudrama and the Interpretation of History," 279–280; *Newsweek*, February 14, 1977.

11. Kenneth K. Hur and John P. Robinson, "The Social Impact of 'Roots,'" *Journalism Quarterly* 55 (Spring 1978): 19; *New York Times*, February 2, 1977.

12. *Newsweek*, February 7, 1977; Alison Landsberg, *Prosthetic Memory: The Transformation of American Remembrance in the Age of Mass Culture* (New York: Columbia University Press, 2004), 101–103; *New York Times*, January 28, 1977.

13. Hur and Robinson, "The Social Impact of 'Roots,'" 19–24.

14. *Newsweek*, February 14, 1977.

15. *New York Times*, March 6, 1977.

16. *New York Times*, March 19, 1977.

17. *New York Times*, March 19, January 28, 1977; Chuck Stone, "Roots: An Electronic Orgy in White Guilt," *The Black Scholar* 7 (May 1977): 40.

18. *New York Times*, June 7, 1977.

19. Hur and Robinson, "The Social Impact of 'Roots,'" 19–24; *New York Times*, April 24, 1977.

20. Fishbein, "*Roots:* Docudrama," 283; Wolper, *Producer*, 235.

21. "There Are Days When I Wish It Hadn't Happened," *Playboy*, March 1979.

22. *Los Angeles Times*, February 8, 1977.

23. *Newsweek*, July 4, 1977.

24. "There Are Days When I Wish It Hadn't Happened."

25. *Ebony*, April 1977.

26. *Ebony*, April 1977.

27. "There Are Days When I Wish It Hadn't Happened."

CHAPTER 10: ROOTS UNCOVERED

1. *New York Times*, March 30, 1977.

2. AH to John Hawkins, December 13, 1976, AHP, MS 1888, box 44, folder 5.

3. *New York Times*, March 30, 1977; *Publisher's Weekly*, April 4, 1977: *Village Voice*, May 30, 1977.

4. AH to John Hawkins, December 13, 1976, AHP, MS 1888, box 44, folder 5.

5.*New York Times,* December 10, 1988.
6.*Sunday Times,* April 10, 1977.
7.*Sunday Times,* April 10, 1977.
8.*New York Times,* April 10, 1977.
9.David A. Gerber, "Haley's Roots and Our Own," *Journal of Ethnic Studies* 5 (1977–78): 99–100.
10.*New York Times,* April 10, 1977.
11.*Times* (London), April 12, 1977.
12.*New York Times,* April 18, 1977.
13.*Village Voice,* May 30, 1977.
14.*New York Times,* April 19, 1977; *Playboy,* March 1979.
15.*New York Times,* April 10, 1977; see *Village Voice,* May 30, 1977, for the suggestion of a "patronizing note."
16.*Los Angeles Times,* April 24, 1977.
17.*Village Voice,* May 30, 1977.
18.*New York Times,* November 14, 1967.
19.*New York Times,* April 24, 1977.
20.Maryemma Graham, *Conversations with Margaret Walker* (Jackson: University Press of Mississippi, 2002), 133–34.
21.Margaret Walker, "How I Wrote Jubilee," in *How I Wrote Jubilee and Other Essays on Life and Literature,* ed. Maryemma Graham (New York: Feminist Press, 1990), 50–65.
22.Charles T. Rowell, "Poetry, History, and Humanism: An Interview with Margaret Walker," *Black World* 25 (1975): 10.
23.Walker, "How I Wrote *Jubilee.*"
24.Margaret Walker Alexander Plaintiff's Affidavit, December 10, 1977, AHP, MS 1888, box 49, folder 6.
25.George Berger to author, March 14, 2015.
26.*Margaret Walker ALEXANDER, Plaintiff, v. Alex HALEY, Doubleday & Company, Inc., and Doubleday Publishing Company, Defendants,* 460 F.Supp. 40 (1978).
27.*New York Times,* January 21, 1940.
28.Courlander to Haley, November 1, 1972, ARC, MS 2032, box 3, folder 28.
29.Joseph Bruchac to author, March 26, 2015.
30.Harold Courlander to Herbert Michelman, January 21, 1975, May 29, 1977, ARC, MS 2032, box 3, folder 8; Courlander to Michelman, February 4, 1977, AHP, MS 1888, box 41, folder 3.
31.AR Notes, 1991, ARC, MS 2032, box 5.
32.*New York Times,* April 23, 1977.
33.*New York Times,* November 9, 1978.
34.Haley direct testimony, 1391–1395, *Courlander v. Haley* trial transcript. ARC, MS 2032, box 5, folder 7.
35.*New York Times,* November 9, 1978.
36.Joseph Bruchac to author, March 26, 2015.
37.This information comes from an anonymous source, a person who witnessed the entire trial and was privy to Judge Ward's comments made in his chambers.
38.*Courlander v. Haley* trial transcript, 1650, ARC, MS 2032, box 6, folders 16 and 20.
39.This information came from a source who chooses to remain anonymous.
40.Courlander trial transcript, p. 1346, AHP, MS 1888, box 39, folder 11.
41.Berger to author, March 14, 2015.
42.This information came from a source who chooses to remain anonymous.

43. *Village Voice,* February 23, 1993; Berger to author, March 16, 2015.
44. *Village Voice,* February 23, 1993.
45. Berger to author, March 14, 2015.
46. AH to Murray Fisher, October 18, 1975, ARC, MS 2032, box 3, folder 28.
47. Donald R. Wright, "Uprooting Kunta Kinte: On the Perils of Relying on Encyclopedic Informants," *History in Africa,* 8 (1981): 205–17.
48. Ibid.
49. Gary B. Mills and Elizabeth Shown Mills, "'Roots' and the New 'Faction': A Legitimate Tool for Clio?" *Virginia Magazine of History and Biography* 89 (January 1981): 3–26.

CHAPTER 11: FIND THE GOOD AND PRAISE IT

1. AR interview with Leonard Jeffries, May 9, 1994, MS 2055, box 1, tape 40; *New York Times,* December 10, 1988.
2. Mallon quoted in Julia Kamysz Lane, "A Brief History of the 'P' Word," *Poets&Writers,* May 1, 2002, http://www.pw.org/content/brief_history_quot pquot_word.
3. Donald Bogle, *Blacks in American Films and Television: An Encyclopedia* (New York: Garland, 1988), 343–344.
4. Ibid.
5. Palmerstown file, AHP, MS 1888, box 64, folder 11 and MS 1888, box 59, folder 1.
6. Bogle, *Blacks in American Films and Television,* 296.
7. Herman Gray, "The Politics of Representation in Network Television," in *Channeling Blackness: Studies on Television and Race in America,* ed. Darnell M. Hunt (New York: Oxford University Press, 2005), 161; C. Richard King, "What's Your Name? *Roots,* Race, and Popular Memory in Post–Civil Rights America," in *African Americans on Television: Race-ing for Ratings,* ed. David J. Leonard and Lisa A Guerrero (Santa Barbara: Praeger, 2013), 79–80.
8. Arjun Appadurai, Carol A. Breckenridge, Lauren Berlant, and Manthia Diawara, "On Thinking the Black Public Sphere," *Public Culture* 7 (1994): xi.
9. *Tennessee* 1 (1988): 28–31; *Los Angeles Times Magazine,* March 16, 1986.
10. *New York Times,* February 14, 1993.
11. AR, "Alex Haley Notes," 1991, ARC, MS 2032, box 5.
12. William Bruce Wheeler to author, March 12, 2015.
13. AR, "Alex Haley Notes," 1991, ARC, MS 2032, box 5.
14. David L. Wolper with David Fisher, *Producer: A Memoir* (New York: Scribner, 2003), 240–241.
15. *Essence,* February 1992.
16. *Los Angeles Times,* February 11, 1992; *Knoxville News-Sentinel,* March 1, 1992.
17. *Jet,* March 2, 1992.
18. *New York Times,* February 14, 1993.
19. *Knoxville New Sentinel,* March 17, 1992.
20. *People,* October 5, 1992.
21. Charles Thomas Galbraith, telephone interview with author, September 2014.
22. Philip Nobile, "Alex Haley's Advice to Ambrose and Goodwin," History News Network, July 8, 2002, http://historynews network.org/article/539.
23. Stanley Crouch, "The 'Roots' of Huckster Haley's Great Fraud," *Jewish World Review,* January 18, 2002, http://www.jewishworldreview.com/cols/crouch011

802.asp; Jack Cashill, *Hoodwinked: How Intellectual Hucksters Have Hijacked American Culture* (Nashville: Nelson Current, 2005), 107–20.

24. Jan Vansina, *Living with Africa* (Madison: University of Wisconsin Press, 1994), 218; Richard Marius, "Alexander Murray Palmer Haley," *Tennessee Encyclopedia,* https://tennesseeencyclopedia.net/entry.php?rec=586.

25. See Nobile's castigation of Gates at http://www.angelfire.com/il2/maplepark library/alley/doc03.html.

26. *Boston Globe,* November 3, 1998; *The Norton Anthology of African American Literature,* ed. Henry Louis Gates, Jr., and Nellie Y. McKay (New York: Norton, 1997).

27. *Alex Haley: The Man Who Traced America's ROOTS* (Pleasantville, NY: Reader's Digest Association, 2007).

28. *Los Angeles Times,* March 7, 2005.

INDEX